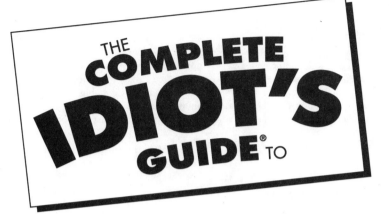

THE

# COMPLETE IDIOT'S GUIDE® TO

# Cooking with Mixes

*by Ellen Brown*

## ALPHA

A member of Penguin Group (USA) Inc.

Most Alpha books are available at special quantity discounts for bulk purchases for sales promotions, premiums, fund-raising, or educational use. Special books, or book excerpts, can also be created to fit specific needs.

For details, write: Special Markets, Alpha Books, 375 Hudson Street, New York, NY 10014.

**Publisher:** *Marie Butler-Knight*
**Product Manager:** *Phil Kitchel*
**Senior Managing Editor:** *Jennifer Chisholm*
**Senior Acquisitions Editor:** *Renee Wilmeth*
**Development Editor:** *Nancy D. Lewis*
**Senior Production Editor:** *Christy Wagner*
**Copy Editor:** *Nancy Wagner*
**Illustrator:** *Chris Eliopoulos*
**Cover/Book Designer:** *Trina Wurst*
**Indexer:** *Angie Bess*
**Layout/Proofreading:** *Ayanna Lacey, Donna Martin*

# Contents at a Glance

# Contents

What the recipe symbols mean:

▲ Fast

● Healthy

■ Make-ahead

# Foreword

Speed-scratch, half-scratch, or convenience cooking—call it what you will, it's the way people cook today. Shortcuts in the kitchen have become the standard route as today's home cooks find themselves increasingly short on time yet long on the desire for great-tasting, nutritious foods. Using top-quality, pre-prepared items to shorten food preparation time is now the norm. Such convenience foods as cut chicken, bagged salad greens, and dry onion soup mix are accepted as basic ingredients.

Enter Ellen Brown, culinary doyenne with three decades of experience in cooking and writing about it. As a teacher, author, marketer, and chef, Ellen has her finger on the culinary pulse of this country's home cooks. And that pulse keeps time with dry mixes—one of the most popular shortcuts available to today's home cook.

A self-confessed former food snob, Ellen Brown admits that there was a time in her life when she would never have cooked with a mix. But times have changed, and so has she. Now mixes are her secret to fast, flavorful cooking.

In *The Complete Idiot's Guide to Cooking with Mixes*, Ellen shows you how, with a little "doctoring," a packaged dry mix can be converted into a personalized signature dish. Ellen takes your hand and leads you through the maze of dry mixes—from soup to sauce to cake—and the ways you can use them in every part of the meal, from appetizer to dessert. First and foremost to Ellen is taste—and the resulting dishes don't have that tell-tale mix taste. No one will know you started with a mix unless you tell them.

In addition to the delicious results, using mixes will streamline your cooking. Dry mixes take the place of time-consuming measuring, chopping, dicing, and slicing, enabling you to jump-start the cooking process. They also help ensure cooking success and consistency.

Ellen begins with sections on secret ingredients and building blocks, in which she teaches you all about the types of mixes, how to stock your pantry, and how to use mixes for basic foods such as stocks, sauces, marinades, rubs, and salad dressings. Then she leads you, chapter by chapter, through every course of the meal: dips and appetizers, hot and cold soups, salads, main courses, vegetables and grains, and sweet treats.

In addition to scores of recipes, *The Complete Idiot's Guide to Cooking with Mixes* is packed with food tidbits, tips, and trivia that are fun to read and will enable you to show off your culinary knowledge with friends and family. Cooking terms are explained, and potential problems are noted in boxes throughout the book. The book also contains a healthy dose of humor, which is a key ingredient in life as well as in cooking.

Let Ellen Brown introduce you to convenience cuisine *à la* dry mixes and set the stage for palate-pleasing, speed-scratch cooking. With the creative, well-tested recipes in *The Complete Idiot's Guide to Cooking with Mixes,* you'll discover that dry mixes are a magical ingredient and you're a kitchen magician. Let the show begin.

Barbara Gibbs Ostmann

Barbara Gibbs Ostmann is co-author of *The Recipe Writer's Handbook* and 11 cookbooks and food writer for *The New York Times* Regional Newspaper Group.

# Introduction

Time is one of our most precious commodities, so we're always looking for shortcuts when cooking. Enter mixes into your culinary world.

These dry products can help you cook every aspect of a meal—from the snacks you put out before dinner to the dazzling desserts that crown the meal. What this book is about is teaching you ways you might not have used mixes before. Mixes aren't magic. But when used in creative ways, you just might think they are.

You might think you know dry mixes. After all, you've made onion dip a few times. But this book is intended to expand the way you view them, and—more important—the way you use them in your daily cooking.

Just think of foods we now expect to find in the supermarket. In your grandmother's day beef was not pre-ground, nor could you buy anything but a whole chicken. Grinding our beef and cutting up our chickens are shortcuts that we now take for granted, but we are always looking for other ways to save time—but not at the expense of flavor.

Dry mixes are another shortcut we take for granted. We know that a soup mix can make soups and dips and a sauce mix can obviously make a sauce. But what you'll see is that a soup mix can also flavor a crispy potato dish and a sauce mix can become the basis for a creamy soup.

The principle underlying all the recipes is commonly called "doctoring." You do it every time you vary preparation instructions from what's on a package. Doctoring means that you are personalizing a product to suit your taste and your needs.

By using a dry mix, there are myriad ingredients that you don't have to stock in your kitchen. Let's use vegetable soup as an example. It lists more than a dozen vegetables, all of which add their inherent flavor to food and together form a harmonious symphony of complex taste.

Even if you haven't used that many savory mixes in cooking, you may have used cake mixes from time to time. In addition to being a shortcut to making a cake from scratch, another benefit to cake mixes—and all mixes—is that you have confidence about the results you'll get when using them.

Because the mix takes the place of measuring, chopping, dicing, and slicing, these dishes take very little "hands on" time to prepare. Most of them ask you to spend only 15 minutes. That's less time than it takes to pick up a pizza.

And the result of your effort is a home-cooked meal of nutritious food.

# How This Book Is Organized

The book is divided into seven parts:

**Part 1, "Secret Ingredients,"** teaches you what mixes are and how they are made. It gives you pointers on how to cook with mixes that go into every part of the meal. In another chapter, you'll learn how to become a more efficient cook. There's a list of what foods stocked in the pantry or kept in the refrigerator will keep you in the express lane at the market, because the number of ingredients you'll need for any recipe will always be few in number.

**Part 2, "Building Blocks,"** gives you recipes and strategies to create basic foods that can be enjoyed on a daily basis. One chapter teaches you quick ways to make homemade stocks to form the foundation for delicious soups, as well as ways to take a basic sauce mix and produce virtuoso variations. Other chapters give you easy recipes for marinades, spice rubs, and salad dressings—all made easy since their base is a soup mix.

**Part 3, "In the Beginning,"** expands your repertoire of great foods to eat before you even sit down at a table. Of course, there is a chapter devoted to dips; they are made from soup mixes as often as soups or other dishes. The remaining chapters of this part are hors d'oeuvres, both hot and cold.

**Part 4, "Stellar Starters,"** showcases hot soups to warm you and cold soups to refresh you. This part also includes small salads with specific dressings that can be served as light meals in larger portions. Most of the recipes in this part are vegetarian or could become so.

**Part 5, "The Main Event,"** is your source of easy new recipes for the center of the plate. One chapter encompasses meat, while the other two chapters in this part are devoted to poultry and seafood.

**Part 6, "Vegetable Patch Panache,"** is a rainbow of colorful and versatile vegetable dishes. The recipes in the first chapter are easy but elegant; vegetables become the star when the main course is simple. The second chapter encompasses recipes for pastas and other vegetarian entrees, all of which can be served as side dishes. And the part ends with a section devoted to potatoes, rice, and other grains.

**Part 7, "Sweet Sensations,"** are all luscious desserts based on cake mixes. The first chapter's recipes are all improvisations on basic cakes, ranging from homey to elegant. The second chapter teaches you how to make luscious bar cookies and drop cookies from cake mixes, and the final chapter presents with a grand finale of desserts that use cake in some fashion but are not in cake form.

At the end of the book is a group of useful appendixes. There's a glossary to add to your knowledge of cooking lingo, a chart to aid in converting measurements to the metric system, and a chart with weights and measures of commonly used ingredients. These appendixes will help you with all your everyday cooking.

## Extra Bites of Information

In every chapter you'll find many boxes that give you extra information that is either interesting, helpful, or both.

**Mix Mastery**

These boxes are cooking tips. Some are specific to the recipe it accompanies. Others will boost your general cooking skills or give you ideas for food presentation. They are meant to make your life easier and make your time in the kitchen more pleasurable.

**Ellen on Edibles**

Cooking has a language all its own, and some terms and ingredients can be intimidating if you don't know what they mean. These boxes are technique and ingredient definitions. A collection of them is then compiled in a glossary at the end of the book.

**Mix with Care**

It's always a good idea to be alerted to potential problems in advance. These boxes provide just such a warning, either about cooking in general or the recipe in particular.

**Dry and Droll**

Check out these boxes for tidbits of food history and amusing quotes about food. They're not essential to cooking. But they're fun to read and share with friends. They'll make you sound like a real gourmet.

## Acknowledgments

While writing a book is a solitary endeavor, bringing it to publication is always a team effort. My thanks go to …

Renee Wilmeth of Alpha Books and Gene Brissie of James Peters Associates for proposing this interesting project.

Christy Wagner, Nancy D. Lewis, and Nancy Wagner for their expert and eagle-eyed editing.

Karen Berman for adding her vast culinary knowledge above and beyond a technical review.

Tigger-Cat Brown, my furry companion who kept me company for endless hours in the kitchen and at the computer, and who critiqued all the fish and seafood dishes.

## Special Thanks to the Technical Reviewer

The technical reviewer for *The Complete Idiot's Guide to Cooking with Mixes* was Karen Berman, a Connecticut-based writer and editor who specializes in food and culture. She is a contributing editor to *Wine Enthusiast* magazine, and her work has appeared in magazines, newspapers, and newsletters. She is the author of an illustrated history book, *American Indian Traditions and Ceremonies*, and has worked in various editorial capacities on numerous cookbooks.

## Trademarks

All terms mentioned in this book that are known to be or are suspected of being trademarks or service marks have been appropriately capitalized. Alpha Books and Penguin Group (USA) Inc. cannot attest to the accuracy of this information. Use of a term in this book should not be regarded as affecting the validity of any trademark or service mark.

# Part 1

# Secret Ingredients

Mixes are the great short cut to great-tasting food. Right there in the package is a base that you can build upon to create a complex-tasting dish in a matter of minutes.

In this part, you'll learn about mixes, what's in them, how they're made, and—most important—how they'll become the secret ingredients for dazzling dishes that come from your kitchen. You'll also find a road map to what other ingredients to stock in your pantry to make cooking with mixes even easier.

# Mixes Unmasked

## In This Chapter

- ◆ What's in dry mixes
- ◆ The role dry mixes play in cooking
- ◆ How to improvise easy dishes based on mixes

Dry mixes are convenience foods that allow you to make homemade dishes in a matter of minutes.

Chances are, you might already have at least one dry mix of some sort in your pantry. After cooking some of the recipes in this book, you will learn that one is not enough!

Dry mixes can be the cornerstones of cooking all aspects of a meal—from dips to desserts. Mixes are time-savers in many ways. Because the ingredients are pre-measured, you know you have the right amount of each one. They also save money, because you don't have to stock the many ingredients contained in the mix.

## Is the Doctor In?

What unites the recipes in this book is that they all include a dry mix of some sort. But you need to expand your horizons when thinking about these mixes. Sure, a soup mix can be augmented with other ingredients and still produce soup. But a soup mix can also make a sauce. In the same way, a gravy mix can be added as the thickening agent to a soup.

On the sweet side, you might already have added a few extra ingredients to a cake mix to personalize the flavor. You'll discover in this book that the same cake mix can become the base layer for bar cookies or the topping for cobblers or other dishes that don't even resemble a cake.

The principle you're using when following these recipes is generically called "doctoring," and you've probably done it thousands of times without thinking about it. "Doctoring" means that you're using a mix in a way not specified in the original instructions or you're adding additional ingredients to a mix that changes its flavor or texture.

After making some of the recipes in this book, you'll become a mix doctor yourself and begin writing your own "prescriptions."

# Testing One, Two, Three

Not all mixes are created equal. You might want to go back to the basics and taste the dish the mix was intended to create before choosing a brand.

In some cases, there is variation in the ingredients themselves. For example, one brand of vegetable soup mix might contain mushrooms and have a far lighter taste than another one that has an undertone of tomato in the broth.

Cake mixes also vary. Some yellow cakes taste more like vanilla, and others have nuances of almond and coconut. Some chocolate cake mixes are more intensely flavored than others, and some devil's food cakes look much more red than others. Bake up a simple layer cake from a few brands if you want to experience this difference firsthand.

Another consideration is price. In soup mixes, one brand has two envelopes to a box while the other leading brand just has one. It's up to you to decide if you think the finished dish is worth the price difference.

There are many recipes, however, that specify a particular mix that is only made by one company although the name might be similar to a mix

**Mix with Care**

None of the recipes in this book were made with a yellow cake mix that requires the addition of butter. If your yellow cake mix calls for butter in the basic preparation, follow that direction. Then pick up with the recipe in this book, because the remainder of the added ingredients might be different from those amounts listed on the box.

produced by another manufacturer. In this case, I strongly urge you to use the specified mix rather than a substitution.

**Dry and Droll** _____

Yes, Virginia, there really is a Mr. Knorr who is the ancestor of the soup and gravy packets in today's supermarkets. Carl Heinrich Knorr was born in Germany in 1800. He began working in the food business by drying and grinding chicory for coffee in 1838. About 30 years later, his sons came into the business and began experimenting with drying vegetables and seasonings. The first Knorr soups were sold in Germany in 1873, and in 1928 the company began exporting to the United States. The Bestfoods division of the consumer giant Unilever purchased the Knorr Company in 1958.

Cake mixes vary in size as well as price. All the desserts in this book were created for a cake mix that makes a two-layer cake. I have not included package weights for the cake mixes because some brands weigh a bit more, but don't substitute a small box that is intended to make a single layer.

# Bubble, Bubble with No Toil and No Trouble

Dry soup mixes contain all the ingredients you'd use if you were making a soup from scratch. They have some sort of stock as the base, and seasonings and other ingredients augment the stock to produce the characteristic flavor.

But don't think that in some mega-kitchen there's a huge vat of soup cooking that then gets *dehydrated*. Scientists in laboratories formulate dry mixes and then pass the formulations on to factories to mix and package.

Sure, some of the foods started out as fresh foods. That's true of all the vegetable bits you see in vegetable soup or the bits of onion in onion soup. There's no way these can be made in a laboratory.

When you read the ingredient listing on the side of a dry mix box, you'll see many words you recognize as foods. But there will also be some terms you won't know—unless you majored in chemistry in college. These are the scientific secrets that go into mixes. Some of them are preservatives, and some are the chemical terms for salts and other common foods, as well as flavorings, aromatics, thickeners, emulsifiers, and leavening agents. (More on these later.)

**Ellen on Edibles** _____

**Dehydration** is the process of removing the natural moisture from foods by drying them at a low temperature. It's one of man's first forms of food preservation and makes the foods far less likely to spoil. Dehydrated foods are lighter and take up less volume than fresh foods. That's why the vegetables in a little packet of dry mix look like so much more once the mix is cooked.

# Getting Soup-er Results

Starting with a soup mix is the quickest way to make a soup, stew, or some other _braised_ dish. The mix takes the place of simmering a stock for many hours and then cooking vegetables in the stock to make a soup. It's all right there.

A constant of most soup mixes is that they contain a large amount of sodium, or what we commonly call salt, so you'll notice that few of the recipes in this book list salt as an ingredient. If you look at the nutritional information on the side of the boxes, you'll see that per serving some soup mixes deliver more than 35 percent of the RDA (Recommended Daily Allowance) for sodium.

When a recipe calls for a soup mix as the basis for a sauce, mixes are an even greater time-saver because the amount of liquid specified is less than what would go into a soup. This short-cuts the cooking time, because the soup does not have to _reduce_.

**Ellen on Edibles** _____

The official term for what we might call stewing or boiling is to **braise**. Braising is a cooking method that cooks food at a low temperature in liquid in a covered pan. The resulting dish is always tender because the long cooking breaks down the fibers within the food.

To **reduce** in cooking is to boil a liquid so it evaporates into the atmosphere, leaving a smaller volume of food behind. This produces a liquid with a thicker consistency and more concentrated flavor than the original.

Because other ingredients are added to the dish, the mix made with less liquid will not taste overly salty. The additional ingredients absorb a good part of the sodium.

While there's often a heavy hand in use with the salt shaker, dry mix makers seem to have overlooked the pepper mill; so always taste the dish right before serving it to see if a bit more black pepper is needed to boost the flavor.

Many soup mixes also contain a thickening agent such as cornstarch or potato starch. Use these mixes to make a sauce thicker than a soup by adding a small amount of liquid, and you have another time-saver when cooking.

An advantage to using dry soup mixes rather than canned condensed soups is that they are far more versatile. Dry soups can be used in mixtures to rub on foods before grilling or broiling, and they can also become the flavoring for coatings when baking or frying foods. Because a can of condensed soup is wet, its functions are more limited.

> **Mix Mastery**
>
> When using soup mixes in coatings and as rubs, it's best to choose mixes that are granular and do not contain large bits of vegetables because the dehydrated vegetables tend to burn when the food is grilled or fried.

# Getting Saucy

The traditional French kitchen has a whole job for the *saucier*, the chef who does nothing but watch over the sauce pots all day. Most of the classic French sauces have to be slowly simmered for a number of hours, and the job of the saucier is to catch them at the perfect moment.

Today, there are a variety of sauce mixes that replicate these rich flavors in a matter of minutes. Like soup mixes, there are no vats of sauce simmering in the factory; most of the ingredients are mixed in dry form.

One of the benefits of using sauce mixes is that many are far more "user friendly" than making the sauces from scratch. One sauce that is now a fixture in our kitchens, which was traditionally made from scratch, is mayonnaise, one of the families of classic French sauces.

My bet is that hollandaise and its cousins and white sauce are the next to become staple convenience foods. It's just too hard to make these classifications of sauces perfectly every time, and the mix does it for you.

# Cake Mix Magic

In cooking, you can take some liberties with quantities of ingredients without endangering the success of the finished dish, but the same cannot be said for baking. Too much of this or too little of that can be the recipe for disaster.

While cooking is an art, baking is both an art and a science. Professional pastry chefs measure recipes by weight in grams rather than by volume (in cups and tablespoons). That way they can be precise to the very gram or ounce.

That's why cake mixes are such a boon to cooks. You save the time needed to precisely measure every ingredient that goes into a cake, plus the cake mix manufacturers add a few tricks of the trade to make the mixes succeed.

All cakes contain sugar, flour, some sort of leavening agent (like baking powder or baking soda), fat, flavoring, eggs (or egg whites in the case of a white cake), and liquids. The dried parts are all there in the cake mix, too.

In addition, cake mixes contain a group of chemicals that we don't stock in our kitchens. They're called *emulsifiers*, and their purpose is to keep the fat and the liquid in a cake batter from separating.

In made-from-scratch cakes, the only emulsifier is the egg yolk. In cake mixes, any number of compounds are used. When you look at the ingredient list and see words like *soy lecithin* and *polysorbate*, recognize that these are not evil chemicals. They are the emulsifiers.

The biggest negative to cooking with cake mixes is what is disparagingly called the "cake mix taste." You know it when you taste it.

That taste is the result of the addition of artificial flavors, specifically vanillin, an artificially created flavor similar to natural vanilla from a vanilla bean. But you'll discover, when cooking the dessert recipes in this book, that by adding assertive flavors and ingredients to the cake mix, you can mask the "cake mix taste."

These ingredients range from citrus zest to pure extracts to liqueurs. Once you've added them, no one will guess that this luscious dessert started in a box.

Cake mixes also contain far more sophisticated leavening agents. Again, there are weird names down in the ranks of the ingredient lists, but they are nothing to fear.

## The Least You Need to Know

- Dry soup mixes can be diluted with a lesser amount of liquid to concentrate the flavor for a sauce or marinade.
- Salt should rarely be added to a dish that contains a dry mix because the mix probably already contains a high amount of sodium.
- Most dishes made with dry mixes do need the addition of black pepper to boost the flavor of the finished dish.
- The addition of ingredients such as citrus zest, liqueurs, and pure extracts can alter the artificial taste of many cake mixes.

# Chapter 2

# The Kitchen Cabinet

## In This Chapter

- ◆ Versatile soup, gravy, and sauce mixes to stock
- ◆ Cake mixes that form the base for dazzling desserts
- ◆ Other foods for the pantry
- ◆ Refrigerator basics

Dry mixes have a long shelf life and take up very little space in a pantry. With a cache of mixes, as well as other pantry staples, you can make most of the recipes in this book with fewer than 10 additional ingredients. That keeps you in the express lane at your local market!

For baking as well as cooking, there are certain refrigerated basics that you probably have on hand already. But I'll list them for you just to make sure.

## Soups to Stock

Here's a list of soup mixes to keep on hand. These are the ones used most frequently in these recipes:

- **Onion soup.** This beefy mix with *caramelized* onions is unquestionably the most popular dry soup mix. Anyone who is old enough to remember when Kennedy was president in the 1960s must remember having an envelope of onion soup around. There is also a beefy onion mix on the market that delivers a more pronounced beef flavor for pot roasts and stews, but it's not necessary to stock them both.

- **Roasted garlic herb.** This mix is what someone in baseball would term a "utility infielder." You can use it in myriad ways, as you soon will see when perusing the recipes in this book. Onions are the first ingredient listed due to their weight, but the overwhelming flavor of the mix is nutty, sweet roasted garlic along with flecks of other vegetables.

- **Savory herb with garlic.** Although the name is similar to roasted garlic herb, the soups are very different. Because it's a powder without any vegetables that need to be reconstituted, it's fast to use and very versatile. The blending of garlic and a variety of aromatic herbs such as thyme and basil adds some bounce to dishes, especially with the addition of other herbs.

- **Vegetable soup.** This is another of the mixes that is used extensively because it contains the basic vegetables used not only for soups but also for stews and sauces. There are two leading brands on the market, so you might want to taste test to find the one you like best.

- **Golden onion soup.** The base for this mix is a chicken stock, and the onions are just lightly *sautéed*. Golden onion soup is used in this book for many creamed soups, as well as chicken and pork dishes.

- **Leek soup.** This thick and rich concoction comes from the European culinary tradition, and it's delicious just as a soup, both hot and cold. If cold and puréed, you can sound really gourmet and serve it as Vichyssoise. It's delicate and contains potato, so it provides the structure for many soups and sauces.

**Ellen on Edibles** _____

**Caramelization** is the process of browning sugar. In the most basic sense, when sugar is heated it goes through various stages and then turns brown when it reaches 350°F. The term also refers to the browning of food to bring out its natural sugars. Because onions bring tears to your eyes, it might come as a surprise to learn that they contain a lot of natural sugar. Cooking the onions slowly releases this sugar and turns the onions brown and sweet. That's why onions need to be caramelized for onion soup.

**Sauté** is a cooking term we've borrowed from the French. Sautéd food is food that is cooked on the stove in a little fat until it caramelizes. The word literally means "to jump," and although we don't want the food to jump around in the pan, we do want to keep it moving at all times. To sauté, cook and stir, usually over medium heat.

- **Tomato with basil soup.** When you want Italian flavors, this is the box to open. It is great for stews, sauces, marinades, and salad dressings.

- **Cream of spinach soup.** There are several cream-of-something dry soup mixes, and the spinach is the most versatile. It makes great dips, soups, delicate sauces, and vegetable dishes.

- **Wild mushroom and chive soup.** My guess is that this mix will replace condensed cream of mushroom soup for the next generation. It has a wonderful, woodsy taste from dehydrated porcini mushrooms, and it's delicious as a sauce for both meat and poultry.

- **Ranch.** Although dressings and dips are the primary uses for this mix, it also makes a good gravy for light meats like chicken and pork.

**Mix Mastery**

The recipes for cream soups that list milk as a preparation ingredient do not specify whether you should use whole milk, 2 percent, or skim milk. After testing all of these, I have decided it really doesn't matter. The thickening agents in the mix create a thick, creamy soup even with skim milk. It's your choice. If you're watching fat grams, go for the skinny milks. Soy milk can be substituted for cow's milk, but don't use water. It makes the dish taste "thin."

# Gravies to Garner

Dry gravy mixes are equally as versatile as soup mixes. They can be transformed into gourmet delights in seconds with very little effort. It's the sauce that makes the difference between a ho-hum dinner on the grill and a feast to serve to company.

Gravy mixes come in small packets that make between 1 and 1½ cups, so if you're making sauce for a crowd, buy accordingly. All gravy and sauce mixes contain some sort of thickener, so they save time as they add flavor because the recipe's final step (thickening) can be trimmed away.

Keep the following sauce mixes on hand:

- **Brown gravy.** Brown gravy has a deep flavor that makes it compatible with all meats and some poultry preparations. Mushroom gravy and onion gravy are also on the market, and if you're very fond of those ingredients, you might want to use them as the base rather than brown gravy.

**Dry and Droll**

What we call brown gravy is dubbed sauce espagnole in the traditional French kitchen. When sauce espagnole is simmered so long that it is reduced in volume by up to 90 percent, it is called demi-glace, a naturally thickened, intensely flavored sauce.

◆ **White sauce or cream sauce.** Different brands have different names for this mix. In from-scratch cooking, a white sauce is made by slowly cooking a *roux* and then adding a liquid. When using a mix, you can stir it into either cold or hot liquid with no fear that the sauce will get lumpy or have the underlying flavor of library paste.

### Ellen on Edibles

**Roux** (pronounced *roo*, like kangaroo) is the French term for flour that is cooked in fat; the resulting mixture thickens sauces and soups. For delicate cream sauces, the goal is to keep the mixture white, but it's the deep-brown roux that gives Cajun and Creole foods their characteristic nutty taste. A dark roux is made with oil or lard instead of butter, because butter would burn long before the right color is reached.

◆ **Hollandaise sauce.** Hollandaise is an emulsion of butter and eggs, flavored with lemon juice, salt, and pepper. Making a proper hollandaise sauce used to cause sweaty palms for even experienced cooks. If the butter wasn't hot enough, the sauce could split, and if the butter was too hot, you ended up with a sauce that had the consistency of lumpy scrambled eggs. But have no fear when adding some butter and water to the mix. In Chapter 3, you'll learn several of the many variations on hollandaise, and how to reproduce them using the basic mix.

## Sweet Dreams

You'll need a basic supply of cake mixes for the dessert recipes in this book. While there are shelves of mixes in even small supermarkets, here are all you'll need:

### Dry and Droll

Angel food cake is light and white, so anything that's dark and rich must be sinful. Right? That's how devil's food cake got its name. The first recipes for it appear in the late nineteenth century.

◆ Two yellow cake mixes that do not contain pudding and that do not call for the addition of butter in the basic preparation.

◆ Two chocolate cake mixes. How much you like chocolate should determine the intensity of the mix. There are light chocolate, milk chocolate, and dark chocolate mixes on the market.

◆ One devil's food cake mix. There is a difference in the formulation between chocolate and devil's food, although in a pinch you could use a chocolate mix.

◆ One white cake mix. Although the cake might not turn out white, white cake mixes have the most innately delicate flavor.

Read the recipe carefully, because occasionally there are spice or lemon cake mixes listed. But you can make almost all the desserts in this book if you stock the mixes listed here.

# Larder Largesse

Very few folks list grocery shopping as one of the ways they like to spend their time. If your pantry is packed with cans and bottles of things you use frequently, the trips can be kept to just the express lane for the perishable items to complete these easy recipes.

## On the Savory Side

Let's start with the basics: flour, granulated sugar, brown sugar, salt, and black pepper. I urge you to buy a pepper mill and grind pepper as you need it. The difference it makes in the flavor of the finished dish is amazing.

In the canned section, keep on hand a few cans of diced tomatoes as well as whole peeled tomatoes, tomato sauce, tomato paste, a few different canned beans (like white beans and kidney beans), chicken stock, beef stock, tuna packed in water, and coconut milk.

Shelf-stable grains and grain-based products are always a quick-cooking lifesaver. In addition to long-grain converted rice, buy some arborio for risotto. The great thing about dried pasta is that if you don't have room in the pantry closet, they can become a kitchen decoration in clear jars on the counter. The "musts" are spaghetti or linguine, orzo, macaroni or small shells, and larger tubes such as penne.

Other dried foods are plain breadcrumbs, Italian-flavored breadcrumbs, and herbed stuffing cubes. Another pantry-friendly food that can help round out a meal is is dried beans. Garbanzo beans, black beans, white beans, and red kidney beans are all inexpensive. Like the pastas, you can always keep the beans in jars on the counter.

**Mix Mastery**

There are hundreds of dried pasta shapes, and most of their Italian names come from their shapes. When substituting one pasta for another specified in a recipe, keep the general dimensions in mind. The rule is that the heartier the sauce, the larger the pasta, so radiatore would be a good substitute for penne.

Once you've made salad dressing a few times, you'll never buy a bottle of it again. Cider vinegar, red wine vinegar, white wine vinegar, and balsamic vinegar should be part of the pantry. A basic vegetable oil and inexpensive olive oil for frying, a good olive oil for dressings or to use as a condiment, and sesame oil are the main ones to balance the vinegar on the shelves.

Other foods to stock are small capers, Worcestershire sauce, hot red pepper sauce, and barbecue sauce.

### Mix with Care

Certain foods can be stored for months in the pantry before they are opened but should be refrigerated after opening. Although many of them are marked with that instruction, others frequently are not. General categories are: mustard, maple syrup, barbecue sauce, Asian condiments such as oyster sauce and hoisin sauce, salad dressings, tortillas, and bottled lemon and lime juice. I also refrigerate expensive olive and nut oils after they've been opened, to retard rancidity.

## Your Flavorful Friend Herb

Dried herbs and spices work very well with the flavor structure of most dry soup and gravy mixes. I prefer whole leaves rather than ground for herbs such as oregano and basil. The ground form of spices like cinnamon and cumin work fine.

### Ellen on Edibles

**Herbes de Provence** is a blend of fragrant herbs used extensively in the south of France and is sold here in many large supermarkets and specialty stores. It contains basil, fennel seed, lavender, marjoram, rosemary, thyme, sage, and summer savory. If you don't have it, equal portions of dried thyme, dried rosemary, and dried basil will approximate the flavor.

The basics used extensively in these recipes are basil, bay leaves, ground cinnamon, ground coriander, ground cumin, dry mustard, ground ginger, *herbes de Provence*, ground nutmeg, oregano, rosemary, sage, and thyme.

The spice blends such as curry powder and chili powder should also be a part of your spice cabinet. Sesame seeds, poppy seeds, and caraway seeds are used for both baking and cooking. They are welcome additions.

## The Chilled Collection

Now that the shelf-stable stuff is accounted for, there are basic foods that you should have in your refrigerator. You probably have most of these on hand at all times anyway. A quart of milk, a pint of half-and-half, a half-pint of heavy cream, a pint of sour cream (or plain nonfat yogurt if you're watching your fat grams), a dozen eggs, and a pound of butter cover the essentials.

In addition, some Parmesan, cheddar, and Swiss cheeses round out the list. While all of them are available pre-shredded, the flavor of cheese dissipates once it's grated, especially for Parmesan, so grate it as you need it.

Carrots, celery, parsley, garlic, and onions are the vegetables used most frequently in these dishes. If you don't eat salad every night, buy the greens in small bags when you need them. Salad greens spoil within a few days.

## Fresh from the Freezer

Packages of frozen mixed vegetables, peas, chopped spinach, pearl onions, and corn come in handy for numbers of recipes. Sheets of puff pastry, filo dough, and a few pre-made pie crusts are other essentials.

## Incidentals

Red wine, white wine, dry sherry, and dry vermouth are all used in these recipes. While you don't have to buy *grand cru* wines for cooking, my rule is that I'd never use a wine in a pot that I wouldn't drink from a glass.

**Mix Mastery**
A rack with pretty glass bottles over the stove is about the worst place to keep dried herbs and spices because both heat and light are foes of these foods. Keep them in a cool, dark place to preserve their potency. The best test for freshness and potency is to smell the contents. If there is not a strong aroma, you need a new bottle.

**Mix with Care**
Onions can be stored in the refrigerator, but they're usually the first food to go if space is at a premium. They can always be stored in a cool, dry place on the counter, but don't store them near potatoes. The gas given off by onions will cause potatoes to sprout and rot faster.

**Ellen on Edibles**
**Grand cru** is a French term that means "great soil." It refers to really fine wine that comes from specific vineyards that have received special classification as such by France's wine classification (appellation) authorities.

**Mix Mastery** _____

Although sherry and vermouth can be stored for months at room temperature once they're opened, red and white wine soon turn to vinegar, even if refrigerated. There are two ways to preserve them for future use: either freeze them right out of the bottle or reduce them and then freeze them. Freezing right out of the bottle is a great way to use them for marinades later on. But if you're adding them to sauces, you might as well take the time to reduce them in advance. Boil the wine until it's reduced by half, then freeze it in a plastic bag or an ice cube tray. Note on the package that the wine has been reduced.

# Foods for Sweet Sensations

I have devoted this part of the pantry inventory to baking needs. I split it up from the other list because, except for a few spices, the foods are very different. And if you're not into making desserts, even though the ones in this book are so incredibly easy, then there's no need to stock most of these items.

## Just the Basics

In addition to the flour, granulated sugar, brown sugar, and salt listed previously, add confectioner's sugar and light brown sugar to the list of basics. Other sweeteners that come in handy are honey and molasses. Buttermilk powder is a convenient pantry food to have on hand. Most recipes that call for buttermilk only use a fraction of the quart. With the powder, you can make up just what you need.

Extracts are important, especially to overcome the "cake mix taste." Buy pure vanilla extract and pure almond extract. They're a bit more expensive but worth every cent. Another good option, especially with chocolate cakes, is instant coffee powder.

**Mix Mastery** _____

It's sometimes difficult to find skinned hazelnuts. If this is the case, toast your hazelnuts, skin on, in a 350°F oven for 5 to 7 minutes or until the skins are browned. Then place them in a linen tea towel and cover them. Rub them back and forth on the counter inside the towel, and the skins should slide right off.

Fruits and nuts are added to many recipes, and the nuts should be stored in the freezer to extend their shelf life. It's best to buy whole nuts and chop them yourself. Walnuts, pecans, and blanched almonds are the best all-purpose baking nuts. You might also want to include skinned hazelnuts and unsalted roasted peanuts in your nut inventory.

Raisins are essential to baking, so if you're only going to stock one dried fruit, make it golden raisins.

Other dried fruits give desserts a more exotic flavor. Dried currants, dried apricots, dried cranberries, and dried cherries are all easy to find. Store dried fruits in airtight plastic bags once the bag has been opened.

Another ingredient that is called for frequently is grated coconut. If possible, buy frozen grated coconut. It's unsweetened, so it can do double duty in Asian recipes as well. If you can't find frozen, you can always find sweetened coconut in the baking aisle.

## And God Created Chocolate

Adding chocolate to a cake mix revolutionizes the taste and form of the mix in myriad ways. Keep chocolate chips on hand for cookies and for folding into batters, and use cocoa powder to mask the "cake mix taste" of all chocolate cakes.

### Dry and Droll

Chocolate is native to Mexico and Central America, and the Aztec king Montezuma was responsible for having introduced it into European civilization. In 1519, he greeted the Spanish explorer Hernán Cortes with a brew called *chocolatl*, which means "fruit water" in the Nahuatl language. The Spanish brought it back to Europe nine years later, and by the mid-1600s, hot chocolate was the chic drink in all royal courts.

For chocolate that is to be grated or melted, keep good-quality unsweetened and bittersweet chocolate on hand. The quality should be good, but you don't have to spend a fortune on imported chocolate—save that for a rich ganache topping or for making chocolate truffles.

White chocolate, although not technically a chocolate because it doesn't contain any chocolate liquor, adds its distinctive flavor and richness to many desserts.

## Refrigerated Resources

In addition to those dairy products listed previously, cream cheese is necessary for baking. Don't buy the whipped cream cheese because it does not measure the same way. Also, beware of reduced-fat or fat-free cream cheese. These might be great to spread on a bagel, but they don't meet the task for a baked dessert.

Citrus fruits are used extensively in baking for both their *zest* and their juice. Lemons, limes, and oranges should be part of your baking pantry. As a backup, small bottles of natural citrus oils are available at specialty food stores. They're not the same as the grated zest, but they are a good substitute in a pinch.

**Ellen on Edibles** _____

**Zest** is the thin, colorful skin on citrus fruits that is bonded to the bitter white pith below, and is the part of the citrus fruit that contains the aromatic oils. The easiest way to remove only the zest is to use a kitchen gadget called a zester. Or you can grate the zest through the small holes on a box grater or use a vegetable peeler and then cut the strips very small.

## The Least You Need to Know

- There are fewer than a dozen soup and sauce mixes to stock to create all the savory recipes in this book.

- By keeping a supply of dried foods in your pantry, the number of items you need to make any of these recipes is fewer than 10, so you'll be shopping in the express lane.

- You can store certain categories of foods in the pantry, but once opened, they should be refrigerated.

- It's not necessary to buy expensive, imported chocolate to make desserts—except when you're making chocolate truffles.

- Only the simplest of dairy products are called for in the recipes in this book.

# Part **2**

## Building Blocks

This part provides you with the foundation for foods. It contains simple stock recipes that can be put up to simmer in a flash because a mix takes the place of much of the slicing and dicing. In the same chapter, you'll find quick fixes for gravy mixes. This gives them distinctive character to dress up grilled and broiled foods.

Marinades, spice rubs, and compound butters add flavor without fuss, and you'll see how easy it is to create these categories of foods when you start with a soup mix as the base. Another category put on the fast track by dry mixes is salad dressings. You can personalize the dressings to suit the spirit of the meal and keep a number on hand.

# Chapter 3

# Stocking Up and Savvy Saucing

## In This Chapter

- ◆ Recipes for easy stocks
- ◆ Ways to enhance basic brown sauce
- ◆ Flavor additions to cream sauce
- ◆ Hollandaise sauce variations

How many times have you seen articles about how homemade stocks give soups and stews a better flavor than those out of the can or from the cube? It's true, and in this chapter, you'll see how easy it is to make them.

Many recipes here start with a package of prepared sauce mix. Think of it as a blank canvas. It has merits of its own, but it really comes alive with the addition of some "paint." The ingredients added to the sauce mix, either as the liquid rather than the water or milk specified or after it's cooked, are the vivid hues.

**Mix Mastery**

When you find those limp carrots or celery stalks in the back of the refrigerator, don't throw them out. Wrap them in plastic wrap and freeze them. They might not be great for nibbling, but they are still good enough to add to the stockpot.

# Stocking Up

In a pinch it's great to have a can to open; however, there is nothing to compare with the rich and complex background flavor that homemade stocks add to soups, stews, and all braised dishes. Making stock is about as difficult as boiling water. Once you get into the habit of making stocks yourself, it will become part of your cooking regimen.

## The Least You Need to Know

♦ Vegetable soup mix can speed up the production of homemade stocks because it contains all the vegetables that are customarily added.

♦ Brown gravy mix is an all-purpose sauce for meats and poultry. Variations to create a more complex flavor and/or add texture can be made within a few minutes.

♦ White sauces, called béchamel in French and cream sauces in some parts of the United States, can be transformed into cheese sauces or flavored with herbs or spices.

♦ Hollandaise is an emulsified sauce made with butter and egg yolks. It is a good topping for vegetables, meats, poultry, and fish and can be seasoned with additional ingredients to create many variations.

♦ Sauce mixes make it easy to serve sauces that can be problematic to make from scratch.

# Chicken Stock

Prep time: less than 10 minutes    •    Cooking time: 2 hours    •    Makes 1 quart

1½ quarts water

2 lb. chicken pieces (bones, skin, wing tips, etc.)

1 envelope vegetable soup mix

2 garlic cloves

6 peppercorns

3 sprigs fresh parsley

3 sprigs fresh thyme or 1 tsp. dried

1 bay leaf

Pour water into a saucepan or stockpot. Add chicken pieces, soup mix, garlic, peppercorns, parsley, thyme, and bay leaf. Stir well and bring to a boil over high heat. When the liquid boils, reduce the heat to low. Skim off the scum that will rise during the first 10 minutes of cooking time. Simmer stock uncovered for 2 hours.

Strain stock through a sieve into a mixing bowl. Press down on the solids with the back of a spoon to extract as much liquid as possible.

Chill stock. Remove and discard the fat layer from the top. Ladle stock into containers, and either use it refrigerated within 4 days or freeze stock for up to 6 months.

**Mix with Care** _____

Skimming stock might not seem like a necessary step, but it's important to the aesthetics of the finished product. The "scum" that rises from chicken and meat stocks can cause the stock to become cloudy once it's finished.

# Brown Chicken Stock

Prep time: less than 15 minutes • Cooking time: 2 hours • Makes 1 quart

2 lb. chicken pieces (bones, skin, wing tips, etc.)

1½ quarts water

1 envelope vegetable soup mix

3 garlic cloves, halved

6 peppercorns

3 sprigs fresh parsley

3 sprigs fresh thyme or 1 tsp. dried

1 bay leaf

Preheat the oven broiler and line a broiler pan with aluminum foil. Arrange chicken pieces in the pan and broil for 3 to 5 minutes on each side or until skin is lightly browned. Transfer chicken to a saucepan or stockpot, and pour in any juice that accumulated in the broiling pan.

### Ellen on Edibles

To **skim** a liquid is to remove whatever is on the very top. To do this, hold a spoon parallel to the surface of the liquid and then gently glide it along the very top. The liquid should either be still or just simmering because it's impossible to skim when it's at a rolling boil.

Add water, soup mix, garlic, peppercorns, parsley, thyme, and bay leaf. Stir well and bring to a boil over high heat. When the liquid boils, reduce the heat to low. *Skim* off the scum that will rise during the first 10 minutes of cooking time. Simmer stock uncovered for 2 hours.

Strain stock through a sieve into a mixing bowl. Press down on the solids with the back of a spoon to extract as much liquid as possible. Discard solids.

Chill stock. Remove and discard the fat layer from the top. Ladle stock into containers, and either use it refrigerated within 4 days or freeze stock for up to 6 months.

# Beef Stock

Prep time: less than 15 minutes   •   Cooking time: 3 hours   •   Makes 1 quart

2 lb. beef shank, or 1 lb. beef stew meat or chuck roast

1½ quarts water

1 envelope vegetable soup mix

3 garlic cloves, halved

6 peppercorns

3 sprigs fresh parsley

3 sprigs fresh thyme or 1 tsp. dried

1 bay leaf

Preheat the oven broiler and line a broiler pan with aluminum foil. Arrange beef in the pan and broil for 3 minutes on each side or until browned. This gives the stock a rich brown color.

Transfer beef to a saucepan or stockpot, and add water, soup mix, garlic, peppercorns, parsley, thyme, and bay leaf. Stir well and bring to a boil over high heat. When the liquid boils, reduce the heat to low. Skim off the scum that will rise during the first 10 minutes of cooking time. Simmer stock uncovered for 3 hours.

Strain stock through a sieve into a mixing bowl. Press down on the solids with the back of a spoon to extract as much liquid as possible. Discard solids.

Chill stock. Remove and discard the fat layer from the top. Ladle stock into containers, and either use it refrigerated within 4 days or freeze stock for up to 6 months.

 **Mix Mastery**

An easy way to freeze stock is in ice cube trays. Measure the volume of an ice cube once it's melted so you'll know how many tablespoons are in each cube. Then you can remove just the right amount for a recipe, and cubes thaw faster than larger blocks in a microwave oven.

# Vegetable Stock

Prep time: less than 10 minutes • Cooking time: 2 hours • Makes 1½ quarts

2 quarts water

1 envelope vegetable soup mix

1 carrot, trimmed, and thinly sliced

2 celery stalks, trimmed and sliced

1 small onion, thinly sliced

3 garlic cloves, halved

6 peppercorns

3 sprigs fresh parsley

3 sprigs fresh thyme or 1 tsp. dried

1 bay leaf

### Ellen on Edibles

Mirepoix (pronounced *meer-eh-PWAH*) is the name for vegetables used to flavor stocks and sauces in classic French cooking. It always contains carrot, onion, celery, and some herbs.

Pour water into a saucepan or stockpot, and add soup mix, carrot, celery, onion, garlic, peppercorns, parsley, thyme, and bay leaf. Stir well and bring to a boil over high heat. When the liquid boils, reduce the heat to low. Simmer stock uncovered for 2 hours or until vegetables are soft.

Strain stock through a sieve into a mixing bowl. Press down on the solids with the back of a spoon to extract as much liquid as possible. Discard solids.

Ladle stock into containers, and either use it refrigerated within 4 days or freeze stock for up to 6 months.

# Seafood Stock

Prep time: less than 15 minutes    •    Cooking time: 2 hours    •    Makes 1½ quarts

2 lobster bodies or 1 lobster body and the shells from 1 lb. raw shrimp

1½ quarts water

1 cup dry white wine

1 envelope vegetable soup mix

6 peppercorns

3 sprigs fresh parsley

3 sprigs fresh thyme or 1 tsp. dried

2 garlic cloves

1 bay leaf

Pull the top shell off 1 lobster body. Scrape off and discard the feathery gills, then break the body into small pieces. Place pieces in a large saucepan or stockpot and repeat with remaining lobster body. Or add shrimp shells, if using.

Pour water and wine into the saucepan or stockpot, and add soup mix, peppercorns, parsley, thyme, garlic, and bay leaf. Stir well and bring to a boil over high heat. When the liquid boils, reduce the heat to low. Simmer stock uncovered for 2 hours.

Strain stock through a sieve into a mixing bowl. Press down on the solids with the back of a spoon to extract as much liquid as possible. Discard the solids.

Ladle stock into containers, and either use it refrigerated within 4 days or freeze stock for up to 6 months.

**Mix Mastery**

Seafood stock is often hard to make if you don't live near the coast. A good substitute is bottled clam juice. Simmer it with white wine and vegetables, as in the Vegetable Stock recipe, to augment its flavor.

# Basic Brown

In fashion, there's always a place for the basic black dress or suit. And in cooking, there's always a role for the basic brown gravy. It adds rich flavor as well as moisture to foods, and it's appropriate for all meats and poultry. But it's a bit too hearty for delicate fish and seafood.

In some of the recipes that follow, the actual amount of liquid used with the gravy mix is different from the quantity of water listed on the package. In other recipes, the sauce is made according to package directions and then additional ingredients are stirred in. These add texture as well as flavor to the smooth gravy.

**Dry and Droll**

The famed nineteenth-century French chef Antonin Carême is credited with classifying sauces into five basic families. Brown sauce is called *sauce espagnole* in French.

There are mixes for mushroom gravy and onion gravy on the market, and if you like those additional ingredients, feel free to substitute them for basic brown. It's also possible to double and triple the recipes given in this chapter if you're feeding a larger crowd.

# Mushroom Tomato Sauce

Prep time: less than 15 minutes • Cooking time: 10 minutes • Makes 4 servings

1 TB. butter

1 TB. olive oil

¼ lb. mushrooms, rinsed, trimmed, and thinly sliced

1 shallot, minced

1 garlic clove, minced

¼ cup dry white wine

1 envelope brown gravy mix

Water as specified on mix package

1 large tomato, seeded and diced

Freshly ground black pepper to taste

Heat butter and olive oil in a skillet over medium heat; add mushrooms. Cook and stir for 3 minutes. Add shallot and garlic. Cook, stirring, for 3 minutes or until shallot is translucent and soft. Add wine and cook until it is reduced in volume by half.

Stir gravy mix into the skillet, and stir in the amount of water specified on the package. Stir well and add tomato. Bring to a boil and simmer sauce over low heat for 5 minutes or until thickened. Season sauce with black pepper to taste.

# Rich Red Wine Sauce

Prep time: less than 10 minutes • Cooking time: 15 minutes • Makes 4 servings

1 shallot, minced

2 tsp. fresh thyme leaves or 1 tsp. dried

1 bay leaf

4 peppercorns

2½ cups dry red wine

1 envelope brown gravy mix

Water as specified on the mix package

Combine shallot, thyme, bay leaf, peppercorns, and wine in a stainless-steel or enameled pan. Bring to a boil over high heat. Reduce heat to medium-high, and boil wine until it is reduced in volume to 1 cup. Strain liquid through a sieve into a bowl and discard solids.

Return reduced wine to the pan, and stir in gravy mix. Add additional water if mix calls for more than 1 cup. Cook sauce according to package directions.

 **Mix with Care**

Wine, vinegar, and other acids should always be boiled in a stainless-steel or enameled steel pan rather than in an aluminum pan. The aluminum will give the dish a metallic taste.

# Mustard Sauce

Prep time: less than 10 minutes • Cooking time: 10 minutes • Makes 4 servings

2 TB. butter

¼ cup finely chopped onion

1 garlic clove, minced

½ cup dry white wine

1 envelope brown gravy mix

Water as specified on mix package

1 to 2 TB. Dijon-style mustard

Freshly ground black pepper to taste

Heat butter in a small saucepan over medium heat; add onion and garlic. Cook and stir for 3 minutes or until onion is translucent. Add wine and cook over high heat until it is reduced in volume to 2 tablespoons.

Add gravy mix and water. Stir well and bring to a boil over medium heat. Stir in mustard, and simmer sauce for 5 minutes. Season sauce with black pepper to taste.

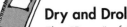 **Dry and Droll**

The "Dijon" of Dijon-style mustard is not only the authentic hometown for this pale yellow mustard with a clean, sharp flavor, but it's also a clue of its ingredients. An authentic Dijon mustard is made with brown mustard seeds, white wine, and unfermented grape juice.

## Game Sauce

Prep time: less than 10 minutes • Cooking time: 10 minutes • Makes 4 servings

½ cup dry white wine

2 TB. cider vinegar

1 shallot, finely chopped

1 envelope brown gravy mix

Water as specified on mix package

2 TB. chopped cornichon or other sweet pickle

1 tsp. chopped fresh tarragon or ½ tsp. dried

Freshly ground black pepper to taste

### Mix Mastery

There are other ways to perk up brown gravy. Use ½ cup Madeira or sherry in place of ½ cup water, stir in 2 tablespoons tomato paste, or—for a luxurious treat—add 1 finely chopped black truffle.

Combine wine, vinegar, and shallot in a stainless-steel or enameled pan. Bring to a boil over high heat. Cook until the liquid is reduced in volume by ¾. Add gravy mix and water and stir well.

Stir in chopped cornichon and tarragon. Bring to a boil over medium heat, and simmer sauce for 5 minutes. Season sauce with black pepper to taste.

# Creamy Creations

White sauce is called cream sauce in some parts of the country. It's the one that is made by cooking flour in butter over low heat and then adding liquid. Here's the catch: If you don't cook the flour long enough, the sauce can be lumpy instead of smooth and can have the decided flavor of library paste. White sauce mix to the rescue! It's foolproof. Right inside the envelope is the perfect thickening agent. As you'll see in other chapters, white sauce is the basis for everything from creamed soups to macaroni and cheese. Here are some variations to keep it in its sauce form.

# Herbed Cream Sauce

Prep time: less than 10 minutes  •  Cooking time: 10 minutes  •  Makes 4 to 6 servings

1 envelope white sauce mix, prepared according to package directions

¼ cup dry white wine

1 TB. chopped fresh parsley

1 tsp. fresh thyme leaves or ½ tsp. dried

1 tsp. chopped fresh tarragon or ½ tsp. dried

1 tsp. chopped fresh oregano or ½ tsp. dried

White pepper to taste

Prepare sauce according to package directions. Add wine, parsley, thyme, tarragon, and oregano. Simmer sauce over low heat for an additional 3 minutes. Season sauce with white pepper to taste.

# Curry Sauce

Prep time: less than 15 minutes  •  Cooking time: 10 minutes  •  Makes 4 to 6 servings

1 envelope white sauce mix

1 TB. butter

2 TB. finely chopped onion

2 TB. finely chopped carrot

2 garlic cloves, minced

1 to 2 TB. curry powder

Freshly ground black pepper to taste

Prepare white sauce according to package directions. Remove from heat and keep sauce in the pot.

Heat butter in a small skillet over medium heat; add onion, carrot, and garlic. Cook and stir for 3 minutes or until onion is translucent and soft. Reduce heat to low and stir in curry powder. Cook and stir for 1 minute.

Scrape mixture into white sauce and stir well. Bring sauce back to a boil and simmer over low heat for 2 minutes. Season sauce with black pepper to taste.

### Mix Mastery

The flavor of most dried herbs and spices is released if the spices are sautéed with a mirepoix or other aromatic vegetables over low heat before adding them to a liquid. Curry powder and chili powder, which are both blends of spices, benefit the most from this pre-cooking.

# Onion Sauce

Prep time: less than 15 minutes • Cooking time: 20 minutes • Makes 4 to 6 servings

1 envelope white sauce mix

2 TB. butter

1 large onion, diced

1 garlic clove, minced

1 tsp. fresh thyme leaves or ½ tsp. dried

1 tsp. chopped fresh rosemary or ½ tsp. dried

Freshly ground black pepper to taste

### Ellen on Edibles

To **sweat** has nothing to do with exercise. It's the term given to cooking vegetables in fat, covered, over low heat. In the case of onions and leeks, the process softens the vegetables and also rids them of any harsh taste. The purpose is to cook them so they're soft and translucent but not to brown them.

Prepare white sauce according to package directions. Remove from heat and keep sauce in the pot.

Heat butter in a small skillet over medium heat; add onion and garlic. Stir onion to coat it with butter. Reduce the heat to low, cover the pan, and *sweat* onions for 10 minutes, stirring occasionally or until soft. Add thyme and rosemary to the pan for the last 5 minutes.

Transfer onion mixture to a food processor fitted with a steel blade or a blender and purée until smooth. Stir onion mixture into white sauce, and simmer sauce over low heat for 2 minutes. Season sauce with black pepper to taste.

# Wild Mushroom Sauce

Prep time: less than 15 minutes  •  Cooking time: 10 minutes  •  Makes 4 to 6 servings

1 envelope white sauce mix

2 TB. butter

1 cup finely diced wild mushrooms such as fresh shiitake or portobello

1 shallot, minced

1 garlic clove, minced

⅓ cup dry sherry

1 TB. chopped fresh parsley

1 tsp. fresh thyme leaves or ½ tsp. dried

Freshly ground black pepper to taste

Prepare white sauce according to package directions. Remove from heat and keep sauce in the pot.

Heat butter in a medium skillet over medium heat; add mushrooms, shallot, and garlic. Cook and stir for 3 to 5 minutes or until mushrooms are soft. Add sherry, parsley, and thyme. Raise heat to high. Cook, stirring, for 2 minutes or until sherry is reduced in volume by half.

Stir mushroom mixture into white sauce, and simmer sauce for 2 minutes over low heat. Season sauce with black pepper to taste.

> **Mix Mastery** _____
>
> Here are some other ingredients you can add to white sauce: ½ cup grated cheddar, Swiss, or Gruyère cheese; 2 to 3 tablespoons prepared horseradish; or 2 to 3 tablespoons prepared mustard.

# Egg-Cetera

Hollandaise and all its relatives are *emulsified* sauces, which can be tricky to make. If the butter is too hot, the egg yolks turn into scrambled eggs. If it's not used immediately, it can be fickle and "break" rather than stay together.

But there are no worries when using a hollandaise sauce mix. The structure of the mix is created so that the sauce actually simmers to blend the flavors. Like brown gravy and white sauce, there are all sorts of hollandaise variations.

> **Ellen on Edibles** _____
>
> **Emulsion** is a mixture of two liquids that don't really want to be together, like oil and water in a salad dressing. The way they are created is to add one liquid to another very slowly, while beating very quickly. Hollandaise sauce and its relatives are emulsions of hot butter with egg yolks. Mayonnaise is an emulsion of egg yolks with oil.

# Béarnaise Sauce

Prep time: less than 15 minutes • Cooking time: 10 minutes • Makes 4 to 6 servings

1 envelope hollandaise sauce mix

¼ cup white wine vinegar

¼ cup dry vermouth

1 shallot, minced

1 TB. chopped fresh tarragon or 2 tsp. dried

Freshly ground black or white pepper to taste

### Mix Mastery

To transform the Béarnaise Sauce into Sauce Choron, whisk 1 tablespoon tomato paste into the prepared sauce along with the tarragon reduction.

Prepare hollandaise sauce according to package directions. Remove from heat and keep sauce in the pot.

Combine vinegar, vermouth, shallot, and tarragon in a small saucepan. Bring to a boil over high heat. Boil the mixture until it reduces in volume to just 2 tablespoons.

Scrape mixture into hollandaise sauce. Stir well and simmer sauce over low heat for 2 minutes. Season sauce with pepper to taste.

# Citrus Hollandaise

Prep time: less than 10 minutes • Cooking time: 10 minutes • Makes 4 to 6 servings

1 envelope hollandaise sauce mix

2 TB. fresh lemon juice

3 TB. fresh orange juice

Water as specified on mix package

1 tsp. grated lemon zest

1 tsp. grated orange zest

Freshly ground black or white pepper to taste

### Mix Mastery

To get the maximum amount of juice from citrus fruits, roll them back and forth on a counter or prick the skin and microwave them on high power for 30 seconds.

Pour sauce mix in a saucepan. Pour lemon juice and orange juice into a measuring cup, and add enough water to reach total amount of water specified on mix package. Prepare hollandaise according to package instructions, and bring to a boil. Stir in lemon and orange zest after sauce thickens. Season sauce with pepper to taste.

# Seafood Hollandaise

Prep time: less than 10 minutes   •   Cooking time: 15 minutes   •   Makes 4 to 6 servings

1½ cups seafood stock or bottled clam juice

½ cup dry white wine

1 TB. lemon juice

1 tsp. fresh thyme leaves or ½ tsp. dried

1 envelope hollandaise sauce mix

to taste

Combine stock, wine, lemon juice, and thyme in ... boil over high heat. Boil mixture until liquid is reduced in volu... a measuring cup and add water, if necessary, to reach total amoun... ckage. Prepare mix according to package directions, and season... ste.

```
08-31-05

03 TX * 7.99   1
03 TX * 7.50   1
03 TX * 5.99   1
01 TX * 5.99   1
     *27.47  ST
      *2.33 TX 1

            4  Q
    *29.80  TL
    *40.00 CA TD
    *10.20 CA CG

  *  12-30
 111-6839
```

# Chapter 4

# Flavor Without Fuss

## In This Chapter

◆ Red wine marinades for meats

◆ White wine marinades for poultry

◆ Light citrus marinades for seafood

◆ Herb and spice rubs for instant flavor

◆ Ways to flavor butter as a topping for foods

Marinades, which have been around for centuries, are used in almost all of the world's cuisines. They are a way to add flavor to foods that are going to be grilled, broiled, or baked without any fuss, because the food is soaked in a liquid until it's ready to cook. Occasionally, for dishes such as sauerbraten, foods are cooked in the liquid in which they are marinated.

But marinating does take time, and in today's pressured world, occasions pop up when there's no time for marinating. That's why herb and spice blends, which are rubbed onto food, have become more popular. Another way to flavor foods without fuss is to make flavored butters and apply these while the food is cooking.

In this chapter, you'll get easy recipes for all these categories as well as tips on how to use them.

# The Slow Soak

Marinating has a dual function: It flavors food, and it also tenderizes it. One of the advantages of making marinades with dry mixes is that the mixes are concentrated so flavor penetrates food quickly.

**Dry and Droll**

In traditional Spanish cooking, wine corks are added to marinades. They're not a flavoring ingredient, but the Spanish cooks maintain that they help tenderize foods.

The easiest way to marinate food is in a heavy plastic bag with a tight-fitting closure or zipper top. You will need less marinade if you use a bag than if you placed the food in a bowl because the marinade surrounds the food in the bag. Another advantage is that part of the process of marinating is turning food so it marinates evenly. Using this method, all you have to do is turn over the bag. Bags also take up less space in the refrigerator than do mixing bowls.

# Time Flies

Each piece of food is unique, but there are some general guidelines for how long food should marinate. It's not advisable to marinate for much longer than these recommended times because the acid—the part of the marinade that tenderizes foods—can break down the fibers too much.

In general, the more delicate the food, the shorter the time it should marinate:

◆ Marinate delicate fish and seafood for no more than 30 minutes per inch of thickness.

◆ Boneless skinless chicken breasts absorb flavor in 3 to 4 hours.

◆ Meats and poultry pieces with skin and bones should marinate for at least 6 to 8 hours and preferably 12 to 18 hours.

There is no magic to marinating overnight. The food is in the dark refrigerator, and it doesn't know the difference. Meats marinated early in the morning are ready to be cooked for dinner the same night.

## The Least You Need to Know

- Marinades tenderize foods as well as flavor them.
- For food safety, never use marinades as a cooking medium, basting sauce, or gravy once you have used it to flavor and tenderize raw foods—unless you cook the marinade for at least 5 minutes.
- Foods should not be left in marinades longer than necessary because they might turn mushy.
- Coat foods with oil before applying a rub so the rub mixture will stick better.
- Spice mixtures can be rubbed onto foods just before cooking so no time is needed for marinating.
- Use soup mixes to create flavored butter, which can be used on grilled foods, in pasta and rice dishes, on toast, and in a variety of other ways.

# Mexican Beer Marinade

Prep time: less than 10 minutes • Makes 2 cups

1 (12-oz.) bottle beer

½ cup lime juice

6 garlic cloves, minced

1 envelope golden onion soup mix

2 TB. *chili powder*

1 tsp. hot pepper sauce or to taste

½ cup olive oil

### Ellen on Edibles

**Chili powder** is a spice blend, only a portion of which is ground dried red chili peppers. The other ingredients are paprika, ground cumin, ground coriander, and cayenne and dried oregano. It's fun to try mixing your own to suit your preference.

Combine beer, lime juice, garlic, soup mix, chili powder, and hot pepper sauce in a mixing bowl. Whisk well. Add olive oil, and whisk well again.

Marinade can be used immediately or refrigerated in an airtight container and used within 4 days.

# Red Wine Marinade for Everything

Prep time: less than 10 minutes • Makes 1½ cups

¾ cup dry red wine

¼ cup balsamic vinegar

1 envelope roasted garlic herb soup mix

2 TB. firmly packed light brown sugar

1 TB. fresh thyme leaves or 2 tsp. dried

1 TB. grated orange zest

1 TB. grated lemon zest

Freshly ground black pepper to taste

½ cup olive oil

Combine wine, vinegar, soup mix, brown sugar, thyme, orange zest, lemon zest, and black pepper in a mixing bowl. Whisk well to dissolve sugar. Add olive oil, and whisk well again.

Marinade can be used immediately or refrigerated in an airtight container and used within 4 days.

# Spicy Margarita Marinade

Prep time: less than 10 minutes • Makes 1½ cups

½ cup orange juice

¼ cup lime juice

¼ cup tequila

¼ cup triple sec or other orange-flavored liqueur

3 garlic cloves, minced

1 jalapeño chili, seeds and ribs removed, and finely chopped

1 envelope golden onion soup mix

1 TB. chili powder

1 tsp. dried oregano

Cayenne to taste

¼ cup olive oil

Combine orange juice, lime juice, tequila, triple sec, garlic, jalapeño, soup mix, chili powder, oregano, and cayenne in a mixing bowl. Whisk well. Add olive oil, and whisk well again.

Marinade can be used immediately or refrigerated in an airtight container and used within 4 days.

### Mix with Care

Many people are fearful of using fresh chilies because cookbooks used to warn you to wear rubber gloves when handling them. That sort of precaution is not necessary (unless you have sensitive skin), but some caveats do apply. Cut chilies on a glass plate rather than on a wooden cutting board to ensure that the volatile oils don't soak in. And the most important thing to remember is to wash your hands very well after handling them.

# Mustard Citrus Marinade

Prep time: less than 10 minutes  •  Makes 1½ cups

½ cup orange juice

½ cup dry white wine

2 TB. lemon juice

2 TB. firmly packed dark brown sugar

2 TB. Dijon-style mustard

2 garlic cloves, minced

1 envelope roasted garlic herb soup mix

Freshly ground black pepper to taste

¼ cup olive oil

Combine orange juice, wine, lemon juice, brown sugar, mustard, garlic, soup mix, and black pepper in a mixing bowl. Whisk well. Add olive oil, and whisk well again.

Marinade can be used immediately or refrigerated in an airtight container and used within 4 days.

**Mix Mastery**

*Whisk* is both a noun and a verb. As a noun, the whisk itself is a cone made up of interlocking wires that converge in a handle. As a verb, to whisk is to use the gadget. It should be rotated in a circular motion through the food in the mixing bowl. This action blends and aerates. That's why you can use a whisk to beat egg whites or whipping cream.

# Provençal Marinade

Prep time: less than 10 minutes   •   Makes 1½ cups

¾ cup dry white wine

4 garlic cloves, minced

1 TB. herbes de Provence, or 1 tsp. dried thyme, 1 tsp. dried rosemary, and 1 tsp. dried basil

1 envelope tomato with basil soup mix

Freshly ground black pepper to taste

½ cup olive oil

Combine wine, garlic, herbes de Provence, soup mix, and black pepper in a mixing bowl. Whisk well. Add olive oil, and whisk well again.

Marinade can be used immediately or refrigerated in an airtight container and used within 4 days.

# Mediterranean Marinade

Prep time: less than 10 minutes   •   Makes 1½ cups

¾ cup dry white wine

¼ cup lemon juice

4 garlic cloves, minced

1 TB. dried oregano

1 tsp. dried thyme

1 envelope roasted garlic herb soup mix

Freshly ground black pepper to taste

½ cup olive oil

Combine wine, lemon juice, garlic, oregano, thyme, soup mix, and black pepper in a mixing bowl. Whisk well. Add olive oil, and whisk well again.

Marinade can be used immediately or refrigerated in an airtight container and used within 4 days.

# Chutney Marinade

Prep time: less than 10 minutes   •   Makes 1½ cups

¾ cup dry sherry

½ cup fruit chutney

¼ cup sesame oil

2 scallions, trimmed and chopped

2 TB. grated fresh ginger

1 envelope golden onion soup mix

Cayenne to taste

### Ellen on Edibles

**Puréeing** is the process of somehow turning food that started solid into a smooth paste or liquid. Purée by mashing, straining, or using a food processor or a blender.

Place sherry and chutney into a food processor fitted with a steel blade or in a blender and *purée* until smooth. Scrape mixture into a mixing bowl, and add sesame oil, scallions, ginger, soup mix, and cayenne. Whisk mixture well.

Marinade can be used immediately or refrigerated in an airtight container and used within 4 days.

# Onion Marinade for Meats

Prep time: less than 10 minutes   •   Makes 1½ cups

1 cup dry red wine

1 envelope onion soup mix

4 garlic cloves, minced

2 TB. chopped fresh parsley

1 TB. fresh thyme leaves or 1 tsp. dried

Freshly ground black pepper to taste

½ cup olive oil

Combine wine, soup mix, garlic, parsley, thyme, and black pepper in a mixing bowl. Whisk well. Add olive oil, and whisk well again.

Marinade can be used immediately or refrigerated in an airtight container and used within 4 days.

# Rub-a-Dub-Dub

Rubs are testimony to the power of ingenious marketing. Since the inception of dried herbs and spices, cooks have coated the surface of foods before they cooked them. Now we call the mixture a "rub."

To make the rub stick well, it's best to coat foods with oil or a spritz of vegetable oil spray before applying the rub. The oil will also ensure that the food has a nice brown tone when it comes off the grill or broiler.

## Barbecue Rub

Prep time: less than 10 minutes   •   Makes ¼ cup

| | |
|---|---|
| 1 envelope roasted garlic herb soup mix | 3 TB. ground coriander |
| ¼ cup firmly packed dark brown sugar | 1 TB. *Chinese five-spice powder* |
| 3 TB. paprika | 1 TB. cayenne |
| 3 TB. ground cumin | |

Combine soup mix, brown sugar, paprika, cumin, coriander, five-spice powder, and cayenne in a jar with a tight-fitting lid. Shake well to combine.

Store rub in a cool dry place, tightly covered, for up to 1 month.

**Ellen on Edibles**

Chinese five-spice powder gives a complex taste and alluring fragrance to any dish. Some of the components are star anise, ground fennel seed, ground cinnamon, allspice, and ground ginger. It's one of the original spice blends.

# Mediterranean Rub

Prep time: less than 10 minutes • Makes ½ cup

1 envelope golden onion soup mix

¼ cup herbes de Provence, or 1 TB. dried thyme, 1 TB. dried rosemary, and 1 TB. dried oregano

1 TB. dry mustard

Coarsely ground black pepper to taste

Combine soup mix, herbes de Provence, mustard, and black pepper in a jar with a tight-fitting lid. Shake well to combine.

Store rub in a cool dry place, tightly covered, for up to 1 month.

# Caribbean Rub

Prep time: less than 10 minutes • Makes ¾ cup

1 envelope savory herb with garlic soup mix

3 TB. curry powder

3 TB. paprika

3 TB. ground cumin

2 TB. ground ginger

1 TB. ground allspice

2 tsp. cayenne

**Dry and Droll**

Curry powder—which is really a combination of spices that usually include turmeric, coriander, cumin, fennel, and ginger—is based on the spice mixtures of India and made its way to the West Indies in the seventeenth century. It became a prized commodity for traders on the "spice route."

Combine soup mix, curry powder, paprika, cumin, ginger, allspice, and cayenne in a jar with a tight-fitting lid. Shake well to combine.

Store rub in a cool dry place, tightly covered, for up to 1 month.

# Steak Rub

Prep time: less than 10 minutes • Makes ½ cup

1 envelope onion soup mix

3 TB. dry mustard

2 TB. granulated garlic or garlic powder

2 TB. coarsely ground black pepper

2 tsp. dried thyme leaves

Combine soup mix, dry mustard, garlic, black pepper, and thyme in a jar with a tight-fitting lid. Shake well to combine.

Store rub in a cool dry place, tightly covered, for up to 1 month.

# Vegetable Chili Butter

Prep time: less than 15 minutes • Makes ½ pound

1 envelope vegetable soup mix

⅓ cup boiling water

½ lb. butter, softened

4 garlic cloves, pushed through a garlic press

2 shallots, finely chopped

2 TB. chili powder

1 TB. ground cumin

Red pepper sauce to taste

Place soup mix in a small mixing bowl, and pour boiling water over it. Stir well and allow mixture to sit for 10 minutes covered.

Transfer mixture to a food processor fitted with a steel blade. Add butter, garlic, shallots, chili powder, cumin, and red pepper sauce. Process until smooth, scraping the inside of the work bowl occasionally. Alternately, beat mixture in a mixing bowl by hand with a wooden spoon or with an electric mixer.

If you're not going to use compound butter immediately, spread mixture on a sheet of plastic wrap or wax paper and form it into a cylinder. Freeze butter for up to 2 months, and slice off slices with a hot knife as needed.

### Mix Mastery

In addition to topping grilled foods, you can use compound butters in other ways. Serve them with corn on the cob, use butters as a garnish for hot soups, make toasted breads with them, or create an instant rice or pasta dish with them and a sprinkling of Parmesan cheese.

**Mix Mastery** _____

If your butter is too hard to blend, do not try to soften it in the microwave oven. A few seconds too long and you've got a melted mess. An easy way to soften butter quickly is to grate it through the large holes of a box grater. It will soften in a matter of minutes at room temperature.

# Butter Is Better

If you're really pressed for time, you can put the food on the grill or under the broiler and make a topping of flavored butter to apply to it while it cooks.

The culinary term for this kind of topping is "compound butter." It really means that butter is mixed with something to give it a special flavor.

# Tomato Butter

Prep time: less than 10 minutes  •  Makes ½ pound

½ lb. butter, softened

1 envelope tomato with basil soup mix

1 TB. dried oregano

1 tsp. dried rosemary

Freshly ground black pepper to taste

Combine butter, soup mix, oregano, rosemary, and black pepper in a food processor fitted with a steel blade. Process until smooth, scraping the inside of the work bowl occasionally. Alternately, beat the mixture in a mixing bowl by hand with a wooden spoon or with an electric mixer.

 **Mix Mastery** _____

If you want to intensify the tomato flavor in this butter, add a few tablespoons chopped sun-dried tomatoes packed in oil.

If you're not going to use compound butter immediately, spread mixture on a sheet of plastic wrap or wax paper and form it into a cylinder. Freeze butter for up to 2 months, and slice off slices with a hot knife as needed.

# Garlic Butter

Prep time: less than 10 minutes  •  Makes ½ lb.

½ lb. butter, softened

1 envelope roasted garlic herb soup mix

4 garlic cloves, put through a garlic press

¼ cup finely chopped fresh parsley

Freshly ground black pepper to taste

Combine butter, soup mix, garlic, parsley, and black pepper in a food processor fitted with a steel blade. Process until smooth, scraping the inside of the work bowl occasionally. Alternately, beat mixture in a mixing bowl by hand with a wooden spoon or with an electric mixer.

If you're not going to use compound butter immediately, spread mixture on a sheet of plastic wrap or wax paper and form it into a cylinder. Freeze butter for up to 2 months, and slice off slices with a hot knife as needed.

 **Mix with Care**

Butters made entirely with dried ingredients can be refrigerated for up to a week without freezing, but those made with fresh ingredients should be frozen and used in portions because the herbs can deteriorate.

# Herb Butter

Prep time: less than 10 minutes  •  Makes ½ pound

1 envelope cream of spinach soup mix

⅓ cup boiling water

½ lb. butter, softened

4 scallions, trimmed and finely chopped

3 TB. chopped fresh dill or 1 TB. dried

2 TB. chopped fresh parsley

1 TB. lemon juice

Freshly ground black pepper to taste

Place soup mix in a small mixing bowl, and pour boiling water over it. Stir well and allow mixture to sit for 10 minutes, covered.

Transfer spinach mixture to a food processor fitted with a steel blade. Add butter, scallions, dill, parsley, lemon juice, and black pepper. Process until smooth, scraping the inside of the work bowl occasionally. Alternately, beat mixture in a mixing bowl by hand with a wooden spoon or with an electric mixer.

If you're not going to use compound butter immediately, spread mixture on a sheet of plastic wrap or wax paper and form it into a cylinder. Freeze butter for up to 2 months, and slice off slices with a hot knife as needed.

# Distinctive Dressings

## In This Chapter

- ◆ New twists on old-fashioned vinaigrette dressings
- ◆ Enticing and flavorful creamy dressings
- ◆ Show-stopping dressings made with cheese

Once you've started making your own salad dressings, you'll never go back to bottled versions. It's so easy to make a variety of dressings that are distinctive as well as delicious.

Dry soup mixes can be the backbone of dressings. They are the framework on which you can improvise and add additional flavors.

The dressings in this chapter are all-purpose dressings for any mixture of fresh greens. They are also delicious on some sliced ripe tomatoes.

## Coat with Care

The first step to a great salad is to select the best lettuces available. You can make your salad as simple as a wedge of crispy iceberg or as complex as small bits of many different "designer greens" like radicchio and mâche.

The next step is to clean the leaves to rid them of all grit. Rinse leaves under cold running water but don't soak them. Soaking can wilt the

**Ellen on Edibles** _____

**Drizzle** is a fancy term for pouring a small amount of liquid slowly over a large area rather than pouring it all in one place. You can drizzle with a measuring cup, but the liquid is more likely to scatter over more territory if you use a spoon.

greens, especially tender ones. While purists maintain that wet leaves should be patted dry with paper towels, I think a salad spinner does a fine job in far less time.

A key to a well-dressed salad is to use a large bowl so the greens can be tossed with the dressing. *Drizzle* a little bit of dressing over the greens and toss them with two spoons or salad servers. The objective is to coat the greens but not drown them. You can always add more dressing, but you can't subtract any.

# Versatile Vinaigrettes

A vinaigrette salad dressing used to be primarily a lip-pursing concoction to toss with greens. Nowadays, chic chefs are also using vinaigrette dressings as sauces for grilled or broiled foods.

The basic proportions for a vinaigrette are three parts oil to one part acid. The acid can be any sort of vinegar, lemon juice, or lime juice.

One of the benefits of making your own vinaigrette is that you can cut back on the oil if you're counting calories or fat grams. You can use stock, vegetable juice, or a nonacidic fruit juice such as orange juice or pineapple juice for up to half the oil.

It takes time for the dehydrated ingredients in the mix to blend into the dressing, so if you want to use it right away, allow it to sit at room temperature for 30 minutes. Unlike commercial vinaigrettes, the oil becomes solid when dressings are refrigerated. If this has happened, let the dressing sit at room temperature for 1 hour before serving.

## The Least You Need to Know

- You can substitute stock or juice for up to half the oil in a vinaigrette dressing to cut back on the calories and fat.

- Substituting mayonnaise for some of the oil in a vinaigrette dressing creates a creamy dressing with the same flavor.

- Although all dressings should be stored in the refrigerator, it's best to allow vinaigrette dressings to sit at room temperature for 1 hour before serving to allow the oil to become liquid.

- Creamy dressing should be served directly from the refrigerator.

- Use "yogurt cheese" in place of sour cream in a creamy dressing to cut back on the fat.

# Basic Mustard Vinaigrette

Prep time: less than 10 minutes    •    Makes 2 cups

4 garlic cloves, finely chopped

2 shallots, finely chopped

1 envelope roasted garlic herb soup mix

2 TB. herbes de Provence, or 2 tsp. dried thyme, 2 tsp. dried oregano, and 2 tsp. dried rosemary

2 TB. Dijon-style mustard

1 TB. granulated sugar

½ cup white wine or red wine vinegar

Freshly ground black pepper to taste

1½ cups olive oil

Combine garlic, shallots, soup mix, herbes de Provence, mustard, sugar, vinegar, and black pepper in a jar with a tight-fitting lid. Shake well. Add oil and shake well again.

Allow dressing to sit for 30 minutes if using immediately or refrigerate for later use. Once refrigerated, dressing will keep for up to 4 days. Allow it to sit at room temperature for 1 hour before using.

 **Mix Mastery**

When making dressings, you want to make sure the soup mix and other seasonings are thoroughly dissolved, so shake ingredients well before adding the oil because seasonings do not dissolve in oil.

# Tomato Balsamic Vinaigrette

Prep time: less than 10 minutes    •    Makes 2 cups

2 shallots, finely chopped

2 garlic cloves, pushed through a garlic press

1 envelope tomato with basil soup mix

½ cup balsamic vinegar

1 TB. dried basil

1 TB. dried oregano

Freshly ground black pepper to taste

1½ cups olive oil

Combine shallots, garlic, soup mix, vinegar, basil, oregano, and black pepper in a jar with a tight-fitting lid. Shake well. Add oil and shake well again.

Allow dressing to sit for 30 minutes if using immediately or refrigerate for later use. Once refrigerated, dressing will keep for up to 4 days. Allow it to sit at room temperature for 1 hour before using.

 **Mix Mastery**

The way you treat garlic determines the intensity of its flavor. Pushing the cloves through a garlic press is the way to extract the most punch. Mincing the cloves once they're peeled produces a milder flavor.

# Creamy Herbed Vinaigrette

Prep time: less than 10 minutes • Makes 2 cups

½ cup cider vinegar

1 envelope roasted garlic herb soup mix

3 scallions, trimmed and finely chopped

2 TB. chopped fresh parsley

2 TB. chopped fresh dill or 2 tsp. dried

Freshly ground black pepper to taste

1 cup mayonnaise

½ cup olive oil

Combine vinegar, soup mix, scallions, parsley, dill, and pepper in a jar with a tight-fitting lid. Shake well. Add mayonnaise and oil, and shake well again.

Allow dressing to sit for 30 minutes if using immediately or refrigerate for later use. Once refrigerated, dressing will keep for up to 4 days. Allow it to sit at room temperature for 1 hour before using.

# Creamy Caesar Dressing

Prep time: less than 10 minutes • Makes 2 cups

1 egg

½ cup lemon juice

4 garlic cloves, pushed through a garlic press

2 TB. Dijon-style mustard

1 TB. anchovy paste (optional)

1 envelope savory herb with garlic soup mix

Freshly ground black pepper to taste

¼ cup mayonnaise

1 cup olive oil

**Dry and Droll** _____
Popular Caesar salad has nothing to do with Rome or its legendary emperor. Restaurateur Caesar Cardini created this salad at his restaurant in Tijuana, Mexico, in 1924. The salad became popular with his Hollywood clientele and was later popularized at such Hollywood bastions as Chasen's.

Bring a small saucepan of water to a boil over high heat. Place egg in boiling water for 60 seconds. Remove egg from the pan with a slotted spoon, and break it into a jar with a tight-fitting lid. Add lemon juice, garlic, mustard, anchovy paste, if using, soup mix, and black pepper. Shake well. Add mayonnaise and oil, and shake well again.

Allow dressing to sit for 30 minutes if using immediately or refrigerate for later use. Once refrigerated, dressing will keep for up to 2 days. Allow it to sit at room temperature for 1 hour before using.

# Southwestern Vinaigrette

Prep time: less than 10 minutes  •  Makes 2 cups

1 envelope vegetable soup mix

⅓ cup boiling water

2 shallots, chopped

3 garlic cloves, minced

¼ cup lime juice

2 TB. chili powder

1 TB. ground cumin

1 tsp. dried oregano

Cayenne to taste

1½ cups olive oil

Place soup mix in a jar with a tight-fitting lid. Pour boiling water over it. Stir, cover the jar, and let the mixture sit for 10 minutes. Add shallots, garlic, lime juice, chili powder, cumin, oregano, and cayenne. Shake well. Add oil and shake well again.

Allow dressing to sit for 30 minutes if using immediately or refrigerate for later use. Once refrigerated, dressing will keep for up to 4 days. Allow it to sit at room temperature for 1 hour before using.

## Mix Mastery

The addition of crunchy croutons really dresses up a simple salad, and they are also a good way to use up stale French bread. Cut the bread into ½-inch cubes, and toss them with olive oil and a dry soup mix such as roasted garlic herb or savory herb with garlic. Bake in a preheated 375°F oven for 10 to 15 minutes, stirring the croutons occasionally until they are brown. Once cooled, the croutons can be stored in an airtight plastic bag for up to 1 week.

# Creamy Concoctions

Creamy dressings that deliver gentle flavor are as popular as vinaigrettes. Although traditional dressings are made with sour cream and mayonnaise, it's possible to keep them lighter by using "yogurt cheese."

To make "yogurt cheese," line a strainer with cheesecloth and pour in a quart of nonfat or low-fat plain yogurt. Allow the mixture to drain over a mixing bowl in the refrigerator for at least 8 hours. You'll find that the liquid has dripped through and you now have about half the original volume of yogurt, which has the consistency of cottage cheese and a flavor akin to sour cream.

Unlike vinaigrette dressings, creamy dressings should be used directly from the refrigerator. There is no oil that needs to liquefy before tossing with the salad.

# Cucumber and Feta Dressing

Prep time: less than 10 minutes • Makes 2 cups

1 envelope leek soup mix

2 cucumbers, peeled, seeded, and cut into a 1-inch *dice*

¼ lb. feta cheese

1 cup sour cream or yogurt cheese

2 garlic cloves

3 TB. chopped fresh dill or 1 TB. dried

Freshly ground black pepper to taste

 **Ellen on Edibles**

To **dice** means to cut ingredients into small cubes. Sometimes the size of the pieces is mentioned in the recipe, but as a general rule, a small dice is ¼ inch, a medium dice is ½ inch, and a large dice is ¾ to 1 inch.

Combine soup mix, cucumbers, feta, sour cream, and garlic in a food processor fitted with a steel blade or in a blender. Purée until smooth. Stir in dill, and season dressing with black pepper to taste.

Refrigerate dressing for at least 30 minutes before serving. Once refrigerated, dressing will keep for up to 4 days.

# Blue Cheese Dressing

Prep time: less than 10 minutes • Makes 2 cups

1 cup mayonnaise

½ cup sour cream or yogurt cheese

1 envelope leek soup mix

3 TB. white wine vinegar

1 cup crumbled blue cheese

Freshly ground black pepper to taste

 **Mix Mastery**

Add both flavor and color to a tossed salad with edible flowers such as nasturtiums and herb blossoms or fresh herbs, such as dill, thyme, and basil.

Combine mayonnaise, sour cream, soup mix, and vinegar in a mixing bowl. Whisk well. Add crumbled blue cheese, and season dressing with black pepper to taste. Whisk well again.

Refrigerate dressing for at least 30 minutes before serving. Once refrigerated, dressing will keep for up to 4 days.

# Green Goddess Dressing

Prep time: less than 10 minutes  •  Makes 2 cups

1 envelope cream of spinach soup mix

½ cup boiling water

1¾ cups mayonnaise

¼ cup tarragon vinegar or white wine vinegar

¼ cup minced fresh parsley

¼ cup minced fresh chives or 2 TB. dried

1 TB. chopped fresh tarragon or 1 tsp. dried

1 TB. anchovy paste (optional)

Freshly ground black pepper to taste

Place soup mix in a small mixing bowl, and pour boiling water over it. Stir well, cover the bowl, and let mixture sit for 10 minutes.

Transfer mixture to a food processor fitted with a steel blade or a blender. Add mayonnaise, vinegar, parsley, chives, tarragon, anchovy paste, if using, and black pepper. Purée until smooth.

Refrigerate dressing for at least 30 minutes before serving. Once refrigerated, dressing will keep for up to 4 days.

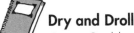

**Dry and Droll**

Green Goddess Dressing was invented at San Francisco's Palace Hotel (now the Sheraton-Palace) as an honor for visiting actor George Arliss, who was in the city appearing in William Archer's play, *The Green Goddess*.

# Parmesan Peppercorn Dressing

Prep time: less than 10 minutes  •  Makes 2 cups

¾ cup mayonnaise

¾ cup sour cream or yogurt cheese

1 envelope roasted garlic herb soup mix

½ cup grated Parmesan cheese

1 TB. coarsely ground black pepper or to taste

**Mix Mastery** _____

Dressings should be refrigerated for at least 30 minutes before using them to allow the ingredients in the mix to fully dissolve and rehydrate in the liquid.

Combine mayonnaise, sour cream, soup mix, Parmesan cheese, and black pepper in a mixing bowl. Whisk well.

Refrigerate dressing for at least 30 minutes before serving. Once refrigerated, dressing will keep for up to 4 days.

# Herbed Ranch Dressing

Prep time: less than 10 minutes  •  Makes 2 cups

1 cup mayonnaise

½ cup sour cream or yogurt cheese

½ cup milk

1 envelope ranch soup mix

3 garlic cloves, pushed through a garlic press

2 TB. herbes de Provence, or 2 tsp. dried thyme, 2 tsp. dried basil, and 2 tsp. dried oregano

Freshly ground black pepper to taste

**Dry and Droll** _____

The Henson family's Hidden Valley Ranch Company is the most likely parentage for ranch dressing, which always has an underlying flavor of buttermilk along with some seasonings. The company started marketing the dressing as a dry mix right after World War II.

Combine mayonnaise, sour cream, milk, soup mix, garlic, herbes de Provence, and black pepper in a mixing bowl. Whisk well.

Refrigerate dressing for at least 30 minutes before serving. Once refrigerated, dressing will keep for 4 days.

# Part

# In the Beginning

You can call them hors d'oeuvres if you're having a fancy cocktail party. You can call them nibbles if you're sitting around on the sofa watching a game with friends. Whatever you call them, this part of the book contains recipes for snack foods.

Naturally there are dips—both hot and cold. Dips are such an important use of dry soup mixes that it lists them right on the front of the box. Dips' first cousins are cheese spreads and cheese balls. You'll find them here, too, along with a wide range of hot and cold hors d'oeuvres (or nibbles, if you prefer).

# Chapter 6

# Divine Dips

## In This Chapter

- ◆ Variations on classic cold dips
- ◆ International dips with flair
- ◆ Warm dips for chilly nights

Look at a box of dry soup mix. Sometimes dips are listed as a use for the mix even before soups. And why not? In 1954, just two years after Lipton introduced its onion soup mix, mixing an envelope of onion soup mix with a pint of sour cream revolutionized entertaining, making it easy to create a tempting hors d'oeuvre.

In this chapter, you'll discover some easy ways to transform basic dips through minor additions. You'll also find recipes for some dips and spreads that will be so good no one will believe they started with an envelope of soup mix.

## Dip Sticks

Hearty potato chips and crunchy corn chips will always hold their place of honor next to the dip bowl. After all, folks don't call those serving sets "chip and dip servers" for nothing. But you might want to vary your appetizer selections and try a few of these easy-to-make options.

**Dry and Droll** _____

Potato chips are the all-American snack. Originally dubbed Saratoga Chips, they were invented in the town of Saratoga, New York, during the mid-nineteenth century. Legend has it that a chef created them for industrial tycoon Cornelius Vanderbilt, who had requested very thinly sliced fried potatoes.

## The Least You Need to Know

- You can serve dips sooner if you combine the mix with boiling water to soften the dry ingredients before completing the recipe.
- Blanche sturdy vegetables like broccoli and asparagus before serving them with dips.
- You can add a variety of ingredients to basic dip recipes to make them special.
- Keep dips hot in small slow cookers, fondue pots, or chafing dishes.

# Pita Toasts

Prep time: less than 10 minutes  •  Cooking time: 10 to 15 minutes  •  Makes 5 dozen pieces

6 white or whole-wheat pita breads

¼ lb. butter, melted

½ envelope roasted garlic herb soup mix

Preheat the oven to 375°F, and line a baking sheet with aluminum foil. Cut each pita bread into five sections and separate the two layers of each section. Arrange the pieces on the baking sheet with the rough side up, in a single layer.

Mix butter and soup mix in a small bowl. Lightly brush pita pieces with butter mixture using a pastry brush. Bake pitas for 10 to 15 minutes or until lightly browned and crisp. Remove the pan from the oven, and store pita toasts in an airtight container once they have cooled.

Pita toasts can be kept at room temperature for up to 1 week.

**Mix Mastery** _____
Pastry brushes are expensive, but paint brushes are cheap. Any natural-bristle paint brush can be used as a pastry brush.

# Crostini

Prep time: less than 10 minutes  •  Cooking time: 10 minutes  •  Makes 3 dozen

1 loaf French or Italian bread, thinly sliced

½ cup olive oil

½ cup grated Parmesan cheese

Preheat the oven to 375°F and line a baking sheet with aluminum foil. Arrange bread slices on the baking sheet in a single layer and brush them lightly with olive oil. Sprinkle slices with Parmesan cheese.

Bake toasts for 10 to 12 minutes or until lightly browned and crisp. Remove the pan from the oven and store toasts in an airtight container once they have cooled.

Toasts can be kept at room temperature for up to 1 week.

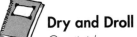

**Dry and Droll** _____
Crostini (pronounced *crow-STEE-nee*), thin slices of bread that are coated with oil before they are baked, are the Italian version of melba toast. In Italian the name comes from the Latin word *crusta*, which means "crust."

# The Crudité Collection

If you're cutting back on calories and fat, an easy way to still enjoy a luscious dip is to use crunchy veggies instead of chips. The pieces should be long enough to be held and dipped but not so long that you get stuck with a lot of veggie left to eat after the dip is gone. And remember—for the sake of hygiene—double-dipping is not acceptable!

Most supermarkets sell baby carrots that are already peeled and celery cut into dipping-size pieces. If you're in a big hurry, add a pint of cherry tomatoes to the mix, and your platter is complete.

Other vegetables make great raw additions. Why not try leaves of Belgian endive; peeled jicama cut into thin strips; and spears of cucumber, zucchini, and yellow squash.

Other vegetables should be *blanched* before using, such as broccoli and cauliflower florets, asparagus spears, green beans, and sugar snap or snow peas.

### Ellen on Edibles

**Blanching** literally means "to whiten," but that's not how the term is used in cooking. Blanching is the process of giving vegetables or fruits a short cooking time. In the case of tomatoes and peaches, the purpose of blanching is to loosen the skins so they slip off easily. In the case of green vegetables, the goal is to cook them just until they are slightly tender but still crisp and to set them a bright green. This also makes their raw flavor more palatable.

To blanch these vegetables, place them in a pot of boiling water. Boil delicate snow peas no more than 30 seconds. Sturdier vegetables like broccoli and asparagus should be boiled for 90 seconds. Drain them and then plunge them into a bowl of ice water for 30 seconds. Remove and drain immediately. This quick chilling stops the cooking action and sets the bright green color.

# Dippity-Do

Dips are easy and can be innovative. You don't need a stove to make them. A mixing bowl and spoon will suffice for making some, while a food processor speeds up preparation of others.

Most recipes tell you to refrigerate mix-based dips for at least a few hours before using them to allow time for dehydrated vegetables and seasonings in the mix to absorb liquid and regain their texture. The larger the pieces, the longer it takes them to turn from crunchy and dry to moist and tender.

Here's a way to shortcut this time: Place the soup mix in a small bowl, and pour ½ cup boiling water over it. Stir well and cover the bowl with a cover or plastic wrap. Allow it to sit for 10 minutes, and then make the dip. The dip will be ready to eat after it has chilled for only 20 minutes.

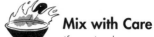

**Mix with Care** _____
If you're heating water in a microwave oven, always use a glass or plastic cup that is at least three times the volume of the liquid, and never cover it.

# Dill and Scallion Dip

Prep time: less than 10 minutes   •   Makes 3 cups

1 cup sour cream or yogurt cheese

1 cup mayonnaise

1 envelope leek soup mix

3 garlic cloves, minced

½ cup lemon juice

½ cup finely chopped scallions

⅓ cup finely chopped fresh dill or 3 TB. dried

Freshly ground black pepper to taste

Combine sour cream, mayonnaise, soup mix, garlic, and lemon juice in a food processor fitted with a steel blade or in a blender. Purée until smooth, and scrape mixture into a mixing bowl. Stir in scallions and dill, and whisk well. Season dip with black pepper to taste.

Dip can be stored in the refrigerator up to 5 days, tightly covered.

# Blue Cheese Dip

Prep time: less than 10 minutes • Makes 3 cups

1½ cups mayonnaise

1 cup sour cream

¼ cup white wine vinegar

1 envelope roasted garlic herb soup mix

½ lb. crumbled blue cheese

Freshly ground black pepper to taste

**Mix Mastery**

Blue cheese encompasses an entire family of cheeses that have a sharp taste and a naturally occurring vein of blue mold. In place of blue cheese you can substitute Italian Gorgonzola or English Stilton.

Combine mayonnaise, sour cream, vinegar, and soup mix in a mixing bowl. Whisk well. Stir in blue cheese, and whisk well again. Season dip with black pepper to taste.

Dip can be stored in the refrigerator for up to 5 days, tightly covered.

# Bloody Mary Dip

Prep time: less than 10 minutes • Makes 3 cups

2 cups sour cream

1 cup mayonnaise

¼ cup lemon juice

¼ cup horseradish

2 TB. Worcestershire sauce

1 envelope tomato with basil soup mix

1 TB. celery seed

1 to 2 tsp. red pepper sauce, or to taste

**Dry and Droll**

The "Bloody Mary" name originated in Paris in the Roaring Twenties. Later, in 1933, it was exported to this side of the Atlantic when tycoon Vincent Astor hired bartender Pete Petiot to run the King Cole Bar at New York's St. Regis Hotel.

Combine sour cream, mayonnaise, lemon juice, horseradish, Worcestershire sauce, soup mix, celery seed, and red pepper sauce in a mixing bowl. Whisk well.

Dip can be stored in the refrigerator for up to 5 days, tightly covered.

# Mediterranean Feta Dip

Prep time: less than 10 minutes  •  Makes 3 cups

2½ cups sour cream or yogurt cheese

¼ cup lemon juice

1 envelope vegetable soup mix

¼ lb. *feta* cheese

1 tomato, cored, seeded, and finely chopped

1 cucumber, peeled and finely chopped

¼ cup finely chopped red onion

1 TB. dried oregano

Freshly ground black pepper to taste

Combine sour cream, lemon juice, soup mix, and feta in a food processor fitted with a steel blade or in a blender. Purée until smooth.

Scrape mixture into a container, and stir in tomato, cucumber, onion, and oregano. Season dip with black pepper to taste.

Dip can be stored in the refrigerator for up to 5 days, tightly covered.

**Ellen on Edibles**

**Feta** is a classic Greek cheese traditionally made from sheep's milk or goat's milk. It is cured and stored in its own salty brine and has a tangy flavor. It crumbles easily to top salads or to mix into dips and also melts well in sauces.

# Mustard Dip

Prep time: less than 10 minutes  •  Makes 3 cups

2 cups sour cream

½ cup mayonnaise

¼ cup Dijon-style mustard

1 envelope golden onion soup mix

1 TB. herbes de Provence, or 1 tsp. dried thyme, 1 tsp. dried rosemary, and 1 tsp. dried basil

Freshly ground black pepper to taste

Combine sour cream, mayonnaise, mustard, soup mix, and herbes de Provence in a mixing bowl. Whisk well. Season dip with black pepper, and whisk well again.

Dip can be stored in the refrigerator for up to 5 days, tightly covered.

# Creamy Salsa Dip

Prep time: less than 10 minutes • Makes 3 cups

2 (8-oz.) pkg. cream cheese, softened

½ cup half-and-half

1 envelope vegetable soup mix

1 cup homemade tomato salsa or refrigerated salsa from the produce aisle of the super-market

½ cup chopped fresh cilantro

Red pepper sauce to taste

 **Mix with Care**

For this recipe, it's important to use the chunky refrigerated salsa usually found in the produce departments of supermarkets rather than jarred salsa. You're after the fresh chopped vegetables.

Combine cream cheese, half-and-half, and soup mix in a food processor fitted with a steel blade or in a blender. Purée until smooth. Scrape mixture into a mixing bowl and stir in salsa and cilantro. Stir well. Season dip with red pepper sauce.

Dip can be stored in the refrigerator for up to 5 days, tightly covered.

# Spinach Dip

Prep time: less than 10 minutes • Makes 3 cups

1 (10-oz.) pkg. frozen chopped spinach, cooked according to package directions

1 envelope cream of spinach soup mix

2 cups sour cream

1 cup mayonnaise

3 TB. lemon juice

4 scallions, trimmed and finely chopped

¼ cup chopped fresh basil or 2 TB. dried

½ cup grated Parmesan cheese

Freshly ground black pepper to taste

Place spinach in a strainer over a mixing bowl and press with the back of a spoon to extract as much water as possible. Reserve liquid and set spinach aside.

Pour reserved liquid into a measuring cup and add enough water to make ½ cup. Bring liquid to a boil and stir in soup mix. Stir well and let mixture sit for 10 minutes.

Combine soup mixture with spinach, sour cream, mayonnaise, lemon juice, scallions, basil, and Parmesan cheese. Stir well. Season dip with black pepper to taste.

Dip can be stored in the refrigerator for up to 5 days, tightly covered.

# Spreads with International Interest

No national cuisine can claim dips and spreads as their own. People around the world love these appetizers. Sour cream, mayonnaise, and yogurt are the most common dip bases in this country, and you'll see cuisines around the world use healthful vegetables as an alternative.

## Tuscan White Bean Dip

Prep time: less than 10 minutes   •   Makes 3½ cups

2 (15-oz.) cans white cannellini beans or navy beans, drained and rinsed

4 garlic cloves

¼ cup olive oil

¼ cup lemon juice

1 envelope roasted garlic herb soup mix

½ cup chopped fresh parsley

2 red bell peppers, seeds and ribs removed, and finely chopped, or ½ cup chopped pimiento

Freshly ground black pepper to taste

Combine beans, garlic, olive oil, lemon juice, and soup mix in a food processor fitted with a steel blade or in a blender. Purée until smooth.

Scrape mixture into a mixing bowl and stir in parsley and red bell pepper. Stir well and season spread with black pepper to taste.

Dip can be stored in the refrigerator for up to 5 days, tightly covered.

### Mix Mastery

Although it's not totally fat-free, this white bean spread is relatively low in fat. Serve it in place of butter or olive oil on the dinner table with bread, the way they do in Italy.

# Hummus

Prep time: less than 10 minutes   •   Makes 3½ cups

2 (15-oz.) cans chickpeas (garbanzo beans), rinsed and drained

4 garlic cloves

½ cup *tahini*, well stirred

¼ cup lemon juice

½ cup mayonnaise

1 envelope roasted garlic herb soup mix

¼ cup finely chopped fresh parsley

Freshly ground black pepper to taste

**Ellen on Edibles**

**Tahini** is a Middle Eastern paste made from sesame seeds. It's what gives hummus its characteristic sesame flavor. The oil always rises to the top, so it's important to stir it well before measuring it.

Combine chickpeas, garlic, tahini, lemon juice, mayonnaise, and soup mix in a food processor fitted with a steel blade or in a blender. Purée until smooth.

Scrape mixture into a mixing bowl, and stir in parsley. Stir well and season spread with black pepper to taste.

Hummus can be stored in the refrigerator for up to 5 days, tightly covered.

# Baba Ghanoush

Prep time: less than 20 minutes   •   Makes 3 cups

2 (1½-lb.) eggplants

¼ cup tahini, well stirred

3 garlic cloves

¼ cup lemon juice

1 envelope vegetable soup mix

3 TB. chopped fresh parsley

Freshly ground black pepper to taste

Preheat the oven to 450°F and line a baking sheet with aluminum foil. Prick eggplants with the tines of a meat fork and place them on the baking sheet. Bake for 20 minutes, turn gently with tongs, and bake for an additional 20 minutes. Remove from the oven. When cool enough to handle, cut them in half and scrape out pulp.

Combine pulp, tahini, garlic, lemon juice, and soup mix in a food processor fitted with a steel blade or in a blender. Purée until smooth.

Scrape mixture into a mixing bowl and stir in parsley. Stir well and season spread with black pepper to taste.

Baba ghanoush can be stored in the refrigerator for up to 5 days, tightly covered.

# Guacamole

Prep time: less than 15 minutes    •    Makes 2½ cups

1 envelope vegetable soup mix

½ cup boiling water

½ cup sour cream

2 TB. lime juice

4 ripe avocados, peeled, pitted and mashed

1 tomato, cored, seeded, and finely chopped

½ small red onion, finely chopped

1 jalapeño or serrano chili, seeds and ribs removed, and finely chopped

½ cup chopped fresh cilantro

Place soup mix in a mixing bowl and pour boiling water over it. Stir well, cover the bowl, and allow soup to sit for 10 minutes. Add sour cream and lime juice, and stir well. Add avocados, tomato, onion, jalapeño, and cilantro. Stir well.

Press a sheet of plastic wrap directly onto the surface of dip, and refrigerate until cold. Dip can be refrigerated for up to 2 days; keep the plastic wrap on the surface to prevent discoloration.

### Mix Mastery

To determine if an avocado is ready to eat, insert a wooden toothpick into the stem end; if it can be inserted with ease, the avocado is ready. After cutting the avocado apart, if you discover that it is not yet ripe, coat the exposed surfaces with butter, margarine, or mayonnaise and allow it to continue ripening at room temperature.

# Hot Options

Twirling strings of luscious, gooey cheese from a bread cube or spearing chunks of sausage in a dip are both images of great communal party treats. Although heat is needed to keep these treats ready to eat, that's not a problem.

The easiest way to keep hot dips hot is by using a 1-quart slow cooker. It tends itself. If the dip is uncovered, set the cooker on low rather than on the keep-warm setting. Other heating options are fondue pots and chafing dishes. Because these have external fuel sources, make sure to place them on heat-proof trays or platters rather than right on table tops.

Bread cubes cut from crusty French or Italian bread are the best choices for hot dips. If you're going the chip route, be sure to use sturdy corn chips or thick potato chips made for dipping.

# Pizza Dip

Prep time: less than 15 minutes • Cooking time: 15 minutes • Makes 3½ cups

1 lb. mild or hot bulk Italian sausage

2 cups tomato sauce

1 envelope tomato with basil soup mix

4 cups (1 lb.) grated mozzarella cheese

1 tsp. dried oregano

1 tsp. dried basil

Freshly ground black pepper to taste

### Mix with Care

When making dips with cheese, stay in the kitchen and stir the pot frequently. Cheese can scorch easily, and the burnt flavor will permeate the whole dip.

Heat a medium skillet over medium-high heat. Add sausage and cook, breaking up any lumps with a fork or the back of a spoon, for 6 to 10 minutes or until it is no longer pink and cooked through. Remove sausage from the skillet with a slotted spoon and transfer it to a saucepan. Add tomato sauce, soup mix, mozzarella, oregano, and basil to the saucepan. Stir well and season with black pepper.

Bring mixture to a boil over medium heat, stirring frequently. Cook, stirring, for 5 minutes or until cheese is melted and mixture has thickened.

# Chili Con Queso

Prep time: less than 15 minutes • Makes 3½ cups

1 cup refrigerated salsa from the supermarket produce aisle, undrained

1 envelope vegetable soup mix

4 cups (1 lb.) shredded Monterey Jack or mild cheddar cheese

4 scallions, trimmed and finely chopped

1 TB. chili powder

2 tsp. ground cumin

Cayenne to taste

Combine salsa, soup mix, cheese, scallions, chili powder, cumin, and cayenne in a saucepan. Stir well.

Bring mixture to a boil over medium heat, stirring frequently. Cook, stirring, for 5 minutes or until cheese is melted and mixture has thickened.

# Refried Bean Dip

Prep time: less than 15 minutes • Cooking time: 10 minutes • Makes 3½ cups

1 (15-oz.) can refried beans

2 cups (½ lb.) shredded Monterey Jack or cheddar cheese

4 scallions, trimmed and thinly sliced

2 tomatoes, cored, seeded, and finely diced

2 garlic cloves, minced

1 (4-oz.) can chopped green chilies

1 envelope roasted garlic herb soup mix

2 TB. chili powder

Cayenne to taste

Combine refried beans, cheese, scallions, tomato, garlic, chilies, soup mix, chili powder, and cayenne in a saucepan. Stir well. Bring mixture to a boil over medium heat, stirring frequently. Reduce heat to low and cook for 10 minutes, stirring frequently, until cheese is melted and mixture has thickened.

 **Mix Mastery**

If you want to serve this dip as the topping for nachos, add half the cheese to the recipe. After the dip is cooked, spread it on large tortilla chips, sprinkle them with the remaining cheese, and pop the nachos under a preheated broiler until the cheese is melted and brown.

# Hot Broccoli Dip

Prep time: less than 15 minutes • Cooking time: 40 minutes • Makes 3 cups

1 (10-oz.) pkg. frozen chopped broccoli, thawed and cooked according to package directions

1 cup mayonnaise

1 cup sour cream

1 cup (¼ lb.) shredded Swiss cheese

1 envelope roasted garlic herb soup mix

Freshly ground black pepper to taste

Preheat the oven to 350°F and spray a 1-quart casserole with vegetable oil spray. Add broccoli, mayonnaise, sour cream, cheese, soup mix, and black pepper. Stir well.

Bake dip uncovered for 40 minutes, stirring occasionally, until hot and bubbly and cheese is melted.

**Mix Mastery**

This is a very versatile hot dip. In place of the broccoli, you can use a package of frozen chopped spinach or artichoke hearts. Chop the artichoke hearts finely before adding them to the mixture.

# Welsh Rarebit Dip

Prep time: less than 15 minutes • Cooking time: 15 minutes • Makes 3 cups

1 (12-oz.) can beer

4 cups (1 lb.) grated sharp cheddar cheese

1 envelope golden onion soup mix

1 TB. prepared mustard

2 tomatoes, cored, seeded, and finely chopped

Cayenne to taste

1 TB. cornstarch

2 TB. cold water

### Dry and Droll

Welsh Rarebit, sometimes called Welsh Rabbit, is a classic dish served in English pubs for high tea. Unlike afternoon tea, which was for the gentry, high tea was the supper for the working class because their main meal of the day was at noontime.

Combine beer, cheese, soup mix, mustard, tomatoes, and cayenne in a saucepan. Stir well. Bring to a boil over medium heat, stirring frequently. Reduce heat to low and cook for 10 minutes, stirring frequently, until cheese is melted and mixture is bubbly.

Mix cornstarch and water in a small cup and stir mixture into the pot. Simmer for 3 minutes or until mixture has thickened.

# Chapter 7

# Cold Creations

## In This Chapter

- ◆ Make-ahead cheese balls and spreads
- ◆ Classy canapés
- ◆ Wraps to roll and slice

There is a whole world of cold hors d'oeuvres and appetizers beyond the dip bowl. In this chapter, you'll find easy recipes for some of them.

Cheese balls and spreads are great at parties, especially because you can make them in advance and freeze them. They thaw quickly, so you have them as an insurance policy for impromptu entertaining.

Canapés today can take the form of a topping for toasts, or they can be pinwheels of goodies rolled up in a flour tortilla and then sliced into bite-size pieces.

## Say Cheese

Cheese spreads and cheese balls are always popular, and soup mixes can add a dimension of flavor to them without any additional work. Dips usually use mayonnaise and sour cream as their base which makes them sturdier, but cheese balls are made with cream cheese or goat's milk cheese that regains its firmness after chilling.

The recipes in this chapter are all best if they are made a day in advance. But the good news is that they all can be frozen, so you can start your "party prep" weeks before the event.

## Presentation Pointers

You can always just pack a cheese spread into a decorative crock and surround it with crackers on a platter, but here are two easy ways to make your creations more decorative.

The first is to line a mixing bowl with plastic wrap and pack the spread into the wrap. Once the spread is chilled and hard, invert and unmold it on a platter and decorate the top as you'd like with fresh chopped herbs or with some of the ingredients that went into the spread.

The second method is to sprinkle some decorative ingredients onto a sheet of plastic wrap or wax paper and form the cheese mixture into a cylinder extending down the center of the wrap on top of the decorations. Using the paper as a guide, form the mixture into a smooth cylinder and refrigerate or freeze it in that format.

## Eating Occasions

In addition to serving cheese spreads as an "assemble-it-yourself" hors d'oeuvre, here are some other ways you can use them, as both appetizers and accents to meals:

**Mix with Care**

Although a hard cheese ball is excellent for presentation, you will have problems spreading it or piping it unless you soften it first. Then the finished creations can go back into the refrigerator.

- On toasts as a garnish for tossed salads
- As fillings for tea sandwiches
- Piped through a pastry bag onto crackers
- As condiments on sandwiches in place of mayonnaise or mustard
- Spread on toast and broiled until cheese is melted for hot canapés

## The Least You Need to Know

- Cheese spreads and cheese balls can be made in advance and frozen.
- Cheese balls have primarily cream cheese or goat's milk cheese as a base so they remain firm.
- Tortilla roll-ups can be made in assembly-line fashion and then cut into pinwheels as hors d'oeuvres.
- Bruschetta are slices of toast that are topped with a cold chopped food.

# Pimiento Cheese

Prep time: less than 15 minutes   •   Makes 3 cups

1 envelope vegetable soup mix

½ cup boiling water

2 garlic cloves, minced

3 cups (¾ lb.) grated sharp cheddar cheese, preferably orange

4 oz. cream cheese, softened

¼ cup mayonnaise

1 (4-oz.) jar pimientos, drained and chopped

2 TB. finely chopped fresh parsley

Cayenne to taste

¼ cup chopped fresh parsley for garnish

Place soup mix in a mixing bowl, and pour boiling water over it. Stir well, cover the bowl, and allow soup to sit for 10 minutes. Transfer to a food processor fitted with a steel blade. Add garlic, cheddar, cream cheese, and mayonnaise and purée until smooth. Add pimientos, parsley, and cayenne to the work bowl, and pulse on and off to blend.

Alternately, uncover dissolved soup mix; add garlic, cheddar, cream cheese, and mayonnaise; and beat on medium speed with an electric mixer until smooth. Then add pimientos, parsley, and cayenne, and mix until distributed.

Pack spread into a crock or use one of the methods listed in the earlier "Presentation Pointers" section. Refrigerate cheese for at least 2 hours or up to 4 days, or freeze it, tightly wrapped, for up to 3 months. Sprinkle the surface with additional chopped parsley before serving.

 **Mix Mastery**

If you're using a food processor to mix the cheeses, there is no need to pre-mince the garlic cloves. They will purée along with the rest of the mixture.

# Easy Garlic Pesto Cheese Ball

Prep time: less than 10 minutes • Makes 3½ cups

1 envelope roasted garlic herb soup mix

2 (8-oz.) pkg. cream cheese, softened

¼ lb. (1 stick) butter, softened

1 (8-oz.) pkg. refrigerated pesto sauce

2 TB. Italian seasoning

Freshly ground black pepper to taste

### Mix Mastery

Here's an alternative way of presenting this spread. Do not add the pesto to the cheese mixture. Place a layer of cheese in a mold and then spread some pesto on top of the cheese layer. Continue in this fashion. When you unmold the cheese, it will have layers.

Combine soup mix, cream cheese, butter, pesto sauce, Italian seasoning, and black pepper in a food processor fitted with a steel blade. Purée until smooth.

Alternately, combine soup mix, cream cheese, butter, pesto sauce, Italian seasoning, and black pepper in a mixing bowl, and beat at medium speed with an electric mixer until smooth.

Pack spread into a crock, or use one of the methods listed in the earlier "Presentation Pointers" section. Refrigerate cheese for at least 2 hours or up to 4 days, or freeze it, tightly wrapped, for up to 3 months. Sprinkle the surface with additional chopped parsley before serving.

# Salmon Spread

Prep time: less than 15 minutes  •  Makes 3½ cups

1 envelope vegetable soup mix

½ cup boiling water

2 (6½-oz.) cans red salmon, drained with skin and bones discarded

2 (8-oz.) pkg. cream cheese, softened

¼ cup lemon juice

¼ cup white horseradish

¼ cup chopped fresh dill or 2 TB. dried

Freshly ground black pepper to taste

Sprigs of fresh dill for garnish

Place soup mix in a mixing bowl and pour boiling water over it. Stir well, cover the bowl, and allow soup to sit for 10 minutes. Transfer soup mixture to a food processor fitted with a steel blade. Add salmon, cream cheese, lemon juice, and horseradish. Purée until smooth. Add dill and black pepper to the work bowl, and pulse on and off to blend.

Alternately, uncover dissolved soup mixture, add salmon, cream cheese, lemon juice, and horseradish, and beat at medium speed with an electric mixer until smooth. Then add dill and black pepper, and mix until distributed.

Pack spread into a crock, or use one of the methods listed in the earlier "Presentation Pointers" section. Refrigerate cheese for at least 2 hours or up to 4 days, or freeze it, tightly wrapped, for up to 3 months. Garnish cheese with dill sprigs before serving.

 **Mix with Care**

It seems that the technology behind pristine canned tuna still eludes salmon canneries. You'll find not only large bones but also tiny, pesky ones, too, as well as skin. The best way to treat canned salmon is to drain it well and then spread it out onto a plate. Then you can pick it over much more easily.

# New England Potted Cheese

Prep time: less than 10 minutes • Makes 3 cups

1 envelope golden onion soup mix

½ cup boiling water

3 cups (¾ lb.) grated cheddar cheese

¼ lb. (1 stick) butter, softened

½ cup ruby port

2 TB. Dijon-style mustard

Freshly ground black pepper to taste

½ cup finely chopped walnuts, toasted in a 350°F oven for 5 minutes, for garnish

### Dry and Droll

Port, a sweet wine fortified with brandy, gets its name from the city of Oporto, Portugal. Because port was very popular with the British nobility, it's not surprising that it gained fans in the American colonies. Traditionally, this port-containing cheese was served at chowder dinners in New England.

Place soup mix in a mixing bowl and pour boiling water over it. Stir well, cover the bowl, and allow soup to sit for 10 minutes. Transfer soup mixture to a food processor fitted with a steel blade. Add cheddar, butter, port, mustard, and black pepper. Purée until smooth.

Alternately, uncover dissolved soup mixture, add cheddar, butter, port, mustard, and black pepper, and beat at medium speed with an electric mixer until smooth.

Pack spread into a crock, or use one of the methods listed in the earlier "Presentation Pointers" section. Refrigerate cheese for at least 2 hours or up to 4 days, or freeze it, tightly wrapped, for up to 3 months. Sprinkle the surface with chopped walnuts before serving.

# Fruity and Nutty Cheese Spread

Prep time: less than 20 minutes   •   Makes 3 cups

1 envelope roasted garlic herb soup mix

1 cup dried cherries or dried cranberries

¾ cup water

1 (8-oz.) pkg. cream cheese, softened

½ lb. goat's milk cheese, softened (or additional cream cheese)

2 TB. lime juice

1 tsp. lime zest

1 cup chopped pecans, toasted in a 350°F oven for 5 minutes

Combine soup mix, dried cherries, and water in a small saucepan. Stir well. Bring to a boil over medium heat. Reduce heat to low, and *simmer* the mixture for 5 to 10 minutes or until reduced in volume to ¼ cup. Allow mixture to cool.

Place cream cheese, goat's milk cheese, and lime juice in a food processor fitted with a steel blade and process until smooth. Alternately, beat with an electric mixer. Stir in fruit mixture, lime zest, and half the pecans.

**Ellen on Edibles** _____
A **simmer** is the lowest point at which water boils. There are bubbles and steam rising, but the liquid is almost all still in the pan.

Pack spread into a crock, or use one of the methods listed in the earlier "Presentation Pointers" section. Refrigerate cheese for at least 2 hours, up to 4 days, or freeze it, tightly wrapped, for up to 3 months. Sprinkle surface with chopped pecans before serving.

# Canapés for Special Occasions

Entertaining today is increasingly informal, but there are some times that you might want to pass some hors d'oeuvres or at least put a platter of individual bite-size pieces on a table. Here are some recipes that fit that bill.

A benefit of these recipes is that they can be produced "assembly-line fashion," so there is little work required for individual presentations.

# Southwest Smoked Salmon Pinwheels

Prep time: less than 20 minutes • Makes 4 dozen

1 envelope vegetable soup mix

½ cup boiling water

1 cup refrigerated salsa from the supermarket produce aisle

1 (8-oz.) pkg. cream cheese, softened

¼ cup chopped fresh cilantro

8 (8-inch) flour tortillas

¾ lb. thinly sliced smoked salmon

3 cups mesclun salad mix or other baby greens, rinsed and dried

Place soup mix in a mixing bowl, and pour boiling water over it. Stir well, cover the bowl, and allow soup to sit for 10 minutes. Place salsa in a strainer, and press with the back of a spoon to extract as much liquid as possible. Uncover soup mixture, and add salsa, cream cheese, and cilantro. Stir well.

Wrap tortillas in plastic wrap, and microwave on high power (100 percent) for 20 to 30 seconds or until soft and pliable.

### Mix Mastery

To serve these pinwheels as a brunch dish instead of as an hors d'oeuvre, tuck in the sides of the tortilla before rolling them. Then cut them in half on the diagonal.

Place tortillas on a work surface in a single layer, and spread each with cream cheese mixture. Arrange smoked salmon slices on bottom half of each tortilla. Place a portion of mesclun on top of salmon.

Roll tortillas firmly but gently, starting at the filled edge. Place rolls on a platter or baking sheet, and refrigerate them for at least 1 hour or up to 6 hours.

Trim off the end of each roll by cutting on the diagonal to remove the portion of tortilla that remains open and empty. Slice each tortilla into 6 slices and serve chilled.

# Smoked Turkey and Sun-Dried Tomato Pinwheels

Prep time: less than 20 minutes   •   Makes 4 dozen

1 envelope roasted garlic herb soup mix

½ cup boiling water

1 (8-oz.) pkg. cream cheese, softened

½ cup finely chopped sun-dried tomatoes

½ cup finely chopped scallions

Freshly ground black pepper to taste

8 (8-inch) flour tortillas

¾ lb. thinly sliced smoked turkey breast

3 cups mesclun salad mix or other baby greens, rinsed and dried

Place soup mix in a mixing bowl, and pour boiling water over it. Stir well, cover the bowl, and allow soup to sit for 10 minutes. Uncover soup mixture, and add cream cheese, sun-dried tomatoes, scallions, and black pepper. Stir well.

Wrap tortillas in plastic wrap, and microwave on high power (100 percent) for 20 to 30 seconds or until soft and pliable.

Place tortillas on a work surface in a single layer, and spread each with cream cheese mixture. Arrange smoked turkey slices on bottom half of each tortilla. Place a portion of mesclun on top of turkey.

Roll tortillas firmly but gently, starting at the filled edge. Place rolls on a platter or baking sheet, and refrigerate for at least 1 hour or up to 6 hours.

Trim off the end of each roll by cutting on the diagonal to remove the portion that remains open and empty. Slice each tortilla into 6 slices and serve chilled.

 **Mix Mastery**

For the roll-up Southwest Smoked Salmon Pinwheels and Smoked Turkey and Sun-Dried Tomato Pinwheels recipes, you can change the meat and use either ham or roast beef, if you prefer.

# Neopolitan Pinwheels

Prep time: less than 20 minutes • Makes 4 dozen

1 envelope tomato with basil soup mix

1 (8-oz.) pkg. cream cheese, softened

½ cup mayonnaise

4 garlic cloves, minced

1 cup (¼ lb.) grated mozzarella cheese

1 TB. *Italian seasoning*

Freshly ground black pepper to taste

1 cup sliced pimiento-stuffed green olives

8 (8-inch) flour tortillas

8 leaves green or red leaf lettuce

½ lb. sliced Mortadella sausage

½ lb. sliced Genoa or hard salami

3 tomatoes, cored, seeded, and chopped

Combine soup mix, cream cheese, mayonnaise, garlic, mozzarella, Italian seasoning, and black pepper in a mixing bowl. Beat mixture with an electric mixer until smooth. Stir in olives and mix well.

Wrap tortillas in plastic wrap, and microwave on high power (100 percent) for 20 to 30 seconds or until soft and pliable.

### Ellen on Edibles

**Italian seasoning** is a pre-mixed blend of dried herbs found in almost all supermarkets. It contains all the characteristic herbs of the cuisine, including oregano, basil, marjoram, thyme, rosemary, savory, and sage.

Place tortillas on a work surface in a single layer, and spread each with cream cheese mixture. Place lettuce leaf on each tortilla, and arrange Mortadella, salami, and tomato on bottom half of each tortilla.

Roll tortillas firmly but gently, starting at the filled edge. Place rolls on a platter or baking sheet, and refrigerate for at least 1 hour or up to 6 hours.

Trim off the end of each roll by cutting on the diagonal to remove the portion of tortilla that that remains open and empty. Slice each tortilla into 6 slices and serve chilled.

# Tomato Bruschetta

Prep time: less than 20 minutes  •  Makes 4 dozen

**For toasts:**

2 loaves French or Italian bread, cut into ½-inch slices

Olive oil spray or vegetable oil spray

**For topping:**

1 envelope roasted garlic herb soup mix

½ cup boiling water

4 cups juiced and seeded diced tomatoes

¼ cup finely chopped red onion

¼ cup chopped fresh basil or 1 TB. dried

¼ cup chopped fresh parsley

3 garlic cloves, minced

¼ cup olive oil

Freshly ground black pepper to taste

Preheat the oven to 400°F, and line two baking sheets with aluminum foil. Arrange bread slices on the baking sheets in a single layer, and spray slices with olive oil spray. Bake toasts for 10 to 12 minutes or until crisp and lightly browned. Toasts can be made up to 4 days in advance and kept in an airtight container once cool.

For the topping, place soup mix in a mixing bowl and pour boiling water over it. Stir well, cover the bowl, and allow soup to sit for 10 minutes. Uncover soup mixture and add tomatoes, onion, basil, parsley, garlic, olive oil, and black pepper. Stir well and refrigerate mixture for 1 hour.

To serve, spoon tomato mixture onto toasts with a slotted spoon.

**Mix Mastery**

The easiest way to prepare tomatoes for this recipe is to cut out the core and then slice the tomatoes in half. Squeeze them over a bowl or the sink, and the seeds will come out easily. Then it's easy to slice them into layers and dice the layers in a stack.

# Garlicky Bean Bruschetta

Prep time: less than 20 minutes • Makes 4 dozen

**For toasts:**

2 loaves French or Italian bread, cut into ½-inch slices

Olive oil spray or vegetable oil spray

**For topping:**

1 envelope roasted garlic herb soup mix

½ cup boiling water

2 (15-oz.) cans cannellini or small white beans, rinsed and drained

½ cup lemon juice

4 garlic cloves, pressed through a garlic press

½ cup finely chopped scallions

½ cup olive oil

Freshly ground black pepper to taste

Preheat the oven to 400°F and line two baking sheets with aluminum foil. Arrange bread slices on the baking sheets in a single layer, and spray slices with olive oil spray. Bake toasts for 10 to 12 minutes or until crisp and lightly browned. Toasts can be made up to 4 days in advance and kept in an airtight container once cool.

**Dry and Droll**

Bruschetta (pronounced *brew-SKEH-tah*) is a generic term in Italian cuisine for slices of toast with a topping. They began as a way to salvage stale bread, but we now frequently buy bread just to make the toast.

For topping, place soup mix in a mixing bowl, and pour boiling water over it. Stir well, cover the bowl, and allow soup to sit for 10 minutes. Uncover soup mixture, and add beans, lemon juice, garlic, scallions, olive oil, and black pepper. Mash bean mixture with a potato masher or the back of a spoon until half the beans are mashed. Stir well and refrigerate mixture for 1 hour.

To serve, spoon bean mixture onto toasts.

# Barbecued Salmon Gravlax with Chili Mayonnaise

Prep time: less than 20 minutes • Makes 8 to 12 servings

**For salmon:**

1½ lb. salmon fillets

1 envelope onion soup mix

½ cup kosher salt

2 cups sugar

2 TB. paprika

2 TB. chili powder

1 TB. ground coriander

1 TB. ground cumin

1 tsp. cayenne

**For Chili Mayonnaise:**

1 cup mayonnaise

2 garlic cloves, minced

2 TB. chili sauce

2 TB. finely chopped onion

1 TB. lemon juice

1 TB. horseradish

2 tsp. chili powder

Crackers or cocktail bread for serving

Rinse salmon fillets under cold water, and pat them dry on paper towels. Combine soup mix, salt, sugar, paprika, chili powder, coriander, cumin, and cayenne in a mixing bowl. Spoon some soup mixture on the bottom of a glass or enameled pan. Place salmon fillets in the pan in a single layer, skin side down. Top with remaining soup mixture. Wrap the pan with plastic wrap and refrigerate it, weighted with cans or heavy plates to press curing mixture into fish. Allow salmon to cure for 3 days, pouring off any accumulated liquid each day.

For Chili Mayonnaise, combine mayonnaise, garlic, chili sauce, onion, lemon juice, horseradish, and chili powder in a mixing bowl. Stir well and refrigerate for at least 6 hours to blend the flavors.

To serve, rinse salmon under cold running water to remove curing coating. Thinly slice salmon on the diagonal, and serve it on crackers or small cocktail breads topped with some Chili Mayonnaise.

### Dry and Droll

Gravlax, "buried fish," is a Scandinavian dish. The combination of salt and sugar cures the fish fillet so it has the texture of a cooked fish, without subjecting it to heat. Gravlax is traditionally flavored with dill, but there are many variations that can be used in the coating, as long as sugar and salt remain the dominant ingredients.

# Chapter 8

# Warm and Wonderful

## In This Chapter

- Hearty hot finger foods
- Nibbles with pastry
- Meatballs to skewer

Hot snacks are a hit at every party, and people don't seem to care if they're a bit messy as long as there's a stack of napkins nearby.

In this chapter, you'll find recipes for hot hors d'oeuvres. Many of these recipes look much more difficult to make than they actually are because we take advantage of various convenience pastries on the market.

## Finger Lickin' Good

Chicken wings and shrimp are foods that are perennially popular with guests of all ages. They are also good choices for entertaining because they can be prepared in advance and kept hot in a slow cooker or reheated in a microwave oven.

## The Least You Need to Know

- ◆ Soup mixes can be used both as a basting sauce and as a marinade for chicken wings.
- ◆ Frozen filo shells, pie crust sheets, and tubes of refrigerated dinner rolls are shortcuts to making hors d'oeuvres encased in pastry.
- ◆ Meatballs can be flavored with soup mixes, and gravy mixes can serve as the basis for hor d'oeuvres sauces.
- ◆ Beef and lamb can be substituted for one another, and ground turkey or chicken can be used in place of pork or veal in meatball recipes.

# Buffalo-Style Chicken Wings

Prep time: less than 15 minutes  •  Cooking time: 15 minutes  •  Makes 2 dozen pieces

12 chicken wings (about 2 lb.)

1 envelope golden onion soup mix

4 garlic cloves

4 TB. butter

2 TB. cider vinegar

2 TB. water

Red pepper sauce to taste

**For serving:**

Blue Cheese Dip (recipe in Chapter 6)

Celery sticks

Preheat the oven broiler, and line a broiler pan with aluminum foil. Cut off wing tips and save them for making stock. Cut each chicken wing into two sections by cutting through the joint. Arrange wing sections in a single layer in the broiler pan.

Combine soup mix, garlic, butter, vinegar, water, and red pepper sauce in a food processor fitted with a steel blade or in a blender. Purée until smooth.

Broil wings for 5 minutes per side or until crisp. Brush ½ butter mixture onto wings, and broil for an additional 2 minutes. Turn wings with tongs, and brush the other side with remaining butter mixture. Broil for an additional 2 minutes. Serve wings with Blue Cheese Dip and celery sticks.

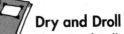

### Dry and Droll

The city of Buffalo, New York, actually celebrates "Chicken Wing Day" on July 29 to commemorate the city's parentage of this now-national sensation. Teressa Bellissimo, owner of the Anchor Bar, invented these wings in 1964 as a treat for her son. She added the blue cheese dressing because it was the bar's house salad dressing.

# Zesty Chicken Wings

Prep time: less than 15 minutes • Cooking time: 40 minutes • Makes 2 dozen

12 chicken wings (about 2 lb.)

1 envelope roasted garlic herb soup mix

¾ cup dry white wine

1 TB. Italian seasoning

Freshly ground black pepper to taste

½ cup olive oil

Cut off wing tips and save them for making stock. Cut each wing into two sections by cutting through the joint. Combine soup mix, wine, Italian seasoning, and black pepper in a heavy resealable plastic bag. Seal the bag, and shake well to dissolve soup mix. Add olive oil and mix well again. Add wing sections, seal the bag, and marinate in the refrigerator for at least 6 hours or up to 18 hours.

**Mix with Care**

To keep food moist, be careful to always use tongs with turning poultry, meat, or fish of any kind. A fork will pierce the food and allow juices to escape.

When you are ready to cook the wings, preheat the oven to 375°F and line a baking pan with aluminum foil. Remove wings from marinade and discard marinade. Arrange wings in the baking pan in a single layer.

Bake wings for 20 minutes or until skin is browned. Turn wings with tongs, and bake for an additional 20 minutes or until wings are crispy.

# New Orleans Barbecued Shrimp

Prep time: less than 20 minutes  •  Cooking time: 10 minutes  •  Makes 6 to 8 servings

2 lb. large raw shrimp, peeled and *deveined*

¼ lb. (1 stick) butter

½ cup olive oil

3 TB. lemon juice

1 envelope roasted garlic herb soup mix

1 TB. dried thyme

1 TB. paprika

2 bay leaves

Cayenne to taste

Slices of French or Italian bread

Rinse shrimp and set aside. Combine butter, olive oil, lemon juice, soup mix, thyme, paprika, bay leaves, and cayenne in a large skillet. Heat mixture over medium heat until butter melts, stirring frequently.

Add shrimp to the pan, and raise heat to high. Cook shrimp, stirring frequently to coat them with sauce, for 5 to 7 minutes or until shrimp are pink and cooked through.

To serve, remove bay leaves from sauce and discard. Place a shrimp and some sauce on each slice of bread.

### Ellen on Edibles

**Deveining** is a simple procedure that should be done to raw shrimp to ensure that the intestinal tract has been removed. Peel the shrimp, and hold it in your hand so you're looking at the top of it. Using a small paring knife, cut through the curved surface of the shrimp from end to end. If there is a vein, it will be a black line in the center. Remove it and rinse the shrimp under cold running water.

# Stuffed Mushrooms

Prep time: less than 20 minutes  •  Cooking time: 30 minutes  •  Makes 2 dozen

24 large mushrooms

1 envelope wild mushroom and chive soup mix

½ cup boiling water

2 TB. butter

2 TB. olive oil

1 small onion, finely chopped

3 garlic cloves, minced

½ cup breadcrumbs

½ cup grated Parmesan cheese

Freshly ground black pepper to taste

Preheat the oven to 400°F, and line a baking sheet with aluminum foil. Rinse mushrooms, trim the bottoms of the stems, and remove the stems and reserve. Arrange mushroom caps on the baking sheet in a single layer, hollow side down, and bake for 10 minutes or until mushrooms exude liquid. Remove the pan from the oven and set aside.

While mushrooms are baking, place soup mix into a mixing bowl and pour boiling water over it. Stir well, cover the bowl, and allow mixture to sit for 10 minutes. Transfer soup mixture to a food processor fitted with a steel blade. Add mushroom stems, and process to chop finely. Alternately, chop finely by hand.

**Mix Mastery**

A melon baller is a good gadget to have around even if you aren't mad for melon. It's a great tool for handling mushrooms because it removes the stem and creates a shallow "bowl" for the stuffing.

Heat butter and oil in a medium skillet over medium heat; add mushroom mixture, onion, and garlic. Cook and stir for 5 minutes or until onion and mushrooms are soft. Stir breadcrumbs, cheese, and black pepper into the pan.

Turn mushroom caps, and mound stuffing in cavities. Bake mushrooms for 20 minutes or until they are soft.

# Crab-Stuffed Mushrooms

Prep time: less than 20 minutes    •    Cooking time: 30 minutes    •    Makes 2 dozen

24 large mushrooms

½ lb. crabmeat, picked over

2 eggs, lightly beaten

¼ cup mayonnaise

¼ cup finely chopped scallions

¼ cup finely chopped red bell pepper

½ envelope (3 TB.) roasted garlic herb soup mix

Cayenne to taste

½ cup breadcrumbs

Preheat the oven to 400°F, and line a baking sheet with aluminum foil. Rinse mushrooms and remove and discard stems. Arrange mushroom caps on the baking sheet in a single layer, hollow side down, and bake for 10 minutes or until mushrooms exude liquid. Remove the pan from the oven and set aside.

While mushrooms are baking, combine crabmeat, eggs, mayonnaise, scallions, red bell pepper, soup mix, and cayenne in a mixing bowl. Stir well. Add breadcrumbs and stir well again.

Turn mushroom caps, and mound stuffing in cavities. Bake mushrooms for 20 minutes or until they are soft.

### Mix with Care

On the list of unpleasant dining experiences is biting into a dish made with succulent crabmeat only to crunch down on a piece of shell or cartilage. The only way to avoid this is to be eagle-eyed when picking over the crabmeat. Spread it out on a dark-colored plate and mix it around with your fingers. That way you'll feel the hard bits and can discard them.

# The Pleasures of Pastry

Hors d'oeuvres encased in pastry are always a hit at a party. They look elegant, and people think you've gone to a lot of trouble to make them—but that doesn't have to be the case. The supermarket has a treasure-trove of options to help you.

One of the best is small filo (also spelled phyllo) cups. Packaged by Athens Foods in a box of 15, you'll find them in the frozen food section. All you have to do is fill and bake them. You can also create great individual hors d'oeuvres with only slightly more work by using refrigerated sheets of pie crust and tubes of dinner rolls.

# Open-Faced Spanakopita

Prep time: less than 20 minutes • Cooking time: 10 minutes • Makes 45 cups

1 (10-oz.) pkg. frozen chopped spinach, thawed and drained

1 envelope cream of spinach soup mix

½ cup heavy cream

½ lb. feta cheese, crumbled

1 egg, lightly beaten

¼ tsp. grated nutmeg

Freshly ground black pepper to taste

3 boxes frozen filo cups

Preheat the oven to 375°F, and line a baking sheet with aluminum foil. Place spinach in a mixing bowl, and stir in soup mix, cream, feta, egg, nutmeg, and black pepper. Stir well and let filling sit for 10 minutes.

Fill filo cups, and arrange them on the baking sheet. Bake pastries for 10 to 12 minutes or until the filling is set.

# English Muffin Pizza Blanca

Prep time: less than 15 minutes • Cooking time: 3 minutes • Makes 4 dozen pieces

8 English muffins

1 envelope leek soup mix

½ cup boiling water

1 cup mayonnaise

½ cup sour cream

1 cup (¼ lb.) grated mozzarella cheese

1 TB. Italian seasoning

Freshly ground black pepper to taste

½ cup sliced pimiento-stuffed green olives

### Mix with Care

Cooking this dish, or any dish with delicate bread, is a time to stay in the kitchen. Only a few seconds makes the difference between nicely toasted and burnt. And the same is true of the topping. Watch the broiler carefully.

Preheat the oven broiler, and line a broiler pan with aluminum foil. Split English muffins, and toast them under the broiler until browned on both sides.

Place soup mix in a small mixing bowl, and pour boiling water over it. Stir well, cover the bowl, and allow mixture to sit for 10 minutes. Stir in mayonnaise, sour cream, cheese, Italian seasoning, and black pepper. Spread mixture on top of English muffin halves. Top with olive slices.

Broil English muffins until the tops are browned, about 2 to 3 minutes. Cut each half into 3 wedges.

# Tomato Sausage Mini-Quiche

Prep time: less than 20 minutes  •  Cooking time: 10 minutes  •  Makes 45 pieces

1 (12-oz.) pkg. bulk pork sausage

3 garlic cloves, minced

2 shallots, minced

1 envelope tomato with basil soup mix

1 TB. herbes de Provence, or 1 tsp. dried thyme, 1 tsp. dried basil, and 1 tsp. dried rosemary

3 eggs, lightly beaten

1½ cups heavy cream

Freshly ground black pepper to taste

3 boxes frozen filo cups

Preheat the oven to 375°F, and line a baking sheet with aluminum foil. Crumble sausage into a skillet placed over medium heat. Cook and stir sausage, breaking up any lumps with a fork or the back of a spoon, for 5 to 7 minutes or until sausage is browned. Remove sausage from the pan with a slotted spoon, and place it in a mixing bowl.

Drain and discard all but 1 tablespoon fat from the skillet. Add garlic and shallots. Cook and stir for 3 minutes or until shallot is translucent and soft. Scrape mixture into the mixing bowl, and add soup mix, herbes de Provence, eggs, cream, and black pepper. Stir well.

Fill filo cups and arrange them on the baking sheet. Bake pastries for 10 to 12 minutes or until the filling is set.

### Dry and Droll

Quiche became a favorite dish on this side of the Atlantic decades ago, but it was hardly new even then. It's a centuries-old dish from the Alsace and Lorraine regions of France. The only constants are that the mixture contains eggs and cream and it's baked in a crust.

# Spicy Moroccan Chicken Turnovers

Prep time: less than 30 minutes • Cooking time: 15 to 20 minutes • Makes 24 turnovers

1 pkg. of 2 refrigerated pie crust sheets, at room temperature

1 envelope golden onion soup mix

½ cup boiling water

3 garlic cloves, minced

1 TB. ground cinnamon

1 tsp. ground turmeric

½ tsp. ground ginger

2 TB. butter

4 eggs, lightly beaten

3 cups finely chopped cooked chicken

¼ cup chopped fresh parsley

½ cup slivered almonds, toasted in a 350°F oven for 5 minutes or until lightly brown

Freshly ground black pepper to taste

Place 1 pie crust sheet between 2 sheets of plastic wrap, and roll it into a 12-inch circle. Cut out 12 (2-inch) circles, using a jar lid as a guide. Repeat with the second sheet of pie crust, and set the circles aside. Preheat the oven to 400°F and line a baking sheet with aluminum foil.

Place soup mix into a small mixing bowl, and pour boiling water over it. Stir well, cover the bowl, and allow mixture to sit for 10 minutes. Stir in garlic, cinnamon, turmeric, and ginger.

### Ellen on Edibles

To **crimp** means to create a decorative edge for pastry. In this case, the crimping also seals the filling inside the dough. If you're making a large pie, the crimping creates a rim on the top of the pie plate so the filling does not boil over.

Heat butter in a medium skillet over medium heat. Add ¾ eggs and scramble until half-set, stirring frequently. Stir in seasoning mixture, chicken, parsley, and almonds. Season mixture with black pepper.

Place 1 tablespoon filling on ½ of each dough circle. Fold dough over filling to make a half-circle, and *crimp* the edges with the tines of a fork. Place turnovers on the baking sheet, brush each with some remaining egg, and cut a small slit in the top.

Bake turnovers for 15 to 20 minutes or until golden brown.

# Beef and Cheddar Pasties

Prep time: less than 20 minutes    •    Cooking time: 15 to 20 minutes    •    Makes 24 pasties

| | |
|---|---|
| 1 envelope onion soup mix | 1 cup (¼ lb.) grated cheddar cheese |
| ½ cup boiling water | 2 tsp. fresh thyme leaves or 1 tsp. dried |
| 1½ lb. ground beef | Freshly ground black pepper to taste |
| 1 small onion, chopped | 3 (8-oz.) pkg. refrigerated crescent rolls |
| 2 garlic cloves, minced | |

Preheat the oven to 375°F, and cover a baking sheet with aluminum foil. Place soup mix into a small mixing bowl, and pour boiling water over it. Stir well, cover the bowl, and allow mixture to sit for 10 minutes.

Place ground beef in a large skillet over medium-high heat. Brown beef for 5 to 7 minutes, breaking up lumps with a fork. Remove beef from the pan with a slotted spoon and set aside. Drain and discard all but 1 tablespoon grease from the pan. Add onion and garlic and cook and stir for 3 minutes or until onion is translucent. Return beef to the pan, and stir in soup mixture, cheese, thyme, and black pepper.

Separate crescent rolls according to package directions. Place 1 heaping tablespoon beef mixture in the center of each roll. Fold over dough, and seal the edges.

Bake pasties for 15 to 20 minutes or until golden brown.

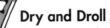

**Dry and Droll**

Pasties were the lunch food of the working classes in England. In particular, they are most closely associated with Cornwall's tin miners. Many times a meat mixture would be placed at one end and fruit would be placed at the other end, so the meal and dessert were in the same pastry package.

# Spear Away

One of the easiest hors d'oeuvres to make is meatballs. They're fast, different, and all that's needed to serve them is a toothpick.

Feel free to improvise with these recipes. Substitute beef and lamb for one another, and use ground turkey or chicken in place of pork or veal.

# Swedish Meatballs

Prep time: less than 20 minutes   •   Cooking time: 25 minutes   •   Makes 3 dozen

2 TB. butter

1 small onion, finely chopped

2 garlic cloves, minced

1 lb. ground pork

1 lb. ground veal, or 1 additional lb. ground pork

2 eggs, lightly beaten

¼ cup milk

½ cup plain breadcrumbs

¼ tsp. grated nutmeg

Salt and freshly ground black pepper to taste

1 envelope white sauce mix

Milk as specified on mix package

½ cup chicken stock

¼ cup chopped fresh dill or 1 TB. dried

Preheat the oven to 500°F. Line a baking sheet with aluminum foil, and spray the foil with vegetable oil spray or rub it with vegetable oil. Melt butter in a small pan over medium heat; add onion and garlic. Cook and stir for 3 minutes or until onion is translucent. Scrape mixture into a mixing bowl.

Add pork, veal, eggs, milk, breadcrumbs, nutmeg, salt, and black pepper. Mix well and form mixture by tablespoons into meatballs. Arrange meatballs on the baking sheet, and bake for 10 minutes or until lightly browned.

While meatballs are baking, prepare white sauce in a large skillet according to package directions. Add stock and dill and stir well. Place meatballs into sauce, and simmer, covered, for 10 to 15 minutes or until cooked through.

### Mix Mastery

Oven-browning meatballs is a great trick to use for all meatball recipes. One of the pitfalls of making meatballs is that they tend to fall apart when browned in a skillet, and using this method helps them retain their shape. Another bonus is that you don't have a messy skillet to wash.

# Bombay Balls

Prep time: less than 20 minutes  •  Cooking time: 15 to 20 minutes  •  Makes 3 dozen

½ cup finely chopped dried apricots

1 envelope golden onion soup mix

¾ cup boiling water

1½ lb. ground lamb

1 TB. curry powder or to taste

Pinch ground cinnamon

3 garlic cloves, minced

1 egg, lightly beaten

⅓ cup plain breadcrumbs

¼ cup chopped fresh parsley

Freshly ground black pepper to taste

Preheat the oven to 400°F, and line a baking sheet with aluminum foil. Place dried apricots and soup mix in a mixing bowl, and pour boiling water over them. Stir well, cover the bowl, and allow mixture to sit for 10 minutes. Add lamb, curry powder, cinnamon, garlic, egg, breadcrumbs, parsley, and black pepper. Mix well and form mixture by tablespoons into meatballs.

Arrange meatballs on the baking sheet and bake for 15 to 20 minutes or until browned.

 **Mix Mastery**

Many foods have formulas of sorts, and meatballs are among them. The reason for using an egg is to keep the meatballs together, as the egg binds them. The purpose of the breadcrumbs is to make the meatballs soft.

# Meatballs in Red Wine Sauce

Prep time: less than 20 minutes   •   Cooking time: 25 minutes   •   Makes 3 dozen

1½ lb. ground beef

1 egg, lightly beaten

¼ cup milk

½ cup Italian-flavored breadcrumbs

½ small onion, finely chopped

3 garlic cloves, minced

2 tsp. Italian seasoning

Salt and freshly ground black pepper to taste

1 envelope brown gravy mix

1 cup dry red wine

½ cup water

Preheat the oven to 500°F. Line a baking sheet with aluminum foil, and spray the foil with veg-etable oil spray or rub it with vegetable oil. Combine beef, egg, milk, breadcrumbs, onion, gar-lic, Italian seasoning, salt, and black pepper in a mixing bowl. Mix well. Form mixture by tablespoons into meatballs, and arrange them on the baking sheet. Bake for 10 minutes or until lightly browned.

While meatballs are baking, whisk gravy mix with wine and water in a large skillet. Bring to a boil over medium heat and stir well. Add meatballs to the skillet, and simmer, covered, for 10 to 15 minutes or until cooked through.

# Part 4

# Stellar Starters

There is no end to the variations on soups that can start with a simple envelope of soup mix. In this part, you'll savor creamy soups made with vegetables, hearty bean soups, and a few poultry and seafood options.

And these are just the hot soups. There is also a chapter of cold soups in this part that will cool you down on the hottest summer day. This part concludes with a chapter on first-course salads. A bonus to these is that they can also be served as an entrée in a larger quantity.

# Chapter 9

# Cozy Hot Soups

## In This Chapter

- ◆ Delicate creamy vegetable soups
- ◆ Hearty vegetable and bean soups
- ◆ Main meal soups with poultry and seafood

On a chilly night, few foods are as comforting as a bowl of steaming soup. Almost every vegetable, from asparagus to zucchini and everything in between, can become the star of a puréed cream soup.

Although these delicate soups are intended as a first course, soups can become the main event when they include big chunks of vegetables, meat, or poultry.

The recipes in this chapter encompass all these options, and they are easier to make than starting from scratch because using a mix shortcuts a few of the steps.

## Creamed to Perfection

Creamed soups are part of the classic French tradition, and long before food processors and blenders, French chefs would painstakingly press the vegetables through strainers to create a satiny texture.

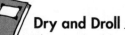

**Dry and Droll** _____
There's an old Spanish proverb: "Of soup and love, the first is best."

But we're lucky enough today to have these time-saving appliances, so making cream soups is reduced to a matter of minutes. The soups in this section can all become vegetarian soups by using vegetable stock instead of chicken stock.

## The Least You Need to Know

◆ Many vegetables can be turned into puréed cream soups using a white sauce as the base.

◆ Beans soups will be flavorful when a soup mix is used as part of the base.

◆ Soups can be a one-dish meal if accompanied by a tossed salad and crusty bread.

◆ The best way to ensure that fish does not overcook in a soup is to turn off the heat once the fish is added and the soup comes back to a boil.

# Cream of Asparagus Soup

Prep time: less than 15 minutes   •   Cooking time: 10 minutes   •   Makes 6 servings

2 (10-oz.) pkg. frozen chopped asparagus, thawed

1 qt. chicken stock or vegetable stock

2 tsp. fresh thyme leaves or ½ tsp. dried

1 envelope white sauce mix

Milk as specified on mix package

Freshly ground black pepper to taste

Combine asparagus, stock, and thyme in a saucepan, and bring to a boil over medium-high heat. Cook asparagus for 5 minutes.

While asparagus is boiling, prepare white sauce according to directions on the package and keep warm.

With a slotted spoon, transfer cooked asparagus to a food processor fitted with a steel blade or a blender, reserving stock in the saucepan. Purée asparagus until smooth. Stir purée back into stock.

Stir white sauce into asparagus soup, and bring to a simmer over medium heat, stirring occasionally. Season soup with black pepper to taste.

**Mix Mastery** _____

You can use this same master recipe for many creamy vegetable soups. Substitute the same amount of broccoli, cauliflower, and peas for the asparagus. You can also add ¾ cup grated cheddar cheese to the white sauce before blending it with the vegetable purée to make the soup a combination of vegetable and cheese.

# Cream of Acorn Squash Soup

Prep time: less than 20 minutes • Cooking time: 1¼ hours • Makes 6 servings

3½ lb. (2 medium) acorn squash

1 envelope white sauce mix

Milk as specified on mix package

1 qt. chicken or vegetable stock

2 TB. chopped fresh parsley

2 TB. molasses

2 TB. bourbon

½ tsp. ground cinnamon

Salt and freshly ground black pepper to taste

Preheat the oven to 350°F. Place squash on a baking sheet and bake, turning it occasionally, for 1 hour or until flesh is tender when pierced with a meat fork. Cut squash in half, discard seeds, and scrape out pulp.

While squash is baking, prepare white sauce according to directions on the package and keep warm.

### Mix Mastery

When choosing acorn squash, pick one heavy for its size with no blemishes on the skin. Butternut squash can be substituted for any recipe calling for acorn squash.

Combine baked squash, stock, parsley, molasses, bourbon, and cinnamon in a saucepan. Bring to a boil over medium-high heat. Reduce the heat to low, and simmer squash for 10 minutes.

With a slotted spoon, transfer squash to a food processor fitted with a steel blade or a blender, reserving the stock mixture in the saucepan. Purée squash until smooth. Stir purée back into stock.

Stir white sauce into squash, and bring to a simmer over medium heat. Season soup with salt and black pepper to taste.

# Cream of Onion Soup

Prep time: less than 30 minutes  •  Cooking time: 45 minutes  •  Makes 6 servings

| | |
|---|---|
| 3 TB. butter | 3 TB. chopped fresh parsley |
| 2 lb. onions, thinly sliced | 2 bay leaves |
| 1 tsp. granulated sugar | 1 TB. fresh thyme leaves or 1 tsp. dried |
| 1 envelope golden onion soup mix | 1 TB. chopped fresh rosemary or 1 tsp. dried |
| 4 cups water | 1 cup half-and-half |
| 1 cup dark beer | Freshly ground black pepper to taste |

Heat butter in a large saucepan over low heat. Add onions, toss to coat, and cover the pan. Cook, stirring occasionally, over low heat for 10 minutes. Uncover the pan, raise the heat to medium, and stir in sugar. Cook, stirring frequently, for 15 to 20 minutes until onions are soft and lightly browned.

Add soup mix, water, beer, parsley, bay leaves, thyme, and rosemary to the pan. Bring to a boil over medium heat. Boil uncovered until liquid is reduced in volume by ¼.

Add half-and-half, and simmer over low heat for 10 minutes. Remove and discard bay leaves, and season soup with black pepper to taste.

**Mix with Care**

Onions frequently stick to the pan when they are being cooked. Stir them frequently, but don't worry if a spot burns. Stir it well, and the color will blend into the other onions.

# Red Pepper Bisque

Prep time: less than 30 minutes • Cooking time: 30 minutes • Makes 6 servings

2 TB. butter

1 small onion, chopped

4 red bell peppers, seeds and ribs removed, and diced

3 garlic cloves, minced

3 cups chicken stock or vegetable stock

1 TB. fresh thyme leaves or 1½ tsp. dried

1 TB. tomato paste

1 bay leaf

1 envelope leek soup mix

1 cup half-and-half

Freshly ground black pepper to taste

Heat butter in a saucepan over medium heat; add onion, red bell peppers, and garlic. Cook and stir for 3 minutes or until onion is translucent. Add stock, thyme, tomato paste, bay leaf, and soup mix. Stir well. Bring soup to a boil, then reduce the heat and simmer, partially covered, for 20 minutes.

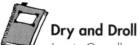

### Dry and Droll

Lewis Carroll wrote "Beautiful soup! Who cares for fish, game, or any other dish? Who would not give all else for two pennyworth only of beautiful soup?"

Remove and discard bay leaf, and with a slotted spoon, transfer vegetables to a food processor fitted with a steel blade or a blender. Purée until smooth. Stir purée back into stock.

Add half-and-half and stir well. Bring soup back to a boil and simmer for 2 minutes. Season soup with black pepper to taste.

# Hearty and Homey

While satiny creamed vegetable soups are understated elegance, the soups in this section of the chapter are down-to-earth favorites. They are brimming with pieces of vegetables and have a depth of flavor from the innate seasonings in the soup mixes.

# Classic Onion Soup Les Halles

Prep time: less than 20 minutes    •    Cooking time: 1 hour    •    Makes 4 servings

3 TB. butter

1 large Bermuda or Vidalia onion, thinly sliced

1 cup dry red wine

4 slices French bread, about ½-inch thick

1 envelope onion soup mix

3 cups water

1 TB. fresh thyme leaves or 1 tsp. dried

1 bay leaf

Freshly ground black pepper to taste

1 cup grated Gruyère or Swiss cheese

¼ cup grated Parmesan cheese

Preheat the oven to 425°F. Combine butter, onion, and wine in an ovenproof baking dish. Bake uncovered, stirring occasionally, for 45 minutes, until onion is soft and most of the liquid has evaporated. While onions are baking, toast bread slices on the other oven rack for 7 to 10 minutes or until lightly browned and crisp.

Transfer onions to a saucepan, and add soup mix, water, thyme, and bay leaf. Stir well and bring to a boil over medium heat. Simmer soup for 10 minutes. Remove and discard bay leaf, and season soup with black pepper to taste.

To serve, preheat the oven broiler. Ladle soup into ovenproof bowls, and top each with a piece of toast. Sprinkle Gruyère and Parmesan cheeses over toast, and broil 6 inches from the broiler element until cheese is melted and brown.

**Dry and Droll**

Onion soup is associated with the old Les Halles market district of Paris, where the bistros were traditionally open 24/7 and served onion soup all day and night long. Most of the market has moved to other quarters, but you can still get a bowl of onion soup there.

# *Minestrone* (Italian Mixed Vegetable and Pasta Soup)

Prep time: less than 30 minutes • Cooking time: 50 minutes • Makes 6 to 8 servings

2 TB. olive oil

1 large onion, diced

3 garlic cloves, minced

1½ cups shredded green cabbage

1 envelope tomato with basil soup mix

3 cups vegetable water

1 carrot, thinly sliced

1 celery stalk, trimmed and thinly sliced

1 tsp. dried thyme

1 tsp. dried oregano

1 bay leaf

2 small zucchini, cut into ½-inch cubes

1 (10-oz.) box Italian green beans, thawed

1 (15-oz.) can white cannellini beans, drained and rinsed

½ cup small elbow macaroni or small pasta shells

Freshly ground black pepper to taste

Parmesan cheese

### Mix Mastery

The great thing about minestrone is that you have an endless variety of vegetables that can be added. Have some peas left over from last night's dinner? Throw them into the soup. Add another kind of bean if you wish, or omit the cabbage if you're not an aficionado. It doesn't matter. The soup will be great.

Heat olive oil in a large saucepan over medium heat; add onion and garlic. Cook and stir for 3 minutes or until onion is translucent. Add cabbage, soup mix, water, carrot, celery, thyme, oregano, and bay leaf.

Bring to a boil over medium heat and simmer, covered, for 20 minutes. Stir in zucchini, green beans, cannellini beans, and pasta. Cook for 20 to 30 minutes or until pasta is cooked and vegetables are tender. Remove and discard bay leaf. Season soup with black pepper to taste, and serve with grated Parmesan cheese.

# Black Bean Soup

Prep time: less than 20 minutes   •   Cooking time: 40 minutes   •   Makes 6 to 8 servings

¼ cup olive oil

1 large onion, diced

1 green bell pepper, seeds and ribs removed, and diced

6 garlic cloves, minced

2 jalapeño chilies, seeds and ribs removed, and diced

1 TB. ground cumin

2 tsp. ground coriander

2 envelopes vegetable soup mix

6 cups water

3 (15-oz.) cans black beans, drained and rinsed

¼ cup chopped fresh cilantro

Freshly ground black pepper to taste

½ cup sour cream for garnish

Lime wedges for garnish

Heat oil in a large saucepan over medium heat. Add onion, green pepper, garlic, and chilies. Cook and stir for 3 minutes or until onion is translucent Add cumin and coriander, and continue to cook for 2 minutes, stirring constantly.

Add soup mix, water, and beans, and bring to a boil over medium heat. Simmer, partially covered, stirring occasionally, for 30 minutes. Purée soup in a food processor fitted with a steel blade or in a blender. Stir in cilantro and season soup with black pepper to taste.

Top each serving with a dollop of sour cream, if desired, and serve garnished with lime wedges.

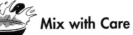

## Mix with Care

Bean soups have a nasty habit of scorching when you're not looking because the beans are heavy and sink to the bottom of the pan. To avoid this, stir bean soups often while they're simmering.

# Split Pea Soup

Prep time: less than 15 minutes  •  Cooking time: 50 minutes  •  Makes 8 to 10 servings

1 lb. green split peas, rinsed

2 envelopes vegetable soup mix

6 cups water

1 ham bone or smoked pork hock (optional)

1 onion, finely chopped

2 garlic cloves, minced

2 TB. chopped fresh parsley

1 TB. fresh thyme leaves or 1 tsp. dried

1 bay leaf

Freshly ground black pepper to taste

### Mix Mastery

Unless you want a vegetarian soup, flavoring any soup with a ham bone is a wonderful addition because it adds a smoky undertaste. Unlike their botanical cousins, dried beans, split peas are among the few legumes that do not require soaking before cooking. Like lentils, they are so small that they virtually fall apart during the cooking time.

Place split peas in a saucepan. Add soup mix, water, ham bone (if using), onion, garlic, parsley, thyme, and bay leaf. Stir well.

Bring soup to a boil over medium heat and simmer, partially covered, for 45 minutes or until split peas have disintegrated. Remove and discard bay leaf. Remove ham bone if used, and cut meat from the bone and set aside.

Transfer soup to a food processor fitted with a steel blade or a blender. Purée until smooth. Season soup with black pepper to taste and stir in reserved ham.

# White Bean Soup with Rosemary and Spinach

Prep time: less than 15 minutes

• Cooking time: 3 hours (including soaking time)

• Makes 6 to 8 servings

2 cups dried navy beans or other small dried white beans

3 TB. olive oil

1 large onion, diced

6 garlic cloves, minced

1 (14½-oz.) can diced tomatoes

½ cup finely chopped carrots

½ cup finely chopped celery

¼ lb. prosciutto, finely chopped

1 envelope roasted garlic herb soup mix

6 cups water

1 TB. fresh thyme leaves or 1 tsp. dried

1 TB. chopped fresh rosemary, or 1 tsp. dried

1 (10-oz.) pkg. frozen leaf spinach, thawed and drained

Freshly ground black pepper to taste

Rinse beans in a colander, and place them in a mixing bowl covered with cold water. Allow beans to soak overnight. Or place beans in a saucepan, and bring to a boil over high heat. Boil 1 minute. Turn off heat, cover the pan, and soak beans for 1 hour. Drain and place beans in a saucepan.

Heat olive oil in a medium skillet over medium heat; add onion and garlic. Cook and stir for 3 minutes or until onion is translucent. Transfer to the saucepan, and stir in tomatoes, carrots, celery, prosciutto, soup mix, water, thyme, and rosemary. Bring to a boil over medium heat, and cook for 1½ to 2 hours or until beans are tender.

With a slotted spoon, transfer ½ of beans to a food processor fitted with a steel blade or a blender. Purée until smooth. Return purée to soup and add spinach. Bring soup back to a boil, and simmer for 5 minutes. Season with black pepper to taste.

> **Dry and Droll**
> Prosciutto has been made for more than 2,000 years in the region of Italy near Parma and must come from Parma, San Daniele, or the Veneto to be authentic. If you've wondered why prosciutto seems to go so well with Parmesan cheese, it might be because the whey from Parmigiano Reggiano is one of the foods the pigs are fed.

# The Main Event

Every culture has robust soups because soups were a great way to make a little bit of meat or fish stretch to feed a crowd. These soups are a meal in a bowl. All that's needed to complete the meal is a tossed salad and some crusty bread. Any of these soups can be doubled or tripled to serve as party fare, too.

# Mexican Tortilla Soup

Prep time: less than 30 minutes  •  Cooking time: 35 minutes  •  Makes 4 to 6 servings

**For soup:**

2 TB. olive oil

2 medium onions, sliced

4 garlic cloves, minced

1 TB. dried oregano

1 TB. dried basil

2 tsp. ground cumin

1 (14½-oz.) can diced tomatoes

1 envelope roasted garlic herb soup mix

3 cups water

2 TB. tomato paste

3 boneless, skinless chicken breast halves, or 6 boneless, skinless chicken thighs cut into ½-inch pieces

1 celery stalk, trimmed and sliced

1 small zucchini, trimmed and cut into ¾-inch dice

1 carrot, sliced

1 medium potato, cut into ½-inch dice

Freshly ground black pepper to taste

**For garnish:**

½ cup vegetable oil

4 (6-inch) corn tortillas, cut into ½-inch strips

1 ripe avocado, peeled, pitted, and diced

1 cup grated Monterey Jack cheese

Heat olive oil in a large skillet over medium heat; add onions and garlic. Cook and stir for 3 minutes or until onion is translucent. Add oregano, basil, and cumin to the pan. Cook for 1 minute, stirring constantly. Add tomatoes and stir well. Purée mixture in a blender or food processor fitted with the steel blade. Scrape purée into a saucepan and add soup mix, water, and tomato paste. Stir well.

### Mix with Care

Fried food that is crisp and not greasy is the result of cooking the right amount of food in properly heated oil. Heat your oil until you see a thin haze and then fry only as much food as will fit in one layer. Filling a pan too full results in food that steams instead of fries.

Add diced chicken, celery, zucchini, carrot, and potato to the saucepan. Bring to a boil over medium heat, and simmer, covered, for 20 to 30 minutes or until chicken is cooked through and potatoes are tender. Season soup with black pepper to taste.

While soup is simmering, heat vegetable oil in a medium skillet over high heat. Add tortilla strips and fry until crisp. With a slotted spoon, remove strips from the pan, and drain on paper towels.

To serve, ladle soup into bowls and garnish each serving with tortilla strips, avocado, and cheese. If dicing avocado in advance, toss with lemon juice to prevent discoloration.

# Nantucket Clam Chowder

Prep time: less than 20 minutes    •    Cooking time: 20 minutes    •    Makes 4 to 6 servings

| | |
|---|---|
| 1 pint fresh chopped clams or 3 (6½-oz.) cans minced clams | 2 large red-skinned potatoes, scrubbed and cut into ½-inch dice |
| 3 TB. butter | 3 TB. chopped fresh parsley |
| 1 large onion, diced | 1 TB. fresh thyme or ½ tsp. dried |
| 2 celery stalks, trimmed and sliced | 1 bay leaf |
| 1 envelope leek soup mix | 1 cup half-and-half |
| 2 (8-oz.) bottles clam juice | Freshly ground black pepper to taste |

Drain clams in a sieve placed over a bowl, pressing down with the back of a spoon to extract as much liquid as possible. Reserve drained juice. Melt butter in a saucepan over medium heat; add onions and celery. Cook and stir for 3 minutes or until onion is translucent.

Stir in reserved clam juice, soup mix, bottled clam juice, potatoes, parsley, thyme, and bay leaf. Bring to a boil over medium heat, and simmer, covered, for 12 minutes or until potatoes are tender. Stir occasionally.

Stir in half-and-half and clams. Simmer for 5 minutes. Remove and discard bay leaf, and season soup with black pepper to taste.

 **Dry and Droll**

In Melville's *Moby Dick*, Ishmael and Queequeg land on Nantucket and are sent to Hosea Hussey's Try Pots Inn. The name of the inn comes from the iron cauldrons used to melt blubber into whale oil. Melville writes that the two had "chowder for breakfast, chowder for dinner, and chowder for supper."

# Provençal Fish Soup

Prep time: less than 30 minutes • Cooking time: 35 minutes • Makes 4 to 6 servings

¼ cup olive oil

1 large onion, diced

2 garlic cloves, minced

1 TB. paprika

1 celery stalk, trimmed and sliced

1 carrot, sliced

2 large potatoes, cut into ½-inch dice

1 (14½-oz.) can diced tomatoes

1 envelope roasted garlic herb soup mix

3 cups seafood stock or bottled clam juice

1 cup dry white wine

½ cup orange juice

2 TB. chopped fresh parsley

1 TB. fresh thyme or ½ tsp. dried

1 TB. grated orange zest

1 lb. halibut, swordfish, or any firm-fleshed white fish fillet, cut into 1-inch cubes

½ lb. medium shrimp, peeled and deveined

Freshly ground black pepper to taste

Thick slices of toasted French or Italian bread

 **Mix Mastery**

Fish needs very little time to cook and is overcooked far more often than undercooked. The best way to cook small cubes, as well as delicate shrimp, is to add it to a pot of simmering liquid. Then cover the pan and bring the soup back to a simmer. Then turn off the heat and let the pot sit undisturbed for 10 minutes.

Heat olive oil in a saucepan over medium heat; add onion and garlic. Cook and stir for 3 minutes or until onion is translucent. Reduce the heat to low and stir in paprika. Cook for 1 minute.

Add celery, carrot, potatoes, tomatoes, soup mix, stock, wine, orange juice, parsley, thyme, and orange zest to the pan. Bring to a boil over medium heat, and simmer, partially covered, for 15 to 20 minutes or until vegetables are tender.

Add fish and shrimp to the pan, and season soup with black pepper to taste. Once liquid comes back to a boil, cover the pot and turn off the heat. Let the pot sit for 10 minutes. Ladle soup over the slices of toast.

# Chapter 10

# Refreshing Cold Soups

## In This Chapter

- ◆ No-cook soups made from raw vegetables and fruits
- ◆ Creamy cold soups
- ◆ Soups to serve either cold or hot

Soup is a food fit for all seasons. Just as a bowl of steamy soup warms us in the winter, a frosty bowl of chilled soup cools us even during the dog days of August.

In this chapter, you'll find a number of easy soup options. Some require no cooking at all, so they're chilled and ready to eat when you are. Others require cooking, so you need to plan for time to chill them. Many of these soups are really versatile. You can either serve them hot from the pan or chill them.

## Keeping Cool

Summer is a time when fresh produce is at its peak. Tomatoes are ripe on the vine, and fruits are ripe for the picking. In this chapter are several great cold soups, which use these fresh fruits and vegetables.

The beauty of these recipes is that most of the work is done by the food processor or blender. You can have them on the table in a matter of minutes.

## The Least You Need to Know

- ◆ There are chilled soups, made from raw vegetables and fruits, that require no cooking.
- ◆ Cream soups can be served hot or cold.
- ◆ Soups should be tasted after chilling to see if they need additional seasoning.

# Gazpacho

Prep time: less than 15 minutes   •   Makes 6 to 8 servings

1 envelope tomato with basil soup mix

1½ cups boiling water

1 medium Bermuda or other sweet white onion, quartered

1 medium cucumber, peeled, seeded, and cut into 1-inch sections

1 green bell pepper, seeds and ribs removed, and diced

1 red bell pepper, seeds and ribs removed, and diced

3 medium to large ripe tomatoes, cored, seeded, and diced

3 large garlic cloves

¼ cup olive oil

1 jalapeño or serrano chili, seeds and ribs removed

¼ cup balsamic vinegar

¼ cup chopped fresh cilantro

Freshly ground black pepper to taste

Combine soup mix and water in a mixing bowl and stir well. Cover the bowl and let mixture sit for 10 minutes.

Place onion, cucumber, green and red bell peppers, and 1 tomato in a food processor fitted with a steel blade, and finely chop, or chop everything finely by hand. Scrape mixture into a large bowl.

Transfer soup mixture to the food processor or to a blender and add remaining 2 tomatoes, garlic, olive oil, jalapeño, and vinegar. Purée until smooth. Stir purée into vegetables, add cilantro, and season soup with black pepper to taste. Chill well.

 **Mix Mastery**

Gazpacho can also become a morning "eye opener." Omit the olive oil and use the soup as you would Bloody Mary mix. Although I like it to have some texture, you can also purée everything if you're serving it as a drink.

# Honeydew Gazpacho

Prep time: less than 15 minutes • Makes 6 servings

½ envelope savory herb with garlic soup mix

1 cup boiling water

1 ripe honeydew melon, seeded and diced

2 cups sliced celery

1 medium onion, diced

2 cucumbers, peeled, seeded, and diced

1 cup sour cream or nonfat yogurt

⅓ cup white wine vinegar

3 TB. chopped fresh mint

Freshly ground black pepper to taste

### Mix Mastery

To judge the ripeness of a melon, smell it for a sweet aroma. Or look at the stem end. If the perimeter of the crater has jagged edges, chances are it was pulled from the vine before it was ripe.

Place soup mix in a mixing bowl, and pour boiling water over it. Stir well, cover the bowl, and allow soup to sit for 10 minutes.

Transfer soup mixture to a food processor fitted with a steel blade or a blender. Add honeydew, celery, onion, cucumbers, sour cream, vinegar, and mint. Purée until smooth, and season with black pepper to taste. Chill well and serve.

# Gazpacho Blanco

Prep time: less than 20 minutes • Makes 6 to 8 servings

1 envelope leek soup mix

2 cups boiling water

⅓ cup white wine vinegar

2 cucumbers, peeled, seeded, and diced

4 garlic cloves

1 green bell pepper, seeds and ribs removed, and diced

4 scallions, trimmed and sliced

2 cups sour cream or plain nonfat yogurt

White pepper to taste

### Dry and Droll

Traditional tomato-based gazpacho comes from the Andalucia region of Spain. The characteristic flavors are garlic and vinegar melded with the vegetables, so this nontomato version still fits the flavor profile.

Place soup mix in a mixing bowl and pour boiling water over it. Stir well, cover the bowl, and allow soup to sit for 10 minutes. Transfer soup to a food processor fitted with a steel blade or a blender, add vinegar, cucumbers, garlic, green pepper, and scallions. Purée until smooth.

Transfer mixture to a mixing bowl, and stir in sour cream. Season soup with white pepper to taste.

# Cold Avocado Soup

Prep time: less than 20 minutes  •  Makes 6 servings

1 envelope golden onion soup mix

2 cups boiling water

4 ripe avocados, peeled, pitted, and cut into pieces

2 TB. lemon juice

2 garlic cloves

¼ cup dry sherry

1½ cups half-and-half

Hot pepper sauce to taste

Place soup mix in a mixing bowl, and pour boiling water over it. Stir well, cover the bowl, and allow soup to sit for 10 minutes.

Transfer soup to a food processor fitted with a steel blade or a blender. Add avocados, lemon juice, garlic, and sherry. Purée until smooth.

Transfer soup to a mixing bowl, and stir in half-and-half. Season soup with hot pepper sauce to taste. Chill well with a sheet of plastic wrap pressed directly onto the surface of soup.

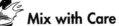 **Mix with Care**

Like potatoes and apples, avocados discolor when they meet air. Rubbing them with lemon juice is a way to prevent this from happening. Another way is to press plastic wrap directly onto the surface of the dish made with avocados.

# Cold and Creamy

One of the advantages to seasoning cold soups with mixes is that they don't have the fat contained in canned or homemade stocks. That means the soups keep a satiny texture once chilled.

Many of these soups are variations on the original flavor of the soup mix, but the directions are different so the soups will chill faster.

# Roasted Garlic Vichyssoise

Prep time: less than 20 minutes • Cooking time: 1¼ hours • Makes 6 servings

| | |
|---|---|
| 1 head garlic | 3 cups water |
| 1 TB. olive oil | 3 cups milk |
| 2 envelopes leek soup mix | Freshly ground black pepper to taste |

Preheat the oven to 350°F. Cut top third off head of garlic, and rub head with olive oil. Wrap head with aluminum foil so only the top is exposed, and bake garlic for 45 minutes to 1 hour or until cloves are soft. When cool enough to handle, press cloves out of the papery husks and set aside.

> **Mix Mastery**
>
> The flavor of garlic varies with how it is treated. It can deliver a powerful punch when raw, but it becomes nutty and sweet when it's sautéed or roasted as in this recipe. The other way garlic is sweet is when the whole cloves are poached in water or stock.

While garlic is baking, combine soup mix and water in a saucepan. Bring to a boil over medium heat, stirring occasionally. Simmer soup for 5 minutes; then set it aside to cool.

Transfer soup and garlic cloves to a food processor fitted with a steel blade or a blender. Purée until smooth. Transfer mixture to a bowl, and stir in milk. Season soup with black pepper to taste and chill well.

# Chilled Dilled Cucumber Soup

Prep time: less than 20 minutes   •   Cooking time: 10 minutes   •   Makes 6 servings

| | |
|---|---|
| 1 envelope white sauce mix | ½ tsp. salt |
| Milk as specified on mix package | ½ cup chopped fresh dill |
| 4 TB. butter | 2 cups milk |
| 4 cucumbers, peeled, seeded, and thinly sliced | Freshly ground black pepper to taste |

Prepare soup mix according to directions on the package. Set aside and keep warm.

Heat butter in a large skillet over medium heat. Add cucumbers and sprinkle them with salt. Cook cucumbers, stirring frequently, for 5 to 7 minutes or until they are soft. Stir in dill and cook for an additional 2 minutes.

Transfer cucumbers to a food processor fitted with a steel blade or a blender. Purée until smooth. Transfer to a mixing bowl. Add prepared white sauce and milk. Stir well and season with black pepper to taste. Serve hot or cold.

**Mix Mastery**

Eating chilled foods dulls the palate, so it's always a good idea to taste food before serving once it's been chilled. You might need more salt and pepper.

# Cream of Pea Soup with Sorrel

Prep time: less than 15 minutes   •   Cooking time: 10 minutes   •   Makes 6 servings

| | |
|---|---|
| 1 envelope leek soup mix | ¼ lb. fresh sorrel, stems discarded, leaves washed and cut crosswise into thin strips |
| 1½ cups water | ½ cup sour cream or plain nonfat yogurt |
| 2 cups milk | Freshly ground black pepper to taste |
| 1 (10-oz.) pkg. frozen peas, thawed | |

Combine soup mix, water, milk, peas, and sorrel in a saucepan. Bring to a boil over medium heat, stirring occasionally. Simmer soup, partially covered, for 10 minutes, stirring occasionally.

Transfer soup to a food processor fitted with a steel blade or a blender. Purée until smooth. Stir in sour cream, and season soup with black pepper to taste. Chill well.

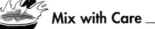

**Mix with Care**

If you plan to serve a cold soup that contains sour cream hot, don't allow it to boil while heating, or the sour cream will curdle.

# Curried Carrot Soup

Prep time: less than 30 minutes • Cooking time: 25 minutes • Makes 6 servings

2 TB. butter

4 scallions, trimmed and chopped

2 TB. grated fresh ginger

1 TB. *curry powder* or to taste

1 envelope roasted garlic herb soup mix

3 cups water

1½ lb. carrots, scrubbed, trimmed, and thinly sliced

1 (14-oz.) can unsweetened coconut milk, stirred well

1 TB. lime juice or to taste

Freshly ground black pepper to taste

**Ellen on Edibles**

Although we might think of **curry powder** as a spice, it's actually a blend of up to 20 spices, which, mixed together, produce the characteristic flavor of Indian cuisine. The color is yellow from turmeric, and other ingredients are ground red chilies, coriander, fenugreek, mustard, ginger, and cinnamon.

Melt butter in a saucepan over medium heat. Add scallions and ginger. Cook and stir for 3 minutes. Stir in curry powder, and cook for 1 minute, stirring constantly.

Add soup mix, water, and carrots to the pan, and bring to a boil over medium-high heat. Simmer soup, covered, for 20 minutes or until carrots are tender.

Transfer mixture to a food processor fitted with a steel blade or a blender. Purée until smooth. Transfer mixture to a mixing bowl, and stir in coconut milk and lime juice. Season soup with black pepper to taste and chill well.

# Bold and Cold

In these last few recipes, we have cooked soups that do not contain any cream. They have delicious and assertive flavors and are also light, so you can serve them before a hearty meal.

# Chilled Borscht

Prep time: less than 20 minutes    •    Cooking time: 30 minutes    •    Makes 6 servings

**For soup:**

1 envelope roasted garlic herb soup mix

5 cups water

2 lb. beets, peeled and coarsely shredded

1 bay leaf

½ cup orange juice

2 cups sour cream or plain nonfat yogurt

Freshly ground black pepper to taste

**For garnish:**

1 cucumber, peeled and chopped

1 bunch scallions, peeled and chopped

Combine soup mix, water, beets, and bay leaf in a saucepan. Bring to a boil over medium-high heat. Reduce the heat to low and simmer soup, covered, for 30 minutes or until beets are tender.

Remove and discard bay leaf, stir in orange juice, and chill soup well. Stir in sour cream and season soup with black pepper to taste.

To serve, ladle chilled soup into bowls, and pass cucumber and scallions separately.

**Dry and Droll**

Borscht is best known as a beet soup, although there are some beetless versions. It can be served cold or hot and can be vegetarian or contain meat. The soup originated in Eastern Europe and was popular with Jewish immigrants from that region. The resorts in New York's Catskill Mountains that featured Jewish entertainers became known as the "Borscht Belt."

# Chilled Tomato Soup

Prep time: less than 20 minutes  •  Cooking time: 15 minutes  •  Makes 6 servings

3 TB. olive oil

3 lb. fresh tomatoes, *skinned*, seeded, and chopped

5 garlic cloves, minced

½ cup chopped fresh basil or 1 TB. dried

1 envelope roasted garlic herb soup mix

5 cups water

Freshly ground black pepper to taste

### Ellen on Edibles ____

**Skinned** is exactly what it sounds like—removing the skin from the tomato. To do this easily, using a sharp knife, carve an X into the bottom of the tomato, plunge it into a pot of boiling water for 10 to 15 seconds, remove it with a slotted spoon, and run cold water over it. The skin will slide right off.

Heat olive oil in a saucepan over medium heat. Add tomatoes and garlic, and cook for 5 minutes. Stir in basil, soup mix, and water. Bring to a boil.

Cook soup, stirring occasionally, for 10 minutes or until tomatoes are very soft. Season soup with black pepper to taste and chill well.

# Small Salads to Perk the Palate

## In This Chapter

- ◆ Mixed vegetable salads
- ◆ Bean salads
- ◆ Salads with fish and meats

Salads of all types are a mainstay of our diets. Although you can always serve a mixture of bright baby greens or a wedge of crunchy iceberg lettuce as a first course, the salads in this chapter provide other options.

These recipes are conceived as units. The dressing for each is created to glorify the salad ingredients, and the use of soup mixes as the seasoning in the dressings makes them far quicker to prepare.

## Light Lunches

Many of the recipes in this chapter can become a light lunch or supper if served in a larger portion. If you want to serve one of these salads as an entrée, double the quantity of the appetizer-size portions that are listed.

Another option is to pair a few salads and make them the whole meal. Select salads with different ingredients, flavors, and textures to add interest to the meal.

# Picnics with Panache

In this chapter, all the recipes for cold salads that do not have hot components are perfect for picnics. The trick is to figure out what to do when. If it's a salad that is dressed in advance, do just that—pack the dish totally finished. If the salad is to be drizzled with dressing just before serving, pack the dressing separately and finish the dish at your picnic site.

## The Least You Need to Know

- ◆ First-course salads can be served as entrées if the portion size is doubled.
- ◆ Cold salads can be taken on picnics either totally complete or with the dressings packed on the side.
- ◆ Some bean and vegetable salads need to be refrigerated before serving to allow the flavor of the dressing to infuse.
- ◆ Canned tuna packed in olive oil delivers more flavor than water-packed tuna.

# Greek Salad

Prep time: less than 15 minutes    •    Makes 6 servings

**For dressing:**

2 TB. savory herb with garlic soup mix

3 TB. water

2 TB. lemon juice

2 TB. red wine vinegar

1 tsp. dried oregano

Freshly ground black pepper to taste

⅓ cup olive oil

**For salad:**

1 large head green leaf lettuce, rinsed, dried, and torn into bite-size pieces

3 large tomatoes, cored, seeded, and cut into ½-inch dice

2 cucumbers, peeled, seeded, and cut into ½-inch dice

½ cup pitted black olives, preferably Kalamata

1 cup crumbled feta cheese

For dressing, combine soup mix, water, lemon juice, vinegar, oregano, and black pepper in a jar with a tight-fitting lid. Shake well. Add oil and shake well again. Dressing can be made up to 4 days in advance and refrigerated. Allow it to sit at room temperature for 1 hour before using.

For salad, combine lettuce, tomatoes, cucumbers, olives, and feta in a salad bowl. Toss with dressing and serve immediately.

 **Mix Mastery**

A melon baller works well to scrape the seeds out of cucumbers. It's also good for removing the core from apples and pears.

# Cherry Tomato and Mozzarella Salad

Prep time: less than 15 minutes • Makes 6 servings

**For dressing:**

2 TB. savory herb with garlic soup mix

3 TB. water

¼ cup balsamic vinegar

Freshly ground black pepper to taste

¼ cup olive oil

**For salad:**

2 pints cherry tomatoes, rinsed, stemmed, and halved

1 lb. fresh mozzarella cheese, cut into ½-inch dice

3 TB. chopped fresh oregano or 2 tsp. dried

2 TB. small pickled *capers*, drained and rinsed

6 large leaves Boston or green leaf lettuce, rinsed and dried

**Ellen on Edibles** _____

**Capers** are the preserved flower buds of a bushy plant that grows near the Mediterranean. They are never eaten fresh but are always salted or pickled. They come in both small and large sizes.

For dressing, combine soup mix, water, vinegar, and black pepper in a jar with a tight-fitting lid. Shake well. Add oil and shake well again. Dressing can be made up to 4 days in advance and refrigerated. Allow it to sit at room temperature for 1 hour before using.

For salad, place cherry tomatoes, mozzarella, oregano, and capers in a mixing bowl. Gently toss salad with dressing. Serve on lettuce leaves.

# Classic Caesar Salad with Herb Croutons

Prep time: less than 15 minutes   •   Makes 6 servings

**For croutons:**

¼ loaf French bread, cut into ½-inch cubes

¼ cup olive oil

½ envelope savory herb with garlic soup mix

Freshly ground black pepper to taste

**For dressing:**

1 egg

½ envelope savory herb with garlic soup mix

4 garlic cloves, minced

¼ cup lemon juice

2 TB. Dijon-style mustard

Freshly ground black pepper to taste

½ cup extra virgin olive oil

**For salad:**

1 large head romaine lettuce, rinsed and broken into 1½-inch pieces

½ cup freshly grated Parmesan cheese

6 to 12 anchovy fillets, drained

Freshly ground black pepper to taste

For croutons, preheat the oven to 375°F, and line a baking pan with aluminum foil. Arrange bread cubes in the pan and toss with olive oil. Sprinkle with soup mix and black pepper, and toss to coat evenly. Arrange cubes in a single layer. Bake for 7 to 10 minutes or until browned. Remove croutons from the oven and set aside.

For dressing, bring a small saucepan of water to a boil over high heat. Add egg and boil for 1 minute. Remove egg from water with a slotted spoon, and break it into a jar with a tight-fitting lid, scraping the inside of the shell to remove any bits of white or yolk still attached to it. Add soup mix, garlic, lemon juice, mustard, and black pepper. Shake well. Add oil and shake well again. Dressing can be made up to 1 day in advance and refrigerated. For salad, toss lettuce with Parmesan, croutons, and enough dressing to coat lightly. Divide the salad among 6 plates, and top each portion with anchovies. Season with black pepper and serve immediately.

**Mix with Care** _____

Some people hesitate to eat raw eggs due to the potential of salmonella bacteria in the egg. If you share this concern, substitute ¼ cup vegetable or chicken stock in the dressing in place of the egg.

# Fennel Salad

Prep time: less than 10 minutes  •  Makes 6 servings

**For dressing:**

2 TB. roasted garlic herb soup mix

¼ cup lemon juice

Freshly ground black pepper to taste

2 garlic cloves, minced

⅓ cup olive oil

**For salad:**

2 fennel bulbs, well chilled

¼ cup chopped fresh parsley

**Mix Mastery**

Fennel is best from August to May. The bulbs should be compact, clean, and bright white or very pale green. Avoid dry-looking bulbs, bulbs with brown spots, or a spreading bulb, which might be too mature and have a woody texture. Although this salad uses the bulb of the fennel, save the stalks and use them as an alternative to celery in salads.

For dressing, combine soup mix, lemon juice, and black pepper in a jar with a tight-fitting lid and shake well. Add garlic and oil and shake well again. Dressing can be made up to 4 days in advance and refrigerated. Allow it to sit at room temperature for 1 hour before using.

For salad, trim stalks and root ends from fennel bulbs. Using a food processor fitted with a thin slicing disk, slice fennel. You can also use a very sharp knife. Place fennel in a salad bowl, and toss with parsley.

Drizzle dressing over fennel, toss, and serve immediately.

# Chiffonade Salad with Gorgonzola Dressing

Prep time: less than 15 minutes    •    Makes 6 servings

**For dressing:**

2 TB. roasted garlic with herb soup mix

¼ cup boiling water

⅓ cup sour cream

⅓ cup mayonnaise

¼ cup chopped fresh parsley

2 TB. white wine vinegar

¼ lb. Gorgonzola or blue cheese, crumbled

Freshly ground black pepper to taste

**For salad:**

½ head romaine lettuce, cored, rinsed, dried, and thinly sliced

1 head radicchio, cored, quartered, and thinly sliced

3 heads Belgian endive, cored and thinly sliced lengthwise

3 hard-cooked eggs, peeled and chopped

¼ cup snipped fresh chives

For dressing, place soup mix in a mixing bowl and pour boiling water over it. Stir well and allow mixture to sit for 10 minutes. Add sour cream, mayonnaise, parsley, and vinegar. Whisk until smooth. Add cheese and stir well. Season with black pepper to taste. Dressing can be made up to 4 days in advance and refrigerated. Allow dressing to sit at room temperature for 1 hour before using.

For salad, combine romaine, radicchio, Belgian endive, eggs, and chives in salad bowl. Toss salad with dressing and serve immediately.

**Ellen on Edibles**

Chiffonade (pronounced *shif-oh-NAHD*) means "made from rags" in French. In cooking, it's not rags that are being shredded but vegetables, such as lettuces, that are cut into very thin strips.

# Gazpacho Salad

Prep time: less than 20 minutes • Makes 6 servings

**For dressing:**

2 TB. tomato with basil soup mix

5 garlic cloves, peeled and minced

1 jalapeño chili, seeds and ribs removed, finely chopped

¼ cup sherry vinegar

¼ cup water

Freshly ground black pepper to taste

⅓ cup olive oil

**For salad:**

1 sweet onion, such as Vidalia or Bermuda, cut into ½-inch dice

2 medium cucumbers, peeled, seeded, and cut into ½-inch dice

1 green bell pepper, seeds and ribs removed, cut into ½-inch dice

1 red bell pepper, seeds and ribs removed, cut into ½-inch dice

6 medium tomatoes, cored, seeded, and cut into ½-inch dice

¼ cup chopped fresh cilantro

6 large leaves Boston or green leaf lettuce, rinsed and dried

### Mix Mastery

It's easier to slice and dice bell peppers from the inside out. Once the seeds and ribs have been removed, place the shiny, slippery skin on your cutting board, and you'll find it's easier to control your knife and cut the size pieces you desire.

For dressing, combine soup mix, garlic, jalapeño, vinegar, water, and black pepper in a jar with a tight-fitting lid. Shake well. Add oil and shake well again. Dressing can be made up to 4 days in advance and refrigerated. Allow it to sit at room temperature for 1 hour before using.

For salad, place onion, cucumbers, green pepper, red pepper, tomatoes, and cilantro into a mixing bowl.

Pour dressing over salad, toss, and refrigerate for 2 to 4 hours, tightly covered. Serve chilled on lettuce leaves.

# Dilled Cucumber Salad

Prep time: less than 15 minutes    •    Makes 6 servings

3 English or 6 large cucumbers, peeled and thinly sliced (seeded if not English cucumbers)

Salt

1 envelope vegetable soup mix

⅓ cup boiling water

1 cup (8 oz.) sour cream or yogurt cheese

2 TB. white wine vinegar

¼ cup chopped fresh dill or 2 TB. dried

Freshly ground black pepper to taste

Lettuce leaves for garnish

6 large Boston or green leaf lettuce leaves, rinsed and dried

Place cucumbers in a colander and sprinkle liberally with salt. Place colander on a plate and let cucumbers sit for 30 minutes, so that they release their liquid. Rinse well under cold running water.

Place soup mix in small bowl. Pour boiling water over it, stir well, cover, and allow mixture sit for 10 minutes. Add sour cream, vinegar, dill, and black pepper. Stir well to combine. Stir cucumbers into dressing, and refrigerate, tightly covered, for 2 to 4 hours. Serve chilled on lettuce leaves.

**Mix with Care**

English cucumbers (also called hothouse cucumbers in some parts of the world) are the long, skinny ones you'll find wrapped in plastic in the produce section. Seeding English cucumbers is not necessary because they have extremely small seeds. If you are using a regular cucumber, increase the count to 6 and scrape out the seeds.

# Mixed Bean Salad

Prep time: less than 20 minutes • Makes 6 servings

**For dressing:**

3 TB. tomato with basil soup mix

¼ cup boiling water

3 TB. red wine vinegar

3 garlic cloves, peeled and minced

1 jalapeño chili, seeds and ribs removed, finely chopped

½ tsp. dried oregano

½ tsp. ground cumin

Freshly ground black pepper to taste

⅓ cup olive oil

**For salad:**

1 cup red kidney beans, rinsed and drained

1 cup chickpeas, rinsed and drained

1 cup cannellini or navy beans, rinsed and drained

1 large tomato, cored, seeded, and chopped

¼ cup diced red onion

2 TB. chopped fresh cilantro

6 large leaves Boston or green leaf lettuce

### Mix Mastery

This combination of beans creates a visually stunning salad, but you can use any combination you prefer. The equivalent to the proportions given in this recipe would be 2 (15-ounce) cans of beans.

For dressing, combine soup mix and boiling water in jar with a tight-fitting lid. Stir well, cover jar, and let mixture sit for 10 minutes. Add vinegar, garlic, jalapeño, oregano, cumin, and black pepper. Shake well. Add oil and shake well again.

For salad, place kidney beans, chickpeas, cannellini beans, tomato, onion, and cilantro into a mixing bowl. Pour in dressing and stir well. Refrigerate salad for 3 to 5 hours and serve on lettuce leaves.

# Black Bean and Papaya Salad

Prep time: less than 20 minutes   •   Makes 6 servings

**For dressing:**

2 TB. savory herb with garlic soup mix

2 garlic cloves, minced

3 shallots, chopped

½ tsp. ground cumin

¼ tsp. ground cinnamon

3 TB. sherry vinegar

2 TB. lime juice

⅓ cup orange juice

Cayenne to taste

⅓ cup olive oil

**For salad:**

2 (15-oz.) cans black beans, rinsed and drained

1 ripe papaya, peeled, seeded, and cut into ¼-inch dice

1 medium *jicama*, peeled and cut into a ¼-inch dice

½ red bell pepper, seeds and ribs removed, and cut into ¼-inch dice

¼ cup chopped fresh cilantro

6 large leaves Boston or green leaf lettuce, rinsed and dried

For dressing, combine soup mix, garlic, shallots, cumin, cinnamon, vinegar, lime juice, orange juice, and cayenne in a jar with a tight-fitting lid. Shake well. Add oil and shake well again. Dressing can be made up to 4 days in advance and refrigerated. Allow it to sit at room temperature for 1 hour before using.

For salad, combine beans with papaya, jicama, red bell pepper, and cilantro in a mixing bowl. Toss salad with dressing, and refrigerate, tightly covered, for at least 1 hour before serving. Serve salad on lettuce leaves.

**Ellen on Edibles**

Jicama (pronounced (*HEE-ka-mah*) is a bulbous root vegetable that's popular in Mexican and Southwestern cooking. It's covered with a thin brown skin that must be peeled off along with the white fibrous layer under it. If you can't find jicama, sweet apples such as Red Delicious can be substituted. Toss the apples with lemon or lime juice to prevent discoloration.

# Salade Niçoise

Prep time: less than 30 minutes    •    Makes 6 servings

**For dressing:**

1 envelope vegetable soup mix

⅓ cup boiling water

⅓ cup cider vinegar

1 TB. Dijon mustard

2 TB. chopped fresh parsley

1 TB. chopped fresh tarragon or 1 tsp. dried

3 garlic cloves, minced

1 shallot, minced

Freshly ground black pepper to taste

Reserved oil from canned tuna in salad

½ cup olive oil

**For salad:**

½ lb. green beans, stemmed

6 large Boston or green leaf lettuce leaves, rinsed and dried

½ lb. baby new potatoes, boiled, sliced, and chilled

½ green or red bell pepper, seeds and ribs removed, and thinly sliced

2 tomatoes, cored and thinly sliced

2 (6½-oz.) cans tuna packed in olive oil, drained, oil reserved

3 hard-cooked eggs, peeled and sliced

⅓ cup pitted black olives

For dressing, combine soup mix and boiling water in a jar with a tight-fitting lid. Stir well, cover jar, and let mixture sit for 10 minutes. Add vinegar, mustard, parsley, tarragon, garlic, shallot, and black pepper. Shake well. Add reserved oil from tuna cans and olive oil, and shake well again. Let dressing sit at room temperature for 1 hour.

### Mix Mastery

Plunging green vegetables into ice water after cooking sets both the color and the texture. The same treatment can be used for broccoli, asparagus, Brussels sprouts, or any green vegetable to retain a crisp-tender texture and vivid color.

For salad, bring a saucepan of water to a boil. Prepare a bowl of ice water. Add green beans to saucepan, and boil for 2 minutes. Drain beans and place them in ice water for 2 minutes to stop the cooking action. Once chilled, drain beans.

Place lettuce leaves on individual salad plates. Arrange beans, sliced potatoes, bell pepper slices, tomato slices, chunks of tuna, hard-cooked egg slices, and olives on plates. Drizzle with dressing and serve.

# White Bean and Tuna Salad

Prep time: less than 15 minutes • Makes 6 servings

2 (15-oz.) cans cannellini beans, rinsed and drained

2 (6½-oz.) cans tuna packed in olive oil, drained, oil reserved

⅓ cup chopped fresh Italian parsley

½ cup finely chopped scallions, white part and 2 inches of green tops

2 TB. roasted garlic herb soup mix

¼ cup lemon juice

2 garlic cloves, minced

Freshly ground black pepper to taste

¼ cup olive oil

6 large leaves Boston or green leaf lettuce, rinsed and dried

Place beans in a mixing bowl. Break tuna into chunks, and add to beans along with parsley and scallions.

Combine soup mix, lemon juice, garlic, and black pepper in a jar with a tight-fitting lid. Shake well. Add reserved tuna oil and olive oil, and shake well again.

Toss salad with dressing, and season with black pepper to taste. Refrigerate salad for 1 to 3 hours to blend flavors. Serve salad chilled on lettuce leaves.

**Mix with Care**

For the success of this dish as well as Salade Niçoise, it is important to use tuna that is packed in oil, preferably olive oil. Water-packed tuna will not deliver as pleasing a flavor or texture.

# Wilted Spinach Salad with Bacon

Prep time: less than 20 minutes • Makes 6 servings

6 strips bacon, cut into ½-inch pieces

½ cup diced red onion

1 Golden Delicious or McIntosh apple, peeled, cored, and chopped

½ envelope savory herb with garlic soup mix

⅓ cup water

3 TB. cider vinegar

1 cup apple juice

3 TB. firmly packed dark brown sugar

1 TB. Dijon-style mustard

Freshly ground black pepper to taste

1 lb. fresh spinach, stemmed, rinsed, and dried

3 hard-cooked eggs, diced

Place bacon in a large skillet over medium heat. Fry until crisp. Remove bacon with a slotted spoon, and drain on paper towels and set aside. Add onion and apple to skillet. Cook and stir for 3 to 5 minutes or until onion is translucent and apple is soft. Add soup mix, water, vinegar, apple juice, brown sugar, and mustard to skillet. Bring to a boil over medium heat, and boil, stirring occasionally, until liquid is reduced in volume by half. Season with black pepper.

Place spinach in salad bowl, and add bacon and eggs. Pour hot dressing over salad, and toss to wilt leaves. Serve immediately.

### Mix Mastery

Spinach can have a lot of grit hidden in the curls of its leaves. The best way to clean it is in a large bowl of cold water, rather than under cold running water. Soak the spinach, rubbing it with your hands to dislodge any dirt, then remove it from the bowl. *Do not* pour the spinach into a colander because the dirt will go right back onto the leaves.

# Bacon, Egg, and Arugula Salad

Prep time: less than 20 minutes    •    Makes 6 servings

**For dressing:**

½ envelope roasted garlic herb soup mix

⅓ cup boiling water

2 shallots, finely chopped

1 tsp. herbes de Provence, or 1 tsp. dried thyme

¼ cup sherry vinegar

Freshly ground black pepper to taste

¾ cup olive oil

**For salad:**

¾ lb. bacon

2 TB. butter

10 eggs

⅓ cup sour cream

Salt and freshly ground black pepper to taste

6 cups arugula leaves, rinsed and stems removed

For dressing, combine soup mix and water in a jar with a tight-fitting lid. Shake well, cover jar, and let mixture sit for 10 minutes. Add shallots, herbes de Provence, vinegar, and black pepper. Shake well. Add oil and shake well again. Dressing can be made up to 4 days in advance and refrigerated. Allow it to sit at room temperature for 1 hour before using.

For salad, cook bacon in a large skillet over medium-high until crisp. Drain bacon on paper towels, and crumble into small pieces. Set aside. Pour bacon grease out of skillet.

Melt butter in the same skillet over low heat. Whisk eggs with sour cream, salt, and black pepper. When butter has melted, add eggs to the pan and cover. After 3 minutes, stir eggs and cover the pan again. Cook until eggs are ¾ set or well done if you prefer.

While eggs are cooking, place arugula in a salad bowl. Toss with dressing. Add bacon and hot eggs to the salad bowl and toss gently. Serve immediately.

### Mix Mastery

An alternative to frying bacon is to bake it in a 325°F oven until crisp. The length of time will depend on the thickness of the bacon, but count on at least 20 minutes.

# Grilled Corn and Sausage Salad

Prep time: less than 30 minutes • Makes 6 servings

**For dressing:**

2 TB. golden onion soup mix

¼ cup boiling water

3 TB. fresh lime juice

3 TB. pure maple syrup

Freshly ground black pepper to taste

¼ cup olive oil

**For salad:**

1 cup mesquite chips

4 ears fresh corn, unshucked

¾ lb. bulk pork sausage

½ cup finely chopped red bell pepper

½ cup finely chopped green bell pepper

3 scallions, white parts and 2 inches of the green tops, finely chopped

3 TB. chopped fresh cilantro

6 large leaves Boston or green leaf lettuce, rinsed and dried

For dressing, place soup mix and water in a jar with a tight-fitting lid. Stir well, cover, and let mixture sit for 10 minutes. Add lime juice, maple syrup, and black pepper. Shake well. Add oil and shake well again. Dressing can be made up to 4 days in advance and refrigerated. Allow it to sit at room temperature for 1 hour before using.

For salad, soak mesquite chips covered in cold water for 30 minutes. Heat a charcoal or gas grill. Remove all but 1 layer of husks from corn, and pull out corn silks. Cover corn in cold water for 10 minutes. Drain mesquite chips, and place on the fire. Grill corn for 10 to 15 minutes, covered with the grill lid or using a sheet of heavy-duty aluminum foil to create a lid. Turn corn with tongs occasionally. When cool enough to handle, discard the husks, and use a sharp serrated knife to cut kernels off cobs. Set aside.

 **Dry and Droll**

Humorist Garrison Keillor of Lake Wobegone fame once quipped that "sex is good, but not as good as fresh, sweet corn."

Cook sausage in a frying pan over medium heat, breaking up lumps with a fork, for 7 to 10 minutes or until browned and no pink remains. Transfer sausage and its fat to a mixing bowl, add corn, red and green bell peppers, scallions, and cilantro and toss.

Toss salad with dressing. Serve salad on lettuce leaves.

# Part 5

# The Main Event

If you consider hors d'oeuvres and appetizers as frills, you'll be ready for the delicate to hearty entrées in this part.

The types of food being cooked divide these chapters. There is a chapter devoted to hearty red and white meats, one for versatile poultry, and one for delicate fish and seafood.

These foods are cooked in a variety of ways, from stews and roasts that take hours to cook to food that grills in a matter of minutes.

# Chapter 12

# From the Plains and Prairies

## In This Chapter

- ◆ Family-pleasing meat loafs and burgers
- ◆ Stews and pot roasts from around the world
- ◆ Recipes featuring lamb, pork, and veal

In this chapter, you'll find recipes that "meat" their mark. Some are delicate, and others are hearty. Some take hours to slowly cook, while others are rapidly cooked on a grill or under a broiler.

Soup mixes and gravy mixes are a boon when cooking all these recipes. In some recipes, a soup mix becomes the basis for an easy marinade. In other recipes, mixes become a no-fuss sauce.

## Safety First

There are naturally occurring bacteria in many raw animal products, and being careful about how these foods are handled before and after you cook them is the key to preventing any food-borne illness. The first test is a simple sniff of the meat. If it has any off odor, discard it, regardless of the "sell by" date on the package.

Unlike poultry, it is not necessary to rinse red meats before cooking them. Any bacteria that might be present on the surface will be destroyed by cooking.

What is important is to wash any cutting boards, knives, countertops, and especially your hands after handling raw meat. Never handle another food, especially those eaten raw like salad greens, without washing your hands because bacteria such as salmonella can be transferred. Also, never place cooked meat on the same platter that held it while raw. This cross-contamination is what causes many illnesses during grill-out season.

Bacteria needs an environment between 40°F and 140°F to grow, so never brown meats and then refrigerate them. Once the surface of meat has been heated, continue the cooking immediately. This also applies to defrosting meats in a microwave oven because the meat is likely to have entered this "danger zone."

Many people like beef and lamb cooked rare—an internal temperature of 145°F, but the U.S. Department of Agriculture recommends that all dishes made with ground beef be cooked until well done—an internal temperature of 170°F.

For centuries, health authorities stressed the importance of cooking pork to well done to guard against trichinosis. That's no longer the case, but experts do advise that pork should be cooked to medium—an internal temperature of 160°F.

# Compatible Animals

Many times you can change the animal without sacrificing the quality of a recipe, as long as the change is in the same flavor and texture family. For example, beef and lamb recipes are interchangeable because they are both hearty meats. In the same way, pork and veal are similar, and both can be substituted for whole pieces of chicken without changing the timing.

Ask yourself this question: Is it a red or a white meat? Even though veal is a young cow, its flavor and texture is more similar to pork or chicken than it is to beef.

# Slow Cook Style

Many of the dishes in this chapter are *braised* stews and roasts. All these recipes are great candidates for cooking in a slow cooker. If you want to adapt a recipe to the slow cooker, follow these general guidelines:

- ◆ Beef and lamb stews cook on low for 8 to 10 hours and on high for 4 to 5 hours.
- ◆ Large pot roasts cook on low for 10 to 12 hours or on high for 5 to 6 hours.

- Veal and pork stews cook on low for 6 to 8 hours or on high for 3 to 4 hours.

- Reduce the amount of liquid in the recipe by ⅓ because there is little evaporation from a slow cooker.

- The hard vegetables in a dish take longer to cook than the meat, so cut them into pieces no larger than ¼ inch.

 **Mix Mastery**

These are general guidelines for converting foods for slow cooker cooking, and you'll find hundreds of recipes for foods in *The Complete Idiot's Guide to Slow Cooker Cooking*. I'm certainly not impartial to the book because I wrote it.

## The Least You Need to Know

- Soup mixes can be used for both marinades and sauces for meats.

- Meat dishes that are braised can also be cooked in a slow cooker.

- Beef and lamb can be substituted for one another. Pork, veal, and chicken are also compatible with each other.

- Meat should not be marinated for longer than the time recommended in the recipe.

# All-American Meat Loaf

Prep time: less than 15 minutes • Cooking time: 1¼ hours • Makes 6 servings

2 TB. vegetable oil

1 onion, chopped

1 carrot, chopped

1 celery stalk, trimmed and chopped

2 garlic cloves, minced

1 envelope onion or beefy onion soup mix

½ cup plain breadcrumbs

½ cup milk

¾ cup ketchup

1 egg, lightly beaten

3 TB. chopped fresh parsley

1 tsp. dried thyme

1½ lb. lean ground beef

Freshly ground black pepper to taste

### Dry and Droll

Our English word *beef* comes from the Latin, *bos*, which means "ox." By the Middle Ages, it had become *beef* or *boef* in English. There were cattle at the Jamestown settlement in Virginia in the early seventeenth century, but the Texas longhorns we use for beef were brought to that state by the Spanish almost a century later.

Preheat the oven to 350°F, and line a 9×13-inch baking pan with aluminum foil. Heat oil in a medium skillet over medium heat; add onion, carrot, celery, and garlic. Cook and stir for 3 to 5 minutes or until onion is translucent and vegetables soften. Set aside to cool.

Combine soup mix, breadcrumbs, milk, ¼ cup ketchup, egg, parsley, thyme, beef, and pepper in mixing bowl. Blend well. Add vegetable mixture, and blend well again.

Transfer meat to a baking dish, and form into a loaf. Spread remaining ½ cup ketchup on top of meat. Bake for 1¼ hours or until an instant-read thermometer inserted into the center of loaf registers 170°F. Let meat loaf sit for 10 minutes. Drain off excess grease and serve immediately.

# Italian Meat Loaf

Prep time: less than 15 minutes    •    Cooking time: 1¼ hours    •    Makes 6 servings

1½ lb. lean ground beef

1 envelope vegetable soup mix

¾ cup *Italian-style breadcrumbs*

½ cup milk

2 eggs, lightly beaten

Freshly ground black pepper to taste

1 (10-oz.) box frozen chopped spinach, thawed

1 cup shredded mozzarella cheese

2 tsp. Italian seasoning, or 1 tsp. dried oregano and 1 tsp. dried basil

Preheat the oven to 350°F, and line a 9×13-inch baking pan with aluminum foil. Combine ground beef, soup mix, breadcrumbs, milk, eggs, and black pepper in mixing bowl. Blend well.

Place meat mixture on a sheet of plastic wrap or wax paper, and form into a 10-inch square. Pat meat down to achieve an even thickness.

Place spinach in a strainer and press with the back of a spoon to extract as much water as possible. Combine spinach with cheese and Italian seasoning, and spread mixture on top of meat. Use the plastic wrap as a guide to roll meat into even cylinder.

Place meat loaf seam side down in the baking pan. Bake for 1¼ hours or until an instant-read thermometer inserted into the center of loaf registers 170°F. Let meat loaf sit for 10 minutes. Drain off excess grease and serve immediately.

**Ellen on Edibles**

Italian-style breadcrumbs are a convenience food that incorporates some herbs and cheese into the breadcrumbs. If you are using plain breadcrumbs, add 1 tablespoon chopped fresh parsley and 1 tablespoon grated Parmesan cheese to a recipe.

# Flavored Burgers

Prep time: less than 15 minutes  •  Cooking time: 10 to 15 minutes  •  Makes 6 servings

**For burgers:**

2 lb. lean ground beef

1 envelope soup mix: your choice of onion, vegetable, roasted garlic herb, beefy onion, or onion mushroom

½ cup water

Freshly ground black pepper to taste

6 hamburger rolls

**For garnishes:**

Sautéed mushrooms and onions

Sliced Swiss or cheddar cheese

Sliced tomato, onion, and pickle

Ketchup, mustard, mayonnaise, or any of the cold dips in Chapter 6

### Mix with Care

Make sure to light the grill or preheat the oven broiler before starting to prepare a simple grilled or broiled dish. A charcoal grill can take up to 30 minutes to heat and a gas grill or oven broiler up to 15 minutes.

Preheat a grill or oven broiler. Combine ground beef, soup mix, water, and black pepper in a mixing bowl. Mix well. Form mixture into 6 patties. Grill or broil to desired doneness, and serve on hamburger rolls with garnishes of your choice.

# Hamburger Stroganoff

Prep time: less than 20 minutes   •   Cooking time: 20 minutes   •   Makes 6 servings

1½ lb. lean ground beef

3 TB. vegetable oil

1 onion, diced

2 garlic cloves, minced

½ lb. white mushrooms, rinsed, stemmed, and sliced

1½ cups water

1 envelope roasted garlic herb soup mix

3 TB. tomato paste

½ cup sour cream

Freshly ground black pepper to taste

Buttered egg noodles for serving

Heat a large skillet over medium heat. Add ground beef, breaking up lumps with a fork. Cook and stir for 5 minutes or until browned. Remove beef from the pan with a slotted spoon and set aside. Drain grease from the pan.

Heat oil in the skillet over medium heat; add onion, garlic, and mushrooms. Cook and stir for 5 minutes or until onion is translucent and mushrooms are soft. Return beef to skillet, and add water, soup mix, and tomato paste. Bring to a boil, reduce heat, and simmer mixture, uncovered, for 10 minutes. Turn off heat, stir in sour cream, and season with black pepper. Serve with buttered egg noodles.

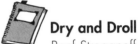

### Dry and Droll

Beef Stroganoff was named for a nineteenth-century Russian diplomat, Count Paul Stroganoff. Many years ago, this dish became one of the hallmarks of what Americans called "continental cuisine."

 **Steak in Red Wine Sauce**

Prep time: less than 15 minutes  •  Cooking time: 10 minutes  •  Makes 4 servings

4 (6- to 8-oz.) fillet, rib eye, or sirloin strip steaks

Salt and freshly ground black pepper to taste

2 TB. olive oil

2 TB. butter

2 shallots, minced

2 garlic cloves, minced

1 envelope brown gravy or mushroom gravy mix

½ cup dry red wine

½ cup water

1 TB. fresh thyme leaves or 1 tsp. dried

Preheat the oven to 200°F. Trim steaks to remove any excess fat and season with salt and black pepper. Heat oil in a skillet over high heat. Add steaks and *sear* on each side for 1 minute. Reduce heat to medium-high, and cook steaks for 2 to 3 minutes on each side for rare or longer if you wish.

**Ellen on Edibles**

**Searing** is the process of browning meat quickly with high heat, either in a skillet or under a broiler. The object of searing is to seal in the meat's juices to keep it moist.

Remove meat from the pan, and place it on a serving platter in oven to keep warm. Pour off grease and place the pan over medium heat; add butter. When butter has melted, add shallots and garlic. Cook and stir for 3 minutes or until shallots are translucent. Add gravy mix, wine, water, and thyme. Stir well, and bring to a boil. Reduce heat to low, and simmer sauce, stirring frequently, for 5 minutes.

Remove steaks from oven, and pour sauce over them.

# Old-Fashioned Beef Stew

Prep time: less than 20 minutes    •    Cooking time: 2 to 3 hours    •    Makes 6 servings

2 lb. beef stew meat

2 TB. vegetable oil

1 onion, chopped

2 garlic cloves, minced

½ lb. white mushrooms, rinsed, trimmed, and halved, if large

3 carrots, cut into ½-inch slices

2 celery stalks, trimmed and sliced

4 large red-skinned potatoes, scrubbed and cut into 1-inch dice

1 turnip, cut into 1-inch dice

1 (10-oz.) box frozen pearl onions, thawed

1 envelope onion or onion mushroom soup mix

1 envelope brown gravy mix

3¾ cups water

2 TB. Worcestershire sauce

2 TB. tomato paste

1 TB. fresh thyme leaves or 1 tsp. dried

1 bay leaf

1 cup frozen peas

Freshly ground black pepper to taste

Preheat the oven broiler, and line a broiler pan with aluminum foil. Place beef cubes in the pan in a single layer, and broil for 3 minutes per side or until cubes are lightly browned. Set aside.

Heat oil in a Dutch oven or large saucepan over medium heat; add onion, garlic, and mushrooms. Cook and stir for 3 minutes or until onion is translucent. Add beef cubes and any juices that accumulated in the broiler pan, along with carrots, celery, potatoes, turnip, pearl onions, soup mix, gravy mix, water, Worcestershire sauce, tomato paste, thyme, and bay leaf.

Bring stew to a boil over medium-high heat. Reduce heat to low, cover the pan, and simmer stew for 2 to 3 hours or until meat is tender. Add peas to the pan and cook for an additional 5 minutes. Remove and discard bay leaf, and season with black pepper to taste.

### Mix Mastery

You can easily adapt dishes like beef stew to suit your taste or to use what vegetables you have on hand. Use parsnips in place of or in addition to carrots and turnips. Add mixed vegetables or cut green beans to the stew instead of green peas. The important thing is to add the foods at the appropriate time so the dish reaches the finish line with everything properly cooked.

# Sauerbraten

Prep time: less than 15 minutes, • Cooking time: 2½ to 3 hours • Makes 6 servings
plus 2 days to marinate

1 envelope roasted garlic herb soup mix

1 cup dry red wine

1½ cups water

½ cup red wine vinegar

2 TB. tomato paste

2 TB. Worcestershire sauce

1 TB. Dijon-style mustard

½ tsp. ground allspice

½ tsp. ground ginger

¼ cup firmly packed dark brown sugar

Freshly packed black pepper to taste

1 onion, thinly sliced

3 garlic cloves, thinly sliced

2 to 3 lb. rump or chuck roast

10 gingersnap cookies, crushed

### Mix with Care

In this recipe, the marinade becomes the braising liquid, which is subject to high heat, so there is no danger of contamination. But the general rule is to always discard marinades; don't use them for basting or dipping sauce. This is especially important when grilling marinated foods. Also, never put the cooked food on the platter you used when the food was raw.

Combine soup mix, wine, water, vinegar, tomato paste, Worcestershire sauce, mustard, allspice, ginger, brown sugar, and black pepper in a heavy sealable plastic bag. Seal and shake well and add onion, garlic, and beef. Marinate in the refrigerator for 2 to 3 days, turning the bag occasionally so meat marinates evenly.

Transfer meat and marinade to a Dutch oven, add gingersnaps, and bring to a boil over medium heat. Reduce the heat to low, cover the pan, and braise for 2½ to 3 hours or until tender. Slice meat across the grain, and spoon gravy over it.

# Beef Brisket in Red Wine Sauce

Prep time: less than 15 minutes   •   Cooking time: 3½ to 4 hours   •   Makes 4 to 6 servings

1 (2 to 2½-lb.) beef brisket

1 envelope brown gravy mix

2 garlic cloves, minced

1 TB. herbes de Provence, or 1 tsp. dried thyme, 1 tsp. dried oregano, and 1 tsp. dried rosemary

1 cup dry red wine

1 cup beef stock

Freshly ground black pepper to taste

Preheat the oven broiler, and line a broiler pan with aluminum foil. Broil brisket for 3 to 5 minutes per side until browned. Set aside. Turn off the broiler, and set the oven temperature to 325°F.

Combine gravy mix, garlic, herbes de Provence, wine, and stock in a Dutch oven and stir well. Place brisket into it. Cover and bake in the oven for 2 hours. Using tongs, turn brisket, cover and cook for an additional 1½ to 2 hours or until brisket is very tender. Season with black pepper to taste. Slice brisket into thin slices across the grain.

### Mix Mastery

If you want a fancier dish, use mushroom gravy instead of brown gravy and add some sautéed mushrooms to the sauce.

# Herb-Basted Prime Rib

Prep time: less than 15 minutes,  •  Cooking time: 1 to 1½ hours  •  Makes 4 to 6 servings
plus 12 hours for marinating

4 lb. standing rib roast

4 garlic cloves, cut into sixths

1 envelope roasted garlic herb soup mix

3 cups dark beer or stout

Freshly ground black pepper to taste

### Mix Mastery

The reason to let meat sit before carving, often referred to as "resting," is so that the juices will reabsorb into the fibers. If a roast is carved immediately out of the oven, it will lose much juice and be drier than if it sits for a time. The amount of time a roast should rest relates to its size. A thin piece of meat can be carved in 5 minutes; a standing rib should sit for 15 minutes.

Using a sharp knife, make 24 1-inch-deep slits at regular intervals over surface of beef. Insert 1 garlic sliver in each. Combine soup mix, beer, and pepper in large sealable plastic bag. Seal and shake well. Place beef in the bag, seal and marinate in the refrigerator 12 to 24 hours, turning the bag occasionally so meat marinates evenly.

Preheat the oven to 450°F. Remove beef from marinade and discard marinade. Place beef on a rack in a roasting pan, and bake for 30 minutes. Reduce heat to 350°F. Roast meat for an additional 30 to 60 minutes or until an instant-read thermometer inserted into center of roast reads 120°F for rare, 125°F for medium rare, or to desired doneness.

Remove beef from the oven and let stand for 15 minutes before carving.

# Braised Lamb Shanks with Winter Vegetables

Prep time: less than 15 minutes • Cooking time: 2½ to 3 hours • Makes 4 to 6 servings

4 to 6 meaty lamb shanks, about 12 oz. each

1 cup dry red wine

½ cup water

1 envelope brown gravy mix

1 carrot, thinly sliced

1 celery stalk, thinly sliced

1 large onion, diced

3 garlic cloves, crushed

2 TB. chopped fresh parsley

1 tsp. herbes de Provence, or 1 tsp. dried thyme

1 bay leaf

Freshly ground black pepper to taste

Preheat the oven broiler, and line a broiler pan with aluminum foil. Broil lamb shanks for 3 to 5 minutes per side or until lightly browned. Set aside. Turn off broiler, and set oven temperature at 350°F.

Combine wine, water, and gravy mix in a Dutch oven or roasting pan and stir well. Add carrot, celery, onion, garlic, parsley, herbes de Provence, and bay leaf. Stir well. Arrange lamb shanks in the pan.

Bake lamb shanks covered for 2½ to 3 hours or until meat is very tender. Remove and discard bay leaf, and season with black pepper.

 **Mix Mastery**

Frequently, lamb shanks have a membrane over the lower part of the bone. It's not really necessary to trim this off, as it will become tender after the long hours of cooking.

# Irish Stew

Prep time: less than 15 minutes • Cooking time: 2 to 2½ hours • Makes 4 to 6 servings

2 lb. lamb meat, cut into 1-inch cubes

2 TB. vegetable oil

1 large onion, diced

2 garlic cloves, minced

1 envelope roasted garlic herb soup mix

2 cups water

2 carrots, diced

1 celery stalk, trimmed and sliced

1 lb. red-skinned potatoes, scrubbed and cut into 1-inch cubes

2 TB. chopped fresh parsley

1 TB. fresh thyme leaves or ½ tsp. dried

1 bay leaf

1 (10-oz.) pkg. frozen mixed vegetables, thawed

Freshly ground black pepper to taste

Preheat the oven broiler, and line a broiler pan with aluminum foil. Broil lamb cubes for 3 to 4 minutes per side or until lightly browned. Set aside.

**Mix with Care**
There is no need to peel thin-skinned red-skinned potatoes as long as they're scrubbed well, but this is not the case if you substitute other potatoes. The skin on russet potatoes will peel off the cubes as they cook, and this isn't very attractive in the pot.

Heat oil in a Dutch oven; add onion and garlic. Cook and stir for 3 minutes or until onion is translucent. Add lamb cubes with any accumulated juices to the pan, along with soup mix, water, carrots, celery, potatoes, parsley, thyme, and bay leaf. Stir well.

Bring mixture to a boil over medium heat. Cover the pan, reduce heat to low, and simmer stew for 2 to 2½ hours or until meat is tender. Add mixed vegetables after 1½ hours cooking time.

Remove and discard bay leaf. Remove 1 cup solids and purée it in a food processor fitted with a steel blade or in a blender. Return purée to stew and season with black pepper.

# Shepherd's Pie

Prep time: less than 30 minutes • Cooking time: 1 hour • Makes 6 to 8 servings

2 lb. lean ground lamb

4 TB. butter

3 TB. olive oil

½ lb. fresh shiitake mushrooms, stemmed and sliced

2 onions, diced

6 garlic cloves, minced

2 cups dry red wine

1 envelope mushroom gravy mix

2 TB. chopped fresh rosemary leaves or 2 tsp. dried

1 TB. fresh thyme leaves or 1 tsp. dried

2 lb. red-skinned potatoes, scrubbed and cut into 1-inch dice

½ cup heavy cream

4 TB. (½ stick) butter

2 cups (½ lb.) grated sharp cheddar cheese

Salt and freshly ground black pepper to taste

1 (10-oz.) box frozen mixed vegetables, thawed

Place a large skillet over medium-high heat. Add lamb, breaking it up with a fork, and brown it well. Using a slotted spoon, transfer lamb to a bowl and drain and discard any fat from the skillet. Heat 2 tablespoons butter and 1 tablespoon oil in the skillet over medium-high heat; add mushrooms. Cook and stir for 3 minutes or until mushrooms are soft. Scrape mushrooms into the bowl with lamb.

Heat remaining butter and oil in the skillet over medium heat; add onions and garlic. Cook and stir for 3 minutes or until onion is translucent and soft. Return lamb and mushrooms to the skillet, and add wine, gravy mix, rosemary, and thyme. Bring to a boil, reduce the heat to low, and simmer mixture, uncovered, for 30 minutes or until thickened. Tilt the pan to spoon off as much grease as possible.

Prepare topping while lamb is simmering. Place potatoes in a saucepan with enough salted water to cover, and bring to a boil over high heat. Reduce heat to medium, and boil potatoes, uncovered, for 12 to 15 minutes or until soft. Drain potatoes. Heat cream, butter, and cheddar cheese in the saucepan over medium heat, stirring occasionally, until cheese is melted. Return potatoes to the saucepan and mash well with a potato masher. Season with salt and black pepper to taste. Set aside.

Preheat the oven to 425°F. Add mixed vegetables to lamb, and bring mixture back to a boil. Simmer for 3 minutes; then scrape mixture into a 9×13-inch baking dish. Spoon potatoes on top of lamb, smoothing them into an even layer. Bake for 15 minutes or until lamb is bubbly and potatoes are lightly browned. Serve immediately.

### Mix Mastery

When baking a casserole such as this one, always place it on a foil-covered baking sheet. It's inevitable that some juices will bubble over the side, and the baking sheet saves cleaning the oven later.

# Grilled Greek-Style Leg of Lamb

Prep time: less than 15 minutes, • Cooking time: 10 to 20 minutes • Makes 4 to 6
plus 12 hours for marinating servings

1 envelope savory herb with garlic soup mix

1 cup dry red wine

1 cup water

4 garlic cloves, minced

2 TB. grated lemon zest

2 TB. dried oregano

2 bay leaves

Freshly ground black pepper to taste

½ cup olive oil

3 lb. boned and butterflied leg of lamb

### Mix with Care

Marinating should always be done according to the specifications of a recipe. There is such a thing as marinating too long. Most marinades contain an acid such as wine or lemon juice, and if food is marinated past the time recommended, the fibers in the food can break down too much.

Combine soup mix, wine, water, garlic, lemon zest, oregano, bay leaves, and black pepper in a large sealable plastic bag. Seal and shake well. Add olive oil, and shake well again. Add lamb and marinate in the refrigerator for 12 to 24 hours, turning the bag occasionally so meat marinates evenly.

Light a charcoal or gas grill. Remove meat from marinade and discard marinade. Grill lamb for 5 to 10 minutes per side, depending on thickness, or until an instant-read thermometer inserted into the thickest part of lamb registers 125°F for medium rare or desired doneness. Remove lamb from grill and allow it to sit for 10 minutes before carving.

# Cranberry-Maple Spareribs

Prep time: less than 15 minutes,   •   Cooking time: 30 minutes   •   Makes 6 servings
plus 12 hours for marinating

| | |
|---|---|
| 1 envelope golden onion soup mix | 1 TB. fresh thyme leaves or 1 tsp. dried |
| 2 cups cranberry juice | ½ tsp. ground allspice |
| ¼ cup frozen orange juice concentrate, thawed | Freshly ground black pepper to taste |
| 4 garlic cloves, minced | 6 lb. baby back ribs, cut into 6 servings |
| 1 shallot, minced | ⅓ cup pure maple syrup |

Combine soup mix, cranberry juice, orange juice concentrate, garlic, shallot, thyme, allspice, and black pepper in a large, heavy, sealable plastic bag. Seal, shake well, and add ribs. Marinate ribs in the refrigerator for 12 to 18 hours, turning the bag occasionally so ribs marinate evenly.

Light a charcoal or gas grill. Remove ribs from marinade and reserve marinade. Grill ribs, turning occasionally, until almost cooked through, about 20 minutes. While ribs are grilling, combine reserved marinade and maple syrup in a small saucepan. Bring to a boil, and boil over medium heat until reduced in volume to ⅓ cup. Brush underside of ribs with glaze, and grill 2 minutes. Turn ribs, brush the other side with glaze, and grill for 2 minutes more.

### Dry and Droll

Early New England settlers sweetened foods with maple syrup because white sugar had to be imported and was, therefore, expensive. Tapping the sugar maple trees native to North America and creating syrup from the sap is another skill the Native Americans taught the settlers.

# Pork Tenderloin with Porcini Mushrooms

Prep time: less than 30 minutes • Cooking time: 25 minutes • Makes 6 servings

2½ lb. pork tenderloin

¼ cup olive oil

2 TB. butter

½ lb. porcini mushrooms, stemmed and thinly sliced

2 garlic cloves, minced

1 envelope roasted garlic herb soup mix

1 cup water

1 cup dry Marsala wine

¼ cup chopped fresh parsley

Freshly ground black pepper to taste

Trim pork tenderloins by cutting off all visible fat and *silverskin*. Cut tenderloin into 1½-inch thick slices. Place slices between 2 sheets of plastic wrap 3 inches apart. Pound pork with flat side of meat mallet or the bottom of a small skillet until ½ inch thick.

Heat 2 tablespoons oil in a large skillet over medium-high heat. Add as many pork slices as will comfortably fit in the skillet in a single layer and brown on both sides, turning pork with tongs. Work in batches if necessary. Transfer pork to a platter and keep warm.

### Ellen on Edibles

**Silverskin** is the almost iridescent membrane that surrounds certain parts of tenderloins. This should be trimmed off because it will be tough and chewy once it's cooked.

Add remaining oil and butter to the skillet; add mushrooms and garlic. Cook and stir for 3 minutes or until mushrooms begin to soften. Add soup mix, water, wine, and parsley and stir well. Return pork to the skillet, and bring to a boil over medium heat. Reduce heat to low, and simmer pork, uncovered, for 15 to 20 minutes or until pork is tender. Season with black pepper to taste.

# Smothered Pork Chops in Onion Gravy

Prep time: less than 30 minutes   •   Cooking time: 2 hours   •   Makes 6 servings

6 (10- to 12-oz.) center cut pork chops

Salt and freshly ground black pepper to taste

¼ cup vegetable oil

4 onions, thinly sliced

½ cup dry white wine

1 envelope golden onion soup mix

2 cups water

Season pork chops with salt and pepper. Heat oil in an oven-proof skillet or Dutch oven over medium-high heat. Brown pork chops well on both sides, remove from the pan, and set aside.

Reduce the heat to low, and add onions to the skillet. Toss to coat with oil, cover pan, and cook for 10 minutes or until onions are soft. Raise heat to medium, and cook, stirring frequently, for about 20 minutes or until browned.

Preheat the oven to 350°F. Add white wine to the skillet, and boil over medium heat until the pan is almost dry. Add soup mix and water and stir well. Return pork chops to the skillet and cover. Bake for 1 to 1½ hours or until meat is tender when pierced by a fork.

 **Mix Mastery**

Veal chops can be cooked exactly the same way as these pork chops. It's always a good idea when taking the time to brown onions to do a larger batch than necessary and freeze the remainder. This step saves time for many recipes in the future.

# Spaghetti with Ragu alla Bolognese (Spaghetti with Meat Sauce)

Prep time: less than 20 minutes  •  Cooking time: 1 hour  •  Makes 8 servings

1 lb. lean ground pork or beef

1 lb. mild or hot bulk Italian sausage

2 TB. olive oil

1 large onion, diced

4 garlic cloves, minced

1 envelope vegetable soup mix

3 (14½-oz.) cans diced tomatoes

½ cup dry red wine

¼ cup chopped fresh parsley

1 TB. Italian seasoning

1 bay leaf

Freshly ground black pepper to taste

6 cups cooked spaghetti or other pasta

1 cup freshly grated Parmesan cheese

Heat a large saucepan over medium-high heat. Add pork and sausage. Cook, stirring and breaking up any lumps with a wooden spoon, for 5 minutes or until browned. Remove meat from the pan with a slotted spoon and set aside. Drain grease from the pan.

### Dry and Droll

Ragu, now referring to any sort of Italian meat sauce, is a term that dates back to the eighteenth century. It comes from the Latin word *gustus*, which means "taste."

Reduce heat to medium, and add oil to the pan. Add onion and garlic. Cook, stirring, for 3 minutes or until onion is translucent and soft. Return meat to the pan and add soup mix, tomatoes, wine, parsley, Italian seasoning, and bay leaf. Bring to a boil. Reduce heat to low, and simmer sauce, uncovered, for 45 minutes, stirring occasionally. Discard bay leaf, and season with black pepper to taste.

Serve sauce over cooked pasta, and pass Parmesan separately.

# Veal with Mushroom Sauce

Prep time: less than 15 minutes   •   Cooking time: 20 minutes   •   Makes 6 servings

| | |
|---|---|
| 2 lb. veal cutlets | 1 envelope wild mushroom and chive soup mix |
| 2 TB. butter | 1 cup water |
| 2 TB. olive oil | ½ cup dry Marsala wine |
| ½ lb. shiitake mushrooms, stemmed and thinly sliced | ½ cup heavy cream |
| 2 garlic cloves, minced | Freshly ground black pepper to taste |

Place veal between two sheets of plastic wrap. Pound with the flat side of a meat mallet or the bottom of a small skillet until ¼-inch thick. Heat butter and oil in a large skillet over medium-high heat. Arrange veal in the skillet in a single layer, and brown on both sides, working in batches if necessary. Remove veal from the skillet and set aside.

Add mushrooms and garlic to the skillet. Cook and stir for 3 minutes or until mushrooms begin to soften. Add soup mix, water, and wine to the skillet. Stir well and return veal to the skillet. Bring to a boil. Reduce heat to low, and simmer veal, uncovered, for 10 minutes or until cooked through. Add cream to the skillet and stir well. Simmer for 3 minutes. Season with black pepper to taste.

 **Mix Mastery**

This recipe also works well for boneless, skinless chicken breasts and thinly sliced pork chops.

# Osso Buco alla Milanese (Braised Veal Shanks)

Prep time: less than 30 minutes  •  Cooking time: 2 hours  •  Makes 6 servings

**For veal:**

6 meaty veal shanks, about 2 inches thick

All-purpose flour for dredging

½ cup olive oil or as needed

4 TB. butter

4 large onions, diced

4 garlic cloves, minced

2 carrots, diced

2 celery stalks, diced

1 envelope tomato with basil soup mix

1½ cups water

½ cup dry white wine

1 TB. herbes de Provence, or 1 tsp. dried thyme, 1 tsp. dried oregano, and 1 tsp. dried rosemary

1 bay leaf

Freshly ground black pepper to taste

**For garnish:**

5 TB. chopped fresh parsley

2 TB. finely minced garlic

2 TB. grated lemon zest

1 TB. grated orange zest

### Dry and Droll

*Osso buco* has become synonymous with *veal shank* in this country as well as in Italy. Unlike lamb shanks, which are almost always braised whole, veal shanks are cut into crosswise slices. *Osso buco* means "pierced bone," and the marrow from the bone is considered such a delicacy that special marrow spoons are served with the dish.

Rub veal shanks with flour, shaking off any excess over the sink or a plate. Heat ¼ cup oil in a Dutch oven over medium-high heat. Place veal shanks into the pan in a single layer, and brown on both sides. Work in batches if necessary. Remove veal shanks from the pan and set aside.

Reduce heat to medium, and add remaining ¼ cup oil and butter to the pan. Add onion, garlic, carrots, and celery. Cook, stirring, for 3 minutes or until onion is translucent and soft. Stir in soup mix, water, wine, herbes de Provence, and bay leaf. Bring to a boil, cover the pan, and simmer shanks over low heat for 1½ to 2 hours or until veal is tender. Remove and discard bay leaf, and season with black pepper to taste.

For the garnish combine parsley, garlic, lemon zest, and orange zest in a small mixing bowl. Serve veal shanks with a sprinkling of mixture.

# From the Coops

## In This Chapter

- ◆ Quick ways to use boneless, skinless chicken breasts
- ◆ Recipes for chicken pieces
- ◆ Hot and cold one-dish meals
- ◆ Ways to cook turkey when it's not Thanksgiving

At last count, more than 95 percent of American households served chicken at least once a week. That's why there's always a need for new chicken recipes, and that's what you'll find in this chapter.

While the convenience and quick cooking time of boneless breasts makes them very popular, whole chicken pieces are more economical and always have their fans, too. You'll find ways to use all types of chicken, as well as a few recipes for increasingly popular turkey.

## Poultry Safety

Since a spate of food-borne illness cases made news some years ago, chicken has come under scrutiny as a carrier of harmful bacteria. You can reduce the risk of contamination by following a few simple safe-handling rules.

Rinse raw poultry under cold, running water when you remove it from the wrapper, and check it for an odor—it should have none. If it has any off smells, discard it.

Keep in mind, however that illness-causing bacteria such as salmonella has no odor, so even if the chicken does not smell bad, you should follow all standard food-safety precautions.

Making sure the poultry reaches the right temperature while cooking is key, because heat kills bacteria. The white meat of chicken cooks more quickly than the dark meat, but both should be cooked to a temperature of 180°F when an instant-read thermometer is inserted into the thickest part of the meat. Once the breasts reach that temperature, allow the thighs and legs to cook for another 5 minutes, regardless of cooking method.

To prevent transferring bacteria from one food to another, use warm water and soap to wash your hands, utensils, and work surfaces after handling raw poultry.

Never put cooked chicken on the same platter that held it raw. If you transport marinated chicken pieces outside to a grill, bring in the platter and wash it well before placing the cooked chicken on it. By the same token, don't prepare other foods—especially those that are to be eaten raw—with the utensils and work surfaces that you used for raw poultry unless you have washed them first.

# The Benefits of Boning

Boneless, skinless chicken breasts are available in all supermarkets, but the price per pound for the edible meat is still less if you bone them yourself. In addition, you can always replenish your cache of bones and skin for making chicken stock by boning the chicken yourself. Make sure your knife is sharp before you start—it makes all the difference.

If possible, buy the chicken breasts whole rather than split. Pull off the skin with your fingers and then make an incision on both sides of the breast bone (just adjacent to the bone), cutting down until you feel the bone resisting the knife.

Treating one side at a time, place the blade of your boning knife against the carcass and scrape away the meat. You will then have two pieces—the large fillet and the small tenderloin.

To trim the fillet, cut away any fat. Some recipes will tell you to pound the breast to an even thickness so it will cook evenly and quickly. Place the breast between two sheets of plastic wrap, and pound with the smooth side of a meat mallet or the bottom of a small, heavy skillet or saucepan.

To trim the tenderloin, secure the tip of the visible tendon with your free hand. Using a paring knife, scrape down the tendon, and the meat will push away.

## The Least You Need to Know

◆ Chicken should always be rinsed under cold running water and patted dry before you cook it.

◆ Boneless, skinless chicken breasts cook more rapidly than chicken pieces that contain bones.

◆ White meat chicken parts take a shorter time to cook than dark meat.

◆ Recipes for whole pieces of chicken can be cooked both on the stove and in the oven.

# Chicken with Mushrooms

Prep time: less than 15 minutes  •  Cooking time: 15 minutes  •  Makes 6 servings

6 boneless, skinless chicken breast halves

2 TB. olive oil

3 TB. butter

2 large porcini mushrooms, rinsed, stemmed, and thinly sliced

2 garlic cloves, minced

1 envelope wild mushroom and chive soup mix

1 cup water

1 cup dry white wine

1 (14½-oz.) can diced tomatoes, drained

2 TB. chopped fresh parsley

Freshly ground black pepper to taste

Rinse chicken and pat dry with paper towels. Heat oil in a large skillet over medium-high heat. Add chicken and brown on both sides, about 3 to 4 minutes per side. Remove chicken from the skillet with tongs and set aside. Reduce heat to medium, and add butter to the pan; add mushrooms and garlic. Cook and stir for 3 to 5 minutes or until mushrooms are soft. Add soup mix, water, wine, tomatoes, and parsley. Bring to a boil, stirring occasionally.

Return chicken to the skillet. Bring to a boil and cook, covered, for 10 to 12 minutes or until chicken is cooked through and no longer pink. Turn chicken midway through cooking with tongs. Season with black pepper to taste.

**Mix Mastery** _____

The best way to store any white or wild mushrooms is in a paper, not a plastic, bag. The inherent moisture in mushrooms can cause them to rot within a few days if sealed in plastic.

# Chicken Breasts Normandy

Prep time: less than 20 minutes   •   Cooking time: 15 minutes   •   Makes 6 servings

6 boneless, skinless chicken breast halves

2 TB. butter

1 Granny Smith apple, peeled, cored, quartered, and thinly sliced

2 tsp. granulated sugar

2 TB. Calvados or apple brandy

1 envelope leek soup mix

1½ cups whole milk

1 TB. fresh thyme leaves or 1 tsp. dried

Freshly ground black pepper to taste

Rinse chicken and pat dry with paper towels. Heat butter in a large skillet over medium heat. Add chicken and brown well on both sides, 3 to 4 minutes per side. Remove chicken from the skillet with tongs and set aside. Add apple to the skillet, and sprinkle with sugar. Cook and stir for 2 minutes or until apples begin to soften.

Add Calvados, soup mix, milk, and thyme to the skillet. Bring to a boil, stirring frequently. Return chicken to the skillet, and bring to a boil. Reduce heat to low, and cook, covered, for 10 to 12 minutes or until chicken is cooked through and no longer pink. Season with black pepper to taste.

### Mix with Care

Apples discolor once they have been exposed to oxygen. The best way to avoid this, should you want to prepare the ingredients for any apple dish in advance, is to toss the apples with some lemon or lime juice. Orange and grapefruit juice do not contain enough acidity to prevent the browning.

# Chicken with Broccoli

Prep time: less than 15 minutes • Cooking time: 15 minutes • Makes 4 servings

4 boneless, skinless chicken breast halves

2 TB. butter

1 envelope cream of broccoli soup mix

2 cups whole milk

2 TB. chopped fresh parsley

1 tsp. herbes de Provence, or 1 tsp. dried thyme

1 (10-oz.) box frozen chopped broccoli, thawed

1 cup grated cheddar cheese

Freshly ground black pepper to taste

### Mix with Care

Stick around after adding the cheese to this dish. Stir until the cheese is melted, but do not let the dish boil or the cheese might scorch. It takes less than 1 minute to melt, so it's easy to prevent this malady.

Rinse chicken and pat dry with paper towels. Melt butter in a large skillet over medium-high heat. Add chicken and brown on both sides, about 3 to 4 minutes per side. Remove chicken from the skillet with tongs and set aside.

Add soup mix, milk, parsley, herbes de Provence, and broccoli to the skillet. Bring to a boil, stirring frequently. Return chicken to the pan, bring to a boil, and simmer, covered, for 10 to 12 minutes or until chicken is cooked through and no longer pink. Add cheese and stir until cheese is melted. Season with black pepper to taste.

# Chicken Curry

Prep time: less than 20 minutes • Cooking time: 20 minutes • Makes 6 servings

**For curry:**

4 boneless, skinless chicken breast halves

3 TB. butter

1 large onion, diced

2 garlic cloves, minced

1 McIntosh apple, peeled, cored, and diced

3 TB. curry powder, or to taste

1 envelope roasted garlic herb soup mix

1 cup canned unsweetened coconut milk

1½ cups water

2 TB. chopped *crystallized ginger*

½ cup heavy cream

Red pepper flakes to taste

3 cups cooked white or brown rice

**Condiments:**

Raisins

Chopped almonds

Sliced scallions

Chutney

Shredded coconut

Rinse chicken under cold water, and pat dry with paper towels. Cut chicken into 1-inch cubes. Heat butter in a large skillet over medium-high heat; add chicken. Cook and stir for 3 minutes until chicken is a creamy beige color. Remove chicken from the skillet with a slotted spoon and set aside.

Reduce heat to medium; add onion, garlic, and apple to the skillet. Cook and stir for 3 minutes or until onion is translucent. Reduce heat to low; add curry powder. Cook and stir for 1 minute.

Add soup mix, coconut milk, water, and ginger to the skillet. Bring to a boil over medium-high heat, stirring frequently. Return chicken to the skillet. Bring to a boil and simmer over low heat, uncovered, for 10 minutes, stirring frequently, or until chicken is cooked through and no longer pink. Add cream and simmer 3 minutes. Season with red pepper flakes, and serve curry over rice. Pass condiments separately.

**Ellen on Edibles**

**Crystallized ginger,** sometimes called candied ginger, is fresh ginger that has been cooked in a large amount of sugar as a preservation method. There is no substitute for it, and dried ground ginger should never be used in its place.

# Hot Fried Chicken Salad

Prep time: less than 30 minutes • Cooking time: 15 minutes • Makes 6 servings

**For chicken:**

6 boneless, skinless chicken breast halves

½ envelope savory herb with garlic soup mix

Freshly ground black pepper to taste

½ cup all-purpose flour

3 eggs

¼ cup milk

2 cups plain breadcrumbs

**For salad:**

1 lb. fresh spinach, washed and stemmed

2 carrots, cut into thin strips

1 red bell pepper, seeds and ribs removed, and cut into thin slices

1 red onion, cut into thin rings

**For dressing:**

3 TB. honey

3 TB. Dijon-style mustard

⅓ cup cider vinegar

½ envelope savory herb with garlic soup mix

Freshly ground black pepper to taste

⅔ cup olive oil

2 cups vegetable oil for frying

Rinse chicken and pat dry with paper towels. Cut chicken into 1½-inch cubes, and season with soup mix and black pepper. Pour flour on a sheet of plastic wrap, beat eggs with milk in a shallow bowl, and pour breadcrumbs on another sheet of plastic wrap. Dip chicken pieces in flour, shaking gently to remove any excess; then dip in egg mixture, and finally in breadcrumbs. Refrigerate for 10 minutes.

For salad, arrange spinach, carrots, red bell pepper, and onion on 6 individual plates or on a serving platter.

## Mix Mastery

Refrigerate foods prior to frying to allow time for the crumbs to adhere. This brief time bonds the flour, egg, and breading so the crumbs are less likely to fall off when the food is fried.

For dressing, combine honey, mustard, vinegar, soup mix, and black pepper in a jar with a tight-fitting lid, and shake well. Add oil and shake well again. Set aside.

To serve, heat vegetable oil in a deep-sided pan over medium-high heat to a temperature of 375°F or until a light haze forms. Add chicken pieces, being careful not to crowd the pan, and fry until golden brown, about 5 minutes. Work in batches if necessary. Remove chicken from oil with a slotted spoon, and drain well on paper towels. Arrange chicken on top of salad, and drizzle dressing over all.

# Self-Basting Roast Chicken

Prep time: less than 15 minutes   •   Cooking time: 1½ hours   •   Makes 6 servings

1 (5- to 6-lb.) roasting chicken, rinsed and patted dry

¼ lb. (1 stick) butter, softened

1 envelope roasted garlic herb soup mix

Freshly ground black pepper to taste

1 cup water

Preheat oven to 375°F. Rinse chicken and pat dry with paper towels. Place chicken in a metal roasting pan on rack. Combine butter, soup mix, and black pepper in a mixing bowl. Stir well. Use your hands to loosen skin on chicken breast and down into joint area between thigh and drumstick. Insert seasoned butter beneath skin on both sides of chicken.

Roast chicken for 1 hour. *Baste* chicken with juices from the pan. Return chicken to oven, and bake for 1 to 1½ hours or until chicken is no longer pink and an instant-read thermometer inserted into the thickest part of the thigh registers 180°F. Baste chicken every 20 minutes with drippings from pan.

Remove chicken to a platter and cover with aluminum foil. To make sauce, remove the rack from the pan, and tilt the pan. Spoon out grease. Add water to the pan, and place it on the stovetop. Bring juices to a boil, scraping the bottom of the pan to dislodge the browned bits from the surface.

Carve chicken, and pass sauce separately.

**Ellen on Edibles**

**Basting** is the process of moistening food with its own juices as it bakes. The easiest way to do this is with a basting brush or a paint brush that is dedicated to basting. Wash the brush well with soap and water, and do not place basting brushes in the dishwasher.

# Chicken Marengo

Prep time: less than 20 minutes • Cooking time: 35 minutes • Makes 4 servings

1 (3- to 3½-lb.) frying chicken, cut into serving pieces

¼ cup olive oil

1 large onion, diced

3 garlic cloves, minced

½ lb. white mushrooms, rinsed, stemmed, and sliced

1 envelope golden onion soup mix

1 cup water

½ cup orange juice

½ cup dry white wine

1 (14½-oz.) can diced tomatoes

1 TB. grated orange zest

1 tsp. dried thyme

1 bay leaf

Freshly ground black pepper to taste

Rinse chicken and pat dry with paper towels. Heat oil in a large skillet over medium-high heat. Add chicken and brown on both sides, 3 to 4 minutes per side. Remove chicken from the skillet with tongs and set aside.

### Dry and Droll

Chicken Marengo was invented to celebrate a victory. When Napoleon's troops won the Battle of Marengo on June 14, 1800, his cook, Dunand, produced this in the camp kitchen. You can make it with veal as well as chicken.

Reduce heat to medium; add onion, garlic, and mushrooms to the skillet. Cook and stir for 3 to 5 minutes or until onion is translucent and mushrooms are soft. Add soup mix, water, orange juice, wine, tomatoes, orange zest, thyme, and bay leaf. Stir well and bring mixture to boil. Return chicken to the skillet, and simmer, covered, for 25 to 30 minutes, or until chicken is cooked through and no longer pink. Remove and discard bay leaf and season chicken with black pepper to taste.

# Coq au Vin (Chicken in Red Wine Sauce)

Prep time: less than 20 minutes   •   Cooking time: 1 hour   •   Makes 6 servings

Some combination of chicken pieces to feed 6: 6 breast halves, 12 thighs or a mix of parts

10 slices bacon, cut into 1-inch sections

½ cup all-purpose flour

1 bunch scallions, trimmed and sliced

½ lb. small white mushrooms, rinsed and trimmed

¼ lb. fresh shiitake mushrooms, stemmed, and quartered if large, halved if small

3 garlic cloves, minced

12 to 18 small red-skinned potatoes, scrubbed and halved (quartered if larger than a walnut)

1 lb. frozen pearl onions, thawed and drained

1 envelope wild mushroom and chive soup mix

½ cup water

1½ cups dry red wine

2 TB. chopped fresh parsley

1 TB. chopped fresh oregano or 1 tsp. dried

1 TB. fresh thyme or 1 tsp. dried

2 bay leaves

Freshly ground black pepper to taste

Preheat the oven to 350°F. Rinse chicken and pat dry with paper towels. Place bacon into a large ovenproof Dutch oven or roasting pan over medium-high heat and cook until crisp. Remove bacon from the pan with a slotted spoon, drain on paper towels, and pour off all but 3 tablespoons fat. Reduce the heat to medium. Dust chicken pieces with flour, and place them into the pan and brown on all sides for about 5 minutes. Remove chicken from the pan with tongs; add scallions, white mushrooms, shiitake mushrooms, and garlic. Cook and stir for 5 minutes or until mushrooms are soft.

Return chicken to the pan, and add potatoes, onions, soup mix, water, wine, parsley, oregano, thyme, and bay leaves. Bring to a boil, then cover the pan, and bake for 1 hour or until potatoes are tender and chicken is cooked through and no longer pink. Remove and discard bay leaves, and season with black pepper to taste.

 **Mix Mastery**

If you're having problems separating strips of bacon, throw the whole amount into a pan as though it were a single slab. Within a few moments, the bacon will have softened enough to make it easy to separate individual slices.

# Chicken with Forty Cloves of Garlic

Prep time: less than 15 minutes  •  Cooking time: 40 minutes  •  Makes 4 servings

1 (3½-lb.) frying chicken, cut into serving pieces

¼ cup olive oil

3 heads garlic, separated into cloves but not peeled

⅓ cup lemon juice

1 envelope golden onion soup mix

2 cups water

Freshly ground black pepper to taste

Preheat oven to 400°F. Rinse chicken pieces and pat dry with paper towels. Heat olive oil in a large oven-proof skillet over medium-high heat. Add chicken pieces and garlic cloves and brown well. Combine lemon juice, soup mix, and water in a mixing bowl.

Using tongs, turn chicken pieces, skin side down, and pour lemon juice mixture into the pan. Bake for 20 minutes. Remove pan from the oven, and, using tongs, turn pieces skin side up. Bake for 15 minutes more for breasts and 20 minutes more for dark meat or until chicken is cooked through and no longer pink. Remove the pan from the oven, and season with black pepper to taste. Place chicken pieces on a serving platter, and scatter garlic cloves around them; spoon sauce from the pan over all.

# Chicken with Spinach and Feta

Prep time: less than 15 minutes  •  Cooking time: 1 hour  •  Makes 6 servings

6 chicken breast halves, with skin and bones

1 (10-oz.) box frozen chopped spinach, thawed and drained

1 envelope cream of spinach soup mix

¾ cup feta cheese, crumbled

¼ cup milk

2 TB. chopped fresh dill or 2 tsp. dried

Freshly ground black pepper to taste

2 TB. olive oil

 **Mix Mastery**

If you're not fond of the sharp taste of feta cheese, substitute mild grated mozzarella for feta in this dish.

Preheat oven to 375°F. Rinse chicken and pat dry with paper towels. Place spinach in a mixing bowl, and add soup mix, feta, milk, dill, and black pepper. Mix well. Stuff mixture under skin of chicken breasts. Rub skin with olive oil, and season with black pepper.

Bake chicken for 45 to 55 minutes or until cooked through and no longer pink.

# Chicken Cacciatore

Prep time: less than 15 minutes  •  Cooking time: 40 minutes  •  Makes 4 servings

1 (3½-lb.) frying chicken, cut into serving pieces

3 TB. olive oil

1 onion, diced

3 garlic cloves, minced

½ green or red bell pepper, seeds and ribs removed, and thinly sliced

¼ lb. white mushrooms, rinsed, stemmed, and sliced

1 envelope tomato with basil soup mix

1½ cups water

2 TB. chopped fresh parsley

1 TB. chopped fresh oregano or 1 tsp. dried

Freshly ground black pepper to taste

Rinse chicken and pat dry with paper towels. Heat oil in large skillet over medium-high heat. Add chicken pieces, and brown on all sides, turning chicken with tongs, for about 5 minutes. Remove chicken from the pan and set aside.

Reduce heat to medium; add onion, garlic, bell pepper, and mushrooms. Cook, stirring, for 3 to 5 minutes or until onion is translucent and mushrooms are soft. Add soup mix, water, parsley, and oregano to the pan. Bring to a boil. Return chicken to the pan, and bring to a boil again. Reduce heat to low, cover the pan, and simmer for 25 to 30 minutes or until chicken is cooked through and no longer pink. Turn chicken pieces midway through cooking time. Remove dish from the oven, and season with black pepper to taste.

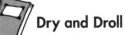

**Dry and Droll**

*Cacciatore* is a catch-all phrase in Italian that means "hunter's style." The sauce always contains tomato, and the food is browned and then simmered in the sauce.

# Oven-Fried Chicken

Prep time: less than 15 minutes    •    Cooking time: 50 minutes    •    Makes 4 servings

1 (3- to 3½-lb.) frying chicken, cut into serving pieces

2 eggs, lightly beaten

2 cups plain breadcrumbs

1 envelope savory herb with garlic soup mix

Freshly ground black pepper to taste

3 TB. vegetable oil

Preheat oven to 375°F, and line a shallow baking pan with aluminum foil. Place a rack in the baking pan.

Rinse chicken and pat dry with paper towels. Place eggs in a shallow bowl. Combine breadcrumbs, soup mix, black pepper, and oil. Spread mixture on sheet of plastic wrap. Dip chicken in egg and then in breadcrumb mixture. Arrange coated chicken pieces on rack.

Bake chicken for 45 to 50 minutes or until chicken is cooked through and no longer pink.

# Biscuit-Topped Chicken Pie

Prep time: less than 20 minutes    •    Cooking time: 25 minutes    •    Makes 4 to 6 servings

4 boneless, skinless chicken breast halves

2 TB. butter

1 envelope golden onion soup mix

1½ cups whole milk

2 tsp. fresh thyme leaves or 1 tsp. dried

2 TB. chopped fresh parsley

1 (10-oz.) pkg. frozen mixed vegetables, thawed

Freshly ground black pepper to taste

1 (4½-oz.) tube refrigerated buttermilk biscuit dough

### Mix Mastery

Pot pies are great recipes for any sort of leftovers. Instead of using raw chicken breasts, you can use 3 cups cubed cooked chicken. In that case, make the sauce and then add the cooked chicken and vegetables at the same time.

Preheat oven to 450°F. Rinse chicken and pat dry with paper towels. Cut chicken into ¾-inch cubes. Heat butter in a skillet over medium heat; add chicken. Cook and stir for 3 minutes or until chicken is a creamy beige color. Add soup mix, milk, thyme, and parsley to the skillet. Bring to a boil, and simmer for 5 minutes. Add vegetables and pepper, and simmer for an additional 5 minutes or until chicken is cooked through and no longer pink. Spoon mixture into and oven-proof casserole, an top with biscuits.

Bake for 10 to 15 minutes or until biscuits are browned.

# *Arroz con Pollo* (Chicken with Rice)

Prep time: less than 30 minutes   •   Cooking time: 30 minutes   •   Makes 6 servings

1 (3- to 3½-lb.) frying chicken, cut into serving pieces with each breast cut into 2 sections

⅓ cup olive oil

2 onions, peeled and chopped

3 garlic cloves, peeled and minced

1 green or red bell pepper, seeds and ribs
removed, and thinly sliced

1½ cups *converted* long-grain rice

2 TB. chili powder or to taste

1 tsp. ground cumin

1 envelope roasted garlic herb soup mix

2 cups water

1 cup frozen peas, thawed

½ cup sliced pimiento-stuffed green olives

Freshly ground black pepper to taste

Preheat oven to 350°F. Rinse chicken and pat dry with paper towels. Heat oil in a large oven-
proof skillet or Dutch oven over medium-high heat. Add chicken and cook for 3 to 4 minutes
per side or until browned. Remove chicken from pan and set aside.

Reduce heat to medium; add onion, garlic, and bell
pepper. Cook and stir for 3 minutes or until onion is
translucent. Add rice. Cook and stir for 2 to 3 minutes
or until grains are opaque. Reduce heat to low; add
chili powder and cumin. Cook and stir for 1 minute.

Add soup mix and water. Bring to a boil over medium-
high heat, and add chicken pieces. Cover and bake for
20 minutes or until chicken is cooked through and no
longer pink and rice has absorbed all liquid. Add peas
and olives, and bake an additional 5 to 7 minutes or
until peas are hot. Season with black pepper to taste.

### Ellen on Edibles

**Converted** rice has been
subjected to a steam pressure process that keeps the grains separate. It takes slightly longer to cook,
which makes it preferable for a
casserole such as this one, because other rice would be mushy
before the chicken is cooked.

# Jambalaya Salad

Prep time: less than 30 minutes  •  Cooking time: 25 minutes  •  Makes 6 servings

**For salad:**

1 envelope tomato with basil soup mix

2 cups water

1 TB. fresh thyme leaves or 1 tsp. dried

1 cup long-grain rice

1 (10-oz.) pkg. frozen peas, thawed

½ lb. cooked shrimp, peeled, deveined, and cut in half lengthwise

3 cooked boneless, skinless chicken breast halves, cut into ½-inch dice

¼ lb. baked ham, cut into ½-inch dice

6 scallions, trimmed and thinly sliced

2 celery stalks, trimmed and thinly sliced

½ red bell pepper, seeds and ribs removed, and chopped

**For dressing:**

¼ cup lemon juice

3 garlic cloves, minced

Salt and cayenne to taste

¼ cup olive oil

For salad, combine soup mix, water, and thyme in a saucepan. Bring to a boil over high heat. Add rice, reduce heat to low, and cook, covered, for 15 to 20 minutes or until soft. Spread hot rice on a baking sheet and chill well.

**Dry and Droll**

Jambalaya is native to the Louisiana bayous, and many experts believe that the name comes from the Spanish word for "ham"— *jamon.*

While rice is cooking, cook peas according to package directions. Drain and chill well. Place rice and peas in a large bowl, and add shrimp, chicken, ham, scallions, celery, and red pepper.

For dressing, combine lemon juice, garlic, salt, and cayenne in a jar with a tight-fitting lid and shake well. Add oil and shake well again. Toss dressing with salad and serve chilled.

# Moroccan Chicken Salad

Prep time: less than 30 minutes  •  Cooking time: 10 minutes  •  Makes 6 servings

**For dressing:**

½ cup orange juice

2 TB. balsamic vinegar

¼ cup chopped fresh cilantro

4 garlic cloves, minced

1 TB. ground cumin

1 tsp. grated orange zest

Salt and freshly ground black pepper to taste

¼ cup olive oil

**For salad:**

4½ cups water

1 envelope vegetable soup mix

2 (10-oz.) boxes plain *couscous*

½ cup dried currants

½ cup chopped dried apricots

4 cooked boneless, skinless chicken breast halves, cut into ½-inch dice

1 (15-oz.) can chickpeas, drained and rinsed

¼ lb. Kalamata olives, pitted and chopped

1 small red onion, peeled and diced

½ small fennel bulb, trimmed and diced

For dressing, combine orange juice, vinegar, cilantro, garlic, cumin, orange zest, salt, and black pepper in a jar with a tight-fitting lid. Shake well. Add oil and shake well again. Set aside. Dressing can be prepared 4 days in advance and refrigerated. Allow it to sit at room temperature for 1 hour before using.

For couscous, bring water and soup mix to a boil in a saucepan over high heat. Add couscous, currants, and apricots. Cover pan, turn off the heat, and let couscous stand for 10 minutes. Fluff mixture with a fork, and transfer it to a mixing bowl. Chill well.

Add chicken, chickpeas, olives, onion, and fennel to couscous. Pour dressing over salad and toss well. Serve chilled.

**Ellen on Edibles** _____

Couscous might resemble a grain, but it's actually a very finely milled pasta popular in North African cuisines. It's very quick to cook. All you have to do is pour boiling water over it, and it absorbs the water and fluffs in a matter of minutes.

# Turkey Stew with Marsala and Sage

Prep time: less than 15 minutes • Cooking time: 25 minutes • Makes 6 servings

4 TB. olive oil

2 lb. turkey breast meat, rinsed and cut into 1-inch cubes

2 TB. butter

½ lb. white mushrooms, rinsed, trimmed, and halved if large

2 medium onions, diced

3 garlic cloves, minced

1 envelope roasted garlic herb soup mix

2 cups water

½ cup dry Marsala wine

2 TB. chopped fresh sage or 2 tsp. dried

Freshly ground black pepper to taste

Heat 2 tablespoons oil in a large skillet over medium-high heat. Add turkey and brown on all sides. Remove turkey with a slotted spoon and set aside. Reduce heat to medium, and add remaining 2 tablespoons olive oil and butter. Add mushrooms, onions, and garlic. Cook and stir for 3 to 5 minutes or until onion is translucent.

### Dry and Droll

Famed French gastronome Brillat-Savarin wrote that "poultry is for the cook what canvas is for the painter."

Add soup mix, water, wine, and sage to pan. Bring to a boil over high heat, and boil until reduced by half, stirring frequently. Return turkey to pan, and cook over low heat, uncovered, for 20 minutes, stirring occasionally. Season with black pepper to taste.

# Cinco de Mayo Turkey Loaf

Prep time: less than 15 minutes • Cooking time: 1 hour • Makes 6 servings

1 egg, lightly beaten

½ cup yellow cornmeal

1 envelope vegetable soup mix

1 cup jarred tomato salsa (mild to hot, depending on your preference)

1½ lb. ground turkey

2 garlic cloves, minced

4 scallions, trimmed and thinly sliced

3 TB. chopped fresh cilantro

Freshly ground black pepper to taste

Preheat oven to 350°F, and line a baking pan with aluminum foil. Combine egg, cornmeal, soup mix, and ½ cup salsa in a large mixing bowl. Mix well. Add turkey, garlic, scallions, cilantro, and black pepper. Mix well again, transfer turkey mixture to a baking dish, and form into a loaf. Spread remaining ½ cup salsa on top.

Bake loaf for 45 minutes to 1 hour or until an instant-read thermometer inserted into the center of the loaf registers 180°F.

**Dry and Droll**

Cinco de Mayo, May 5, commemorates the Mexican defeat of the French at the Battle of Puebla in 1862. The French did install a European monarchy in Mexico a year later, but it only lasted until 1867.

# Chapter 14

# From the Seas and Lakes

## In This Chapter

- ◆ Hearty fish stews
- ◆ Fish fillets with delicate sauces
- ◆ Grilled fish with exotic toppings
- ◆ Quickly prepared shellfish

Eating more fish and seafood is part of today's healthier lifestyle, and in this chapter, you'll find some enticing and easy recipes to add to your repertoire.

Fish is relatively low in calories, and many species, such as salmon, contain what is now considered to be "good fat," or omega-3 fatty acids, which have been proven to be beneficial to health and can reduce cholesterol, specifically the LDL, or "bad cholesterol."

## Finishing with Fish

Cooking fish has but one large pitfall—overcooking. It can make moist fillets dry and turn tender seafood rubbery. That's why many of these dishes cook the sauce or stew base for a long period of time and add the fresh fish at the very last minute.

A good general rule is to grill or broil fish fillets or steaks for 10 minutes per inch of thickness. Fish continues to cook after it's taken away from the heat as the heat from the exterior penetrates inward. So if a fish steak is still slightly translucent in the center when taken off the grill, it will become opaque—the sign that the fish is cooked through—after it sits for a few minutes.

# Substituting Species

Fish falls into basic families, and depending on where you live, you can always find something fresh. The biggest group of fish is the "firm-fleshed white fish." The cod family, including scrod, haddock, and whiting, are native to the North Atlantic, as do halibut and striped bass Grouper come from southern waters, as does red snapper. Other options are sea bass, striped bass, turbot, and orange roughy.

All these species of fish are mildly flavored and thick enough to hold together when cooked in a sauce or on the grill. Species such as sole and flounder are delicate and should be pan-fried or baked.

Swordfish, tuna, and salmon steaks are best suited for grilling and broiling, while salmon fillets can be pan-fried or poached as well as cooked by these methods.

## The Least You Need to Know

- Take care to not overcook either fish or seafood.
- Substitute any firm-fleshed white fish such as cod, halibut, or grouper for one another.
- Grill or broil fish for 10 minutes per inch of thickness.
- Cook shrimp until pink and cooked through.

# Nantucket Seafood Chowder

Prep time: less than 20 minutes   •   Cooking time: 40 minutes   •   Makes 4 to 6 servings

2 TB. bacon fat or vegetable oil

1 large onion, diced

1 carrot, peeled and thinly sliced

1 celery stalk, trimmed and sliced

1 envelope leek soup mix

3 cups seafood stock or bottled clam juice

½ cup heavy cream

1 lb. red-skinned potatoes, scrubbed and cut into ½-inch dice

2 TB. chopped fresh parsley

½ tsp. dried thyme

1 bay leaf

1 lb. cod, halibut, or other firm-fleshed white fish, cut into 1-inch cubes

½ lb. bay scallops

1 (10-oz.) box frozen corn kernels, thawed

6 slices bacon, cooked until crisp and crumbled (optional)

Freshly ground black pepper to taste

Heat bacon fat in a large saucepan or stockpot over medium heat; add onion, carrot, and celery. Cook and stir for 3 minutes or until onion is translucent. Add soup mix, stock, and cream. Stir well and add potatoes, parsley, thyme, and bay leaf.

Bring to a boil over medium heat, stirring occasionally. Reduce heat to low, and simmer stew, partially covered, for 15 to 20 minutes or until potatoes can be pierced easily with the tip of a sharp knife.

Add fish, scallops, corn, and bacon (if using). Bring to a boil, and simmer 3 minutes. Cover pan, turn off heat, and let mixture sit for 10 minutes. Remove and discard bay leaf and season with black pepper to taste.

**Dry and Droll** _____

There are many theories as to the derivation of the word *chowder*. One is that is comes from the French *chaudière*, which is the large cauldron into which Breton fishermen threw their catch to create a communal stew. There is also an English ancestry that maintains that chowder is a variation of an old Cornwall word *jowter*, which was a fish peddler.

# Bouillabaisse (French Seafood Stew)

Prep time: less than 30 minutes • Cooking time: 45 minutes • Makes 4 to 6 servings

¼ cup olive oil

1 large onion, diced

2 garlic cloves, minced

1 TB. paprika

1 celery stalk, trimmed and sliced

1 carrot, peeled and sliced

2 large potatoes, peeled and cut into ½-inch dice

1 envelope tomato with basil soup mix

1 (14½-oz.) can diced tomatoes, drained

2 cups seafood stock or bottled clam juice

1 cup dry white wine

½ cup orange juice

2 TB. chopped fresh parsley

1 TB. fresh thyme leaves or ½ tsp. dried

1 TB. grated orange zest

1½ lb. halibut, swordfish, or any firm-fleshed white fish, cut into 1-inch cubes

½ lb. medium raw shrimp, peeled and deveined

Freshly ground black pepper to taste

Heat oil in a large saucepan or stockpot over medium heat; add onion and garlic. Cook and stir for 3 minutes or until onion is translucent. Reduce heat to low, and stir in paprika. Stir for 1 minute.

### Mix Mastery

Feel free to personalize the types of fish used. Clams, oysters, scallops, shrimp, and stronger fish such as tuna all work well. It's up to you. Just make sure the fish is at least ¾-inch thick.

Add celery, carrot, potatoes, soup mix, tomatoes, stock, wine, orange juice, parsley, thyme, and orange zest. Bring to a boil over medium heat, stirring occasionally. Reduce heat to low, and simmer mixture, uncovered, for 20 to 30 minutes or until vegetables are tender.

Add fish and shrimp, bring to a boil over medium heat, and simmer for 3 minutes. Cover the pan, turn off heat, and let mixture sit for 10 minutes. Remove and discard bay leaf, and season stew with black pepper to taste.

# Seafood Gumbo

Prep time: less than 20 minutes  •  Cooking time: 1 hour  •  Makes 6 servings

¼ cup plus 3 TB. vegetable oil

¼ cup all-purpose flour

1 cup water

3 onions, diced

1 green or red bell pepper, seeds and ribs removed, and diced

2 celery stalks, trimmed and sliced

4 garlic cloves, minced

1 (10-oz.) box frozen sliced okra, thawed

1 (14½-oz.) can diced tomatoes, juice reserved

1 envelope roasted garlic herb soup mix

3 cups seafood stock or bottled clam juice

1 TB. fresh thyme leaves or 1 tsp. dried

1 TB. chopped fresh basil or 1 tsp. dried

2 bay leaves

1 lb. snapper, cod, halibut, or other firm-fleshed white fish, cut into 1-inch cubes

½ lb. medium shrimp, peeled and deveined

½ pint shucked oysters, or ¼ lb. additional shrimp

Cayenne to taste

Cooked white rice

Heat ¼ cup oil in a large saucepan or stockpot over medium-high heat. Whisk in flour, and reduce heat to medium. Whisk flour constantly for 5 to 7 minutes or until resulting roux is walnut brown. Whisk in water, and continue to whisk until mixture is thick and smooth. Set aside.

Heat remaining 3 tablespoons oil in a medium skillet over medium heat; add onions, bell pepper, celery, and garlic. Cook and stir for 3 minutes or until onion is translucent. Transfer vegetables to roux and then add okra, tomatoes and their juice, soup mix, seafood stock, thyme, basil, and bay leaves.

Bring to a boil over medium heat. Reduce heat to low and simmer uncovered for 45 minutes or until vegetables are tender. Add fish, shrimp, and oysters. Bring mixture back to a boil, and simmer for 3 minutes. Turn off heat, cover the pan, and let mixture rest 10 minutes or until fish is cooked through and edges of oysters have curled. Remove and discard bay leaves, and season with cayenne. Serve gumbo over white rice.

**Dry and Droll**

Gumbo, from the Ethiopian African *gombo*, which is the word for "okra," is a Louisiana culinary classic that dates back to the French and Spanish settlers and their African slaves. It can contain fish, meats, or poultry, but the constant that gives it its name is okra. Okra is what thickens it.

# Spicy Southwest Shrimp

Prep time: less than 15 minutes • Cooking time: 10 minutes • Makes 6 servings

2 lb. large raw shrimp, peeled and deveined

¼ lb. bacon, finely sliced

2 medium onions, diced

5 garlic cloves, minced

3 jalapeño chilies, seeds and ribs removed, finely chopped

1 TB. ground cumin

1 (15-oz.) can pinto beans, drained and rinsed

½ envelope tomato with basil soup mix

1 cup seafood stock or bottled clam juice

¼ cup olive oil

2 TB. chopped fresh cilantro

2 tsp. fresh thyme leaves or ½ tsp. dried

Freshly ground black pepper to taste

Lime juice to taste

**Mix Mastery**

When cutting chili peppers, rub the hand not holding the pepper with vegetable oil to avoid getting the potent chili oil on your skin. Then carve down the sides of the pepper and remove the flesh. The seeds will remain attached to the ribs, and you can discard the whole unit.

Rinse shrimp and set aside. Place bacon in a saucepan over medium-high heat. Cook bacon until almost crisp, then add onions and garlic. Lower heat to medium. Cook and stir for 2 minutes. Add jalapeño and cumin, and continue to cook for 1 minute. Add beans, soup mix, and stock. Bring to a boil, reduce heat to low, and simmer for 10 minutes.

When sauce has almost completed simmering, place a large skillet over high heat, and heat oil until hot. Add shrimp and sear on both sides, for 30 seconds per side. Transfer bean mixture to the pan, and add cilantro and thyme. Lower heat to medium, and cook for about 2 minutes or until shrimp are cooked through and pink in color. Season with black pepper and lime juice to taste.

# Seafood Jambalaya

Prep time: less than 30 minutes   •   Cooking time: 30 minutes   •   Makes 6 servings

2 TB. vegetable oil

¼ lb. *andouille* sausage, thinly sliced

1 onion, diced

3 garlic cloves, minced

1 green or red bell pepper, seeds and ribs removed and thinly sliced

2 celery stalks, trimmed and thinly sliced

1 (14½-oz.) can diced tomatoes, juice reserved

1 envelope roasted garlic herb soup mix

2 cups seafood stock or bottled clam juice

2 cups water

3 TB. chopped fresh parsley

1 tsp. dried thyme

1 bay leaf

1½ cups uncooked converted long-grain white rice

1½ lb. medium shrimp, peeled and deveined

¾ lb. halibut, cod, or other firm-fleshed white fish, cut into ¾-inch dice

Cayenne to taste

Heat oil in a large Dutch oven over medium heat; add sausage. Cook and stir for 3 minutes, or until sausage is browned. Remove sausage from pan with slotted spoon; set aside. Add onion, garlic, bell pepper, and celery to pan. Cook and stir for 3 minutes or until onion is translucent. Add tomatoes and their juice, soup mix, stock, water, parsley, thyme, bay leaf, and rice. Stir well. Bring to a boil over medium heat, then reduce heat to low and cook, covered, for 20 minutes, or until rice is tender and liquid is absorbed.

Add shrimp and fish to dish, and season with cayenne to taste. Cook for 3 minutes on low heat, covered, then turn off heat and let mixture sit for 10 minutes. Remove and discard bay leaf.

**Ellen on Edibles** _____

Andouille (pronounced *ahn-DEW-ee*) is a spicy, smoked Louisiana pork sausage used frequently in Cajun cooking. If it's not available, use another smoked pork sausage such as kielbasa, and add a bit of extra cayenne when seasoning the dish to compensate.

# Shrimp Creole

Prep time: less than 20 minutes • Cooking time: 45 minutes • Makes 4 to 6 servings

3 TB. olive oil

6 scallions, trimmed and chopped

2 celery stalks, trimmed and chopped

½ green bell pepper, seeds and ribs removed, and finely chopped

3 garlic cloves, minced

1 TB. dried oregano

1 TB. paprika

1 tsp. ground cumin

½ tsp. dried basil

1 envelope tomato with basil soup mix

2 cups seafood stock or bottled clam juice

2 bay leaves

1½ lb. large raw shrimp, peeled and deveined

Cayenne to taste

### Mix with Care

A great time saver is to double or triple sauce recipes like this one and freeze some for a future meal. But do not freeze the seafood because it will fall apart when it's thawed and reheated. Freezing makes all liquids expand, and when that happens within the fish, the delicate cell walls break down.

Heat oil in a medium saucepan over medium heat; add scallions, celery, green bell pepper, and garlic. Cook and stir for 3 minutes or until scallions are soft. Reduce heat to low, and stir in oregano, paprika, cumin, and basil. Cook for 1 minute, stirring constantly.

Stir in soup mix, stock, and bay leaves. Bring to a boil over medium heat, stirring frequently. Reduce heat to low, and simmer sauce, covered, for 30 minutes or until vegetables are soft. Add shrimp and bring to a boil over medium heat. Simmer for 3 minutes, turn off heat, and let mixture sit for 10 minutes. Remove and discard bay leaves. Season with cayenne to taste.

# Sautéed Scallops with Leeks and Bacon

Prep time: less than 30 minutes   •   Cooking time: 25 minutes   •   Makes 6 servings

2 lb. bay scallops or sea scallops cut into quarters

2 TB. butter

9 leeks, white parts only, washed well, trimmed and cut into a fine julienne

2 garlic cloves, minced

1 envelope leek soup mix

2 cups half-and-half

½ lb. bacon

Freshly ground black pepper to taste

Rinse scallops, pat dry with paper towels, and set aside. Melt butter in a skillet over low heat. Add leeks and garlic, and cook, covered, over low heat for 10 minutes, stirring occasionally. Add soup mix and half-and-half, raise the heat to medium, and cook until mixture is reduced in volume by ⅔, stirring occasionally.

While sauce is cooking, fry bacon in a large skillet until crisp. Remove bacon from pan, reserving the grease. Drain bacon on paper towels, and crumble. Add bacon to sauce, and season with pepper.

Discard all but 2 tablespoons bacon grease from the skillet. Set it over high heat, and when grease begins to smoke, add scallops. Cook and stir for 2 minutes or until scallops are opaque in the center. Season with black pepper to taste.

To serve, divide leek mixture among 6 plates and top with scallops.

**Dry and Droll**

The English word *scallop* comes from the French *escalope*, which refers to the shell in which the mollusk lives.

# Steamed Mussels Marinara

Prep time: less than 15 minutes • Cooking time: 25 minutes • Makes 6 servings

5 lb. mussels, scrubbed and *debearded*

¼ cup cornmeal

3 TB. olive oil

1 onion, chopped

4 garlic cloves, minced

1 envelope tomato with basil soup mix

½ cup dry white wine

1 cup water

½ cup chopped fresh basil or 2 TB. dried

3 TB. chopped fresh parsley

3 TB. chopped fresh oregano or 1 TB. dried

Freshly ground black pepper to taste

Place mussels in a mixing bowl. Cover with cold water, and stir in cornmeal. Let mussels sit for 30 minutes, then drain and rinse.

Heat oil in a Dutch oven over medium heat; add onion and garlic. Cook and stir for 3 minutes or until onion is translucent. Stir in soup mix, wine, water, basil, parsley, oregano, and black pepper. Bring to a boil over medium heat. Reduce heat to low, cover and simmer sauce for 15 minutes, stirring occasionally.

Add mussels to the pan, and raise heat to medium-high. Cover and steam mussels for 3 minutes. Stir to redistribute mussels, and steam for an additional 3 to 5 minutes or until mussels have opened. Discard any mussels that did not open.

### Ellen on Edibles

**Debearding** is a process unique to mussels. Regardless of provenance, all mussels have a fibrous beard that needs to be removed. The easiest way to do this is to grasp the mussel between your thumb and index finger. Using your other hand, rub a dull knife blade over the beard to loosen it. Then put down the knife and give the beard a tug to pull it free. Then scrub the mussels with a stiff brush under cold running water.

# Grilled Lobster with Herb Butter Sauce

Prep time: less than 15 minutes  •  Cooking time: 15 minutes  •  Makes 6 servings

6 (1½-lb.) live lobsters

½ envelope savory herb with garlic soup mix

⅓ cup boiling water

¼ lb. butter

4 garlic cloves, minced

2 TB. lemon juice

2 TB. chopped fresh parsley

2 tsp. herbes de Provence

1 tsp. grated lemon zest

Freshly ground black pepper to taste

Bring a lobster pot or large stockpot of salted water to a rolling boil. Add lobsters, head first, and cover the pot. When water returns to a boil, cook lobsters for 8 minutes. Remove lobsters with tongs, and run cold tap water over them to cool them.

Light a charcoal or gas grill. Place a lobster on a large work surface with the top of its shell up. Cut lobster in half lengthwise. Remove and discard black vein running down the tail and sand sac located at the top of the head. Repeat with remaining lobsters.

Combine soup mix and water in a small bowl and stir well. Melt butter in a small saucepan over low heat. Add garlic, lemon juice, parsley, herbes de Provence, lemon zest, and black pepper. Stir well, add soup mixture, and stir again.

Place lobsters on grill rack, cut side up. Cover grill and cook for 2 minutes. Drizzle lobsters with ½ butter mixture, cover the grill, and cook for 3 minutes more or until meat in tail is firm. Remove lobsters from the grill, and drizzle with remaining butter mixture.

## Mix Mastery

Although there is no difference in the flavor of a male or female lobster, the bright red roe from the females adds a rosy color to stocks and can be sprinkled over salads as a garnish. To learn how to identify the female, ask your fishmonger to show you two lobsters of similar size—one male and one female—side by side. The one with the broader abdomen and tail is the female. The female also has smaller, more flexible swimmerets, which are the first pair of legs at the base of the tail.

# Crab-Stuffed Fish Fillets

Prep time: less than 15 minutes • Cooking time: 20 minutes • Makes 6 servings

Vegetable oil spray

6 (4- to 6-oz.) thin sole or flounder fillets

2 cups herbed stuffing crumbs (not cubes)

½ envelope vegetable soup mix

¼ lb. crabmeat, picked over to remove all shell fragments

¼ lb. butter, melted

⅔ cup mayonnaise

1 tsp. herbes de Provence, or 1 tsp. dried thyme

Salt and freshly ground black pepper to taste

Preheat the oven to 375°F, and grease a baking pan with vegetable oil spray. Rinse fish fillets and set aside.

### Mix Mastery

If you can't find flounder or sole fillets, you can use a thicker fish such as halibut. Instead of folding the fish over the stuffing, cut a pocket in the center of the fillets and stuff the pocket. Secure it closed with toothpicks.

Combine stuffing crumbs, soup mix, crabmeat, ½ melted butter, mayonnaise, and herbes de Provence in a mixing bowl. Mix well.

Spoon stuffing mixture on one side of each fish fillet. Fold fillet over stuffing, and secure it closed with toothpicks. Arrange fillets in baking pan, sprinkle with salt and black pepper, and drizzle remaining butter over fish.

Bake for 15 to 20 minutes or until fish is cooked through.

# Southwestern Crab Cakes

Prep time: less than 15 minutes   •   Cooking time: 15 minutes   •   Makes 6 servings

2 eggs, lightly beaten

½ cup mayonnaise

½ cup cracker meal

1 envelope vegetable soup mix

1 TB. chili powder

1 tsp. ground cumin

1½ lb. crabmeat, picked over to remove all shell fragments

2 red bell peppers, seeds and ribs removed, and very finely chopped

2 green bell peppers, seeds and ribs removed, and very finely chopped

3 scallions, trimmed and chopped

¼ cup chopped fresh cilantro

Vegetable oil spray

Preheat the oven to 450°F. Cover a baking sheet with heavy-duty aluminum foil, and spray the foil with vegetable oil spray.

Combine eggs, mayonnaise, cracker meal, soup mix, chili powder, and cumin in a mixing bowl, and whisk until well blended. Gently fold in crabmeat, red and green bell peppers, scallions, and cilantro.

Form mixture into 12 balls and then flatten them into patties ½-inch thick on baking sheet. Spray tops of patties with vegetable oil spray. Bake for 12 to 15 minutes or until lightly browned on top.

**Mix with Care**

Cilantro is a very delicate herb and bruises easily. The best way to preserve it is to pick off the leaves, rinse them, and place them on a moist paper towel. Roll the paper towel tightly, then wrap the towel in plastic wrap.

# Sole Florentine

Prep time: less than 15 minutes • Cooking time: 25 minutes • Makes 6 servings

2 lb. sole or flounder fillets

2 (10-oz.) boxes frozen leaf spinach, thawed

3 TB. butter

2 shallots, chopped

1 envelope cream of spinach soup mix

1½ cups whole milk

½ cup grated Swiss cheese

Freshly ground black pepper to taste

Preheat the oven to 350°F, and spray a 9×13-inch baking pan with vegetable oil spray. Rinse fish fillets and set aside. Place spinach in a colander, and press with the back of a spoon to extract as much liquid as possible. Place spinach in baking pan, spreading it evenly with a wooden spoon.

 **Mix Mastery** _____

Swiss cheese is traditional for this dish, but you can also use cheddar or Gruyère to vary the flavor. However, it is important that the cheese does not overpower the delicate fish.

Heat butter in a small saucepan over medium heat; add shallots. Cook and stir for 3 minutes or until shallots are translucent. Stir in soup mix and milk. Bring to a boil over medium heat, stirring frequently. Reduce heat to low, and simmer for 5 minutes, stirring frequently. Stir in cheese, and simmer until cheese is melted. Season with black pepper to taste.

Stir ¾ sauce into spinach and spread it evenly with a wooden spoon. Place fish on top of spinach, and spread remaining sauce on top of fish. Bake for 20 to 25 minutes or until sauce is bubbly and fish is cooked through.

# Grilled Swordfish with Smoked Cheddar Sauce

Prep time: less than 15 minutes    •    Cooking time: 20 minutes    •    Makes 6 servings

2 TB. butter

½ cup chopped onion

2 garlic cloves, minced

1 envelope white sauce mix

Milk as specified on mix package

1½ cups grated smoked cheddar cheese

1 tomato, cored, seeded, and finely chopped

6 (8-oz.) swordfish steaks

Salt and freshly ground black pepper to taste

Light a charcoal or gas grill. Melt butter in a medium saucepan over medium heat; add onion and garlic. Cook and stir for 3 minutes or until onion is translucent. Add sauce mix and milk to the pan and stir well. Bring to a boil, and simmer for 5 minutes. Add cheese and tomato, and cook until cheese is melted, stirring frequently.

Season fish steaks with salt and black pepper, and grill for 3 to 5 minutes per side, depending on thickness or until fish is still slightly translucent in the center. To serve, ladle some sauce into the center of a heated plate, and top with a fish steak.

### Dry and Droll

George Brown Goode's *History of the American Fisheries* was a landmark book when the government published it in 1887. Goode writes that fishing for swordfish dates back to the 1840s in New England's waters. "Its flesh is excellent food, and it is captured by harpoon according an exciting and even dangerous sport ... with the harpooner taking a position at the end of the bowsprit."

# Aegean Grilled Halibut

Prep time: less than 15 minutes • Cooking time: 10 minutes • Makes 6 servings

6 (8-oz.) halibut steaks

½ envelope roasted garlic herb soup mix

¼ cup water

⅓ cup lemon juice

Grated zest of 1 lemon

6 garlic cloves, minced

¼ cup chopped fresh parsley

2 TB. dried oregano

1 TB. fresh thyme leaves or 1 tsp. dried

½ cup olive oil

Freshly ground black pepper to taste

 **Mix Mastery**

One way to add additional flavor to foods if you're cooking on a charcoal grill is to soak sprigs of fresh woody herbs such as thyme and rosemary in water and place them on the hot coals. This technique works with fish, meat, and poultry.

Rinse halibut and set aside. Combine soup mix, water, lemon juice, lemon zest, garlic, parsley, oregano, and thyme in a heavy, sealable plastic bag. Seal bag and shake well. Add oil and shake well again. Add fish steaks, and marinate in the refrigerator for 2 to 3 hours.

Light a charcoal or gas grill. When the fire is hot, remove fish from marinade and discard marinade. Grill fish for 3 to 5 minutes per side or until slightly translucent in the center. Season with black pepper to taste.

# Grilled Jerk Tuna

Prep time: less than 15 minutes  •  Cooking time: 6 minutes  •  Makes 6 servings

2 lb. tuna steaks

1 envelope savory herbs with garlic soup mix

¼ cup boiling water

¼ cup lime juice

2 TB. granulated sugar

½ tsp. ground allspice

½ tsp. ground ginger

Cayenne to taste

½ cup olive oil

Rinse tuna and refrigerate. Combine soup mix and water in a small mixing bowl. Stir well, cover, and let sit for 10 minutes. Add lime juice, sugar, allspice, ginger, and cayenne. Mix well. Add oil and mix well again. Spread mixture on all surfaces of tuna, and place tuna in a heavy, sealable plastic bag. Seal and place tuna in the freezer for 30 minutes.

Light a charcoal or gas grill, and heat until very hot. Remove fish from marinade and discard marinade. Grill tuna for 2 to 3 minutes per side, depending on thickness, for rare tuna or longer for desired doneness.

### Mix Mastery

Tuna is one fish that is really best enjoyed rare and not cooked through. If you don't believe in eating undercooked fish for potential health concerns, this recipe can also be made with salmon, swordfish, or halibut. The best way to ensure that the fish will be rare is to marinate it in the freezer and deep-chill it before grilling.

# Grilled Salmon with Spicy Pecan Butter

Prep time: less than 15 minutes • Cooking time: 10 minutes • Makes 6 servings

6 (6- to 8-oz.) salmon fillets

2 TB. olive oil

Salt and freshly ground black pepper to taste

1 jalapeño chili, seeds and ribs removed

¾ cup pecans, toasted in a 350°F oven for 5 minutes

4 sprigs fresh parsley

4 sprigs fresh cilantro

¼ lb. butter, softened

2 TB. lemon juice

½ envelope roasted garlic herb soup mix

1⅓ cups dry white wine

4 shallots, finely chopped

⅓ cup half-and-half

Light a charcoal or gas grill. Rub salmon with olive oil, sprinkle with salt and black pepper, and set aside. Combine jalapeño, toasted pecans, parsley, cilantro, butter, and lemon juice in a food processor fitted with a steel blade. Chop finely, using the on-and-off pulsing action.

Place soup mix, wine, and shallots into a small saucepan, over medium-high heat, and cook until the liquid is reduced in volume by half. Add half-and-half, reduce heat to medium, and reduce in volume by half again. Slowly whisk in pecan-butter mixture. Season with black pepper to taste.

Grill salmon for 10 minutes per inch of thickness. To serve, top grilled salmon with pecan-butter sauce.

### Mix Mastery

A vegetable peeler and a pair of tweezers are the best ways to get rid of those pesky little bones in fish fillets. Run a peeler down the center of the fillet, starting at the tail end. It will catch the larger pin bones, and with a twist of your wrist, you can pull them out. For finer bones, use your fingers to rub the flesh lightly and then pull out the bones with the tweezers.

# Part 6

# Vegetable Patch Panache

Even the most devoted carnivore will enjoy the recipes in this part. The first chapter is a group of vegetable dishes that take advantage of all seasons. They'll dress up the plate if the entrée is simple.

Vegetarian entrées is the theme of another chapter, and all these dishes can be served as side dishes if the portions are smaller. This part ends with recipes glorifying potatoes, rice, and other grains.

# Chapter 15

# Reds, Whites, and Greens

## In This Chapter

◆ International vegetable medleys
◆ Spruced-up hearty root vegetables
◆ Getting the most from delicate summer crops

Only one component on an entrée plate should be the star. If you're cooking an elaborate entrée, probably the best sidekick is a simply prepared steamed vegetable to add a contrasting color as well as nutrition to the plate. But if your entrée is a simple grilled or broiled dish, then the vegetable and other side dishes can be a bit more elaborate.

Vegetables come in a rainbow of colors, as well as flavors and textures. The recipes in this chapter will give you some new ideas of how to boost their flavor with soup and sauce mixes.

## Soup-ing Up Flavors

The recipes in this chapter are for specific dishes, but here are some more general ways to use soup and sauce mixes with vegetables. Spinach, broccoli, cauliflower, carrots, and green beans are good choices for these procedures:

- Use white sauce mix to make any creamed vegetable. You can add cheese or seasoning to the sauce or just use it as is. One envelope of white sauce will be enough for two boxes of frozen vegetables.

- Use leek soup mix as an alternative to white sauce. If the mix is made with 1½ cups whole milk, it creates a creamy sauce with a subtle leek flavor.

- Use tomato with basil soup mix to give vegetables an Italian and tomato flavor. Dilute it with 1½ cups water for the right sauce consistency and intensity of flavor.

## The Least You Need to Know

- It's worth spending time on elaborate vegetable dishes when the entrée is simple and does not have a sauce of its own.

- White sauce mix and leek soup mix can create cream sauces for a number of different vegetables.

- Root vegetables such as carrots, parsnips, and celery root are hard and require long cooking times.

# Ratatouille

Prep time: less than 20 minutes   •   Cooking time: 30 minutes   •   Makes 4 to 6 servings

1 (¾-lb.) eggplant, trimmed and cut into ¾-inch cubes

Salt

½ cup olive oil

1 onion, diced

3 garlic cloves, minced

1 small zucchini, trimmed and cut into ¾-inch cubes

1 small summer squash, trimmed and cut into ¾-inch cubes

½ envelope tomato with basil soup mix

1 cup water

1 TB. herbes de Provence, or 1 tsp. dried thyme, 1 tsp. dried oregano, and 1 tsp. dried rosemary

Freshly ground black pepper to taste

Place eggplant in a colander, and sprinkle it liberally with salt. Put a plate on top of eggplant, and weight it with cans. Place the colander on a plate or in the sink. Let eggplant sit for 30 minutes, then rinse cubes and pat dry on paper towels.

Heat ¼ cup oil in a large skillet over medium heat; add onion and garlic. Cook and stir for 3 minutes or until onion is translucent. Scrape mixture into a mixing bowl and set aside.

Add remaining ¼ cup oil to the skillet; add eggplant cubes, zucchini, and summer squash. Cook and stir for 3 minutes or until eggplant is starting to soften. Return onion to the pan, and add soup mix, water, and herbes de Provence. Stir well.

Bring to a boil over medium-high heat, stirring occasionally. Reduce heat to low, and simmer, uncovered, for 15 to 20 minutes or until eggplant is soft. Season with black pepper to taste. Ratatouille can be served hot, at room temperature, or chilled.

 **Mix with Care**

Even though you rinsed the eggplant, it still provides a fair amount of salt to the dish. Taste it carefully before adding additional salt.

# Caponata

Prep time: less than 20 minutes • Cooking time: 25 minutes • Makes 6 to 8 servings

1 (1-lb.) eggplant, peeled and cut into ½-inch cubes

Salt

⅓ cup olive oil

2 celery stalks, trimmed and diced

1 onion, diced

4 garlic cloves, minced

½ envelope roasted garlic herb soup mix

¼ cup red wine vinegar

1 tsp. granulated sugar

1 (15-oz.) can diced Italian plum tomatoes, juices reserved

1 TB. tomato paste

¼ cup green olives, pitted, slivered, and rinsed well

2 TB. small capers, drained and rinsed

Freshly ground black pepper to taste

Place eggplant in a colander, and sprinkle liberally with salt. Put a plate on top of eggplant cubes, and weight the plate with cans. Place the colander on a plate or in the sink. Let eggplant sit for 30 minutes, then rinse cubes, and pat dry on paper towels.

> ### Mix Mastery
> Like many recipes, this one calls for 1 tablespoon tomato paste. I buy tomato paste that comes in a tube, which will keep refrigerated for a few weeks. If you do open a can, freeze the remaining sauce in 1-tablespoon portions in an ice cube tray. Then store the small cubes in a heavy plastic bag for up to six months.

Heat half the oil in a large skillet over medium heat; add celery, onion, and garlic. Cook, stirring, for 3 minutes or until onion is translucent and soft. Remove vegetables from the pan with a slotted spoon and set aside.

Pour remaining oil into the skillet; add eggplant cubes. Cook, stirring, for 5 minutes or until lightly browned. Return celery mixture to the skillet, and add soup mix, vinegar, sugar, tomatoes and their juices, tomato paste, olives, and capers. Bring to a boil, reduce heat to low, and simmer uncovered, stirring frequently, for 15 minutes or until vegetables are cooked but still retain texture. Season with black pepper to taste, and serve at room temperature or chilled.

# Green Beans with Mushroom Sauce

Prep time: less than 15 minutes   •   Cooking time: 15 minutes   •   Makes 6 servings

1½ lb. green beans, trimmed and cut into 1-inch pieces

3 TB. butter

2 shallots, chopped

2 garlic cloves, minced

½ lb. fresh shiitake mushrooms, stemmed and sliced

½ cup Marsala wine

1 envelope wild mushroom and chive soup mix

1½ cups heavy cream

Freshly ground black pepper to taste

Bring a large pot of salted water to a boil over high heat. Prepare a bowl of ice water. Add green beans to boiling water, and cook for 3 minutes or until just tender. Drain beans and plunge them into the ice water for 2 minutes to stop the cooking action. Drain again and set aside.

Melt butter in a medium skillet over medium heat; add shallots and garlic. Cook and stir for 3 minutes or until shallots are translucent. Increase heat to medium-high and add mushrooms. Cook and stir for 3 minutes or until mushrooms are tender. Raise heat to high, add Marsala, and boil for 2 minutes or until liquid evaporates. Stir in soup mix and cream, reduce heat to medium, and simmer for 3 minutes or until reduced in volume by ⅓. Transfer beans back to pan to heat through in hot sauce. Season with black pepper to taste.

 **Mix Mastery**

Most string beans today do not need to have the strings removed because that trait has been bred out of most species. But some farm-fresh beans do need help. It's easy: Just snap off the stem end and use the stem to pull off the string.

# Zucchini Pancakes

Prep time: less than 20 minutes • Cooking time: 10 minutes • Makes 6 servings

2 lb. zucchini

Salt to taste

½ envelope savory herb with garlic soup mix

2 eggs, lightly beaten

2 garlic cloves, minced

2 TB. chopped fresh basil or 2 tsp. dried

1 cup Italian-flavored breadcrumbs

Freshly ground black pepper to taste

1 cup vegetable oil

Trim ends off zucchini, and grate zucchini through the largest holes of a box grater. Place shreds in a colander and sprinkle liberally with salt. Allow zucchini to drain over a mixing bowl for 30 minutes. Rinse well; then, using your hands, squeeze out as much liquid as possible. Set aside.

 **Mix Mastery**

Zucchini is Italian in origin and its native name was retained when it was integrated into American cooking. Choose small zucchini because they tend to have a sweeter flavor and the seeds are still tender and less pronounced.

Preheat the oven to 200°F, and line a baking sheet with aluminum foil. Combine soup mix, eggs, garlic, basil, and breadcrumbs in a mixing bowl. Stir in zucchini, and season with black pepper.

Heat oil in a large skillet over medium-high heat. Add zucchini mixture in ¼ cup mounds, and flatten them to thin pancakes with the back of a spatula. Make only a single layer at a time; work in batches if necessary. Fry pancakes for 2 to 3 minutes on each side or until cooked through and lightly browned. Drain pancakes on paper towels. Keep pancakes warm in oven on a baking sheet. Repeat with remaining mixture, adding more oil as necessary.

# Corn Pudding

Prep time: less than 15 minutes    •    Cooking time: 45 minutes    •    Makes 6 servings

5 eggs

6 TB. butter, melted, plus more for greasing the pan

1½ cups half-and-half

1 envelope vegetable soup mix

¼ cup all-purpose flour

3 cups fresh corn kernels, about 5 or 6 ears, or 2 (10-oz.) boxes frozen corn, thawed

4 scallions, trimmed and chopped

½ red bell pepper, seeds and ribs removed, and finely chopped

2 garlic cloves, minced

2 TB. chopped fresh parsley

2 tsp. fresh thyme leaves or ½ tsp. dried

Freshly ground black pepper to taste

Preheat the oven to 350°F. Butter a 2-quart soufflé dish or ovenproof casserole, and bring a pot of water to a boil.

Whisk eggs with 6 TB. melted butter, half-and-half, soup mix, and flour. Stir in corn, scallions, red bell pepper, garlic, parsley, thyme, and black pepper. Pour mixture into the prepared soufflé dish, and place the soufflé dish in a roasting pan.

Pour boiling water into the roasting pan so it extends halfway up the sides of the soufflé dish to create a *bain marie*. Bake for 45 minutes or until top is browned and a knife inserted in the center comes out clean. Allow pudding to sit for 5 minutes before serving.

### Ellen on Edibles

**Bain marie** is the French term for a water bath that cooks food gently by surrounding it with simmering water. The water temperature is actually lower than the oven temperature because water only reaches 212°F, so delicate custards set without getting rubbery.

# Creamed Corn

Prep time: less than 15 minutes  •  Cooking time: 20 minutes  •  Makes 6 servings

6 ears fresh corn, shucked

2 TB. butter

6 scallions, trimmed and thinly sliced

1 envelope leek soup mix

1½ cups whole milk

Freshly ground black pepper to taste

### Mix Mastery

The method given for cooking fresh corn on the cob in this recipe is the all-time best, foolproof way to cook corn perfectly; it's never overcooked. Although the corn must sit in the pan for 10 minutes, one of the nice parts of this method is that it will stay hot for up to 1 hour.

Bring a large pot of salted water to a boil. Add corn and cover. When water returns to a boil, turn off heat, and let corn sit for 10 minutes. Remove corn from the pan with tongs, and when cool enough to handle, cut kernels off cobs. Scrape cobs with the back of a knife to extract as much liquid and pulp as possible.

Heat butter in a medium saucepan over medium heat; add scallions. Cook and stir for 3 minutes or until scallions are soft. Add soup mix, and stir in milk. Bring to a boil over medium heat, stirring frequently. Reduce heat to low, and simmer, uncovered, for 5 minutes.

Stir corn into pan, and simmer for 5 minutes. Season with black pepper to taste.

# Braised Red Cabbage

Prep time: less than 15 minutes • Cooking time: 1 hour • Makes 6 to 8 servings

| | |
|---|---|
| 1 (2 lb.) head red cabbage, cored and shredded | 1 envelope golden onion soup mix |
| 2 TB. red wine vinegar | 1 cup dry red wine |
| 2 TB. granulated sugar | 1 cup water |
| 2 TB. butter | 1 cinnamon stick |
| 1 onion, chopped | 1 bay leaf |
| 1 McIntosh or Golden Delicious apple, peeled, cored, and chopped | ⅓ cup red currant jelly |
| | Freshly ground black pepper to taste |

Place cabbage in a large bowl. Sprinkle with vinegar and sugar and toss. Allow cabbage to sit at room temperature for 1 hour.

Heat butter in a large saucepan over medium heat; add onion and apple. Cook, stirring, for 3 minutes or until onion is translucent and soft. Add soup mix, wine, water, cinnamon stick, and bay leaf. Bring mixture to a boil, and stir in cabbage with any juices from the bowl.

Cover the pan, and cook cabbage over low heat for 45 to 60 minutes, stirring occasionally, or until cabbage is tender. Remove and discard cinnamon stick and bay leaf, and stir in jelly. Cook, uncovered, over medium heat for 10 minutes or until the liquid reduces and becomes syrupy. Season with black pepper to taste.

 **Dry and Droll**

Cabbage is one of the oldest vegetables in recorded history although its stature has ranged from lowly to esteemed, depending on the culture. The philosopher Diogenes remarked to a young man that "If you lived on cabbage you would not be obliged to flatter the powerful." The retort was that, "If you flattered the powerful you would not be obliged to live on cabbage."

# Roasted Root Vegetables

Prep time: less than 15 minutes  •  Cooking time: 1¼ hours  •  Makes 6 servings

1 lb. red-skinned potatoes, scrubbed and cut into 1-inch pieces

1 lb. carrots, peeled and cut into 1-inch pieces

½ lb. *celery root*, peeled and cut into 1-inch pieces

½ lb. parsnips, peeled and cut into 1-inch pieces

2 onions, cut into 1-inch pieces

1 envelope savory herb with garlic soup mix

½ cup olive oil

3 TB. chopped fresh rosemary or 1 TB. dried

Freshly ground black pepper to taste

**Ellen on Edibles** _____

Although **celery root,** also called celeriac, looks ugly and brown, the flesh underneath that skin is white and delicate. It has a crunch similar to a water chestnut when raw and turns velvety and smooth when cooked. The flavor is reminiscent of ribs of celery, though more distinct and pronounced.

Preheat the oven to 400°F, and line a large baking sheet with aluminum foil.

Place potatoes, carrots, celery root, parsnips, and onions on baking sheet. Mix together soup mix, oil, and rosemary in a small bowl. Drizzle oil mixture over vegetables and toss to coat them evenly. Spread them over the baking sheet in an even layer.

Bake for 1 to 1¼ hours, stirring occasionally, until vegetables are browned and tender. Season with black pepper to taste.

# Spinach-Stuffed Tomatoes

Prep time: less than 15 minutes • Cooking time: 40 minutes • Makes 6 servings

6 large ripe tomatoes

1 (10-oz.) box frozen chopped spinach, thawed

2 TB. butter

6 scallions, trimmed and sliced

1 envelope leek soup mix

1½ cups whole milk

Freshly ground black pepper to taste

½ cup freshly grated Parmesan cheese

Preheat the oven to 375°F, and line a baking pan with aluminum foil. Slice core ends off tomatoes, and scoop out pulp and seeds, leaving hollow "shells." Invert tomatoes on paper towels to drain.

Place spinach in a sieve, and press with the back of a spoon to extract as much water as possible. Set aside. Heat butter in a saucepan over medium heat and add scallions. Cook and stir for 3 minutes or until scallions are soft. Add soup mix, and stir in milk. Bring to a boil over medium heat, stirring frequently. Reduce heat to low, and simmer mixture for 5 minutes, stirring frequently.

Stir spinach into mixture, and season with black pepper. Place tomatoes on the baking pan, hollow side up, and spoon spinach mixture into hollow tomato shells. Sprinkle tomatoes with cheese. Bake for 30 to 40 minutes or until tomatoes are soft and filling is hot.

 **Mix Mastery**

Cream of spinach soup can be used for this recipe, but if there is actual spinach in the filling, the leek soup creates a more complex flavor that enhances the spinach. This principle is true for many vegetable dishes. The background flavor allows the star to shine.

# Cauliflower au Gratin

Prep time: less than 15 minutes • Cooking time: 1 hour • Makes 6 servings

1 (1½ lb.) head cauliflower, stem, leaves, and core removed

3 TB. unsalted butter, plus more for greasing pan

1 shallot, finely chopped

1 envelope white sauce mix

Milk as specified on mix package

1 cup grated Swiss cheese

Freshly ground black pepper to taste

¼ cup grated Parmesan cheese

3 TB. breadcrumbs

Bring a large pot of salted water to a boil over high heat. Cut cauliflower head into 1-inch florets. Boil florets for 8 to 10 minutes or until tender. Drain and set aside.

Preheat the oven to 375°F. Butter a medium baking dish or gratin pan. Melt 3 tablespoons butter in a saucepan over medium heat and add shallots. Cook and stir for 3 minutes or until shallots are translucent. Add sauce mix, and whisk in milk. Bring to a boil over medium heat, and simmer, stirring frequently, for 5 minutes. Add Swiss cheese, and season with black pepper to taste.

Arrange cauliflower in gratin dish, and top with sauce. Combine Parmesan cheese and breadcrumbs. Sprinkle mixture over sauce. Bake gratin for 30 to 40 minutes or until lightly browned and bubbly.

# Ginger-Glazed Carrots

Prep time: less than 15 minutes • Cooking time: 15 minutes • Makes 6 servings

1½ lb. carrots, peeled and cut on the diagonal into ¼-inch slices

1 cup orange juice

½ envelope golden onion soup mix

3 TB. butter

3 TB. firmly packed dark brown sugar

2 TB. grated fresh ginger

1 tsp. grated orange zest

2 scallions, trimmed and finely chopped

Freshly ground black pepper to taste

Place carrots, orange juice, soup mix, butter, brown sugar, ginger, and orange zest in a large skillet. Bring to a boil over medium heat, and cook carrots, covered, for 4 minutes. Uncover the pan and simmer for 10 minutes, stirring occasionally, or until liquid is almost evaporated and carrots are coated in a sweet glaze.

Sprinkle carrots with chopped scallions, and season with black pepper to taste.

# Refried Beans

Prep time: less than 20 minutes • Cooking time: 15 minutes • Makes 6 to 8 servings

½ cup vegetable oil or bacon fat

2 large red onions, diced

6 garlic cloves, minced

2 (15-oz.) cans red kidney beans, rinsed and drained

½ envelope roasted garlic herb soup mix

½ cup water

½ (4-oz.) can diced mild green chilies

½ cup refrigerated tomato salsa from the produce aisle of the supermarket

Cayenne to taste

**Mix with Care** _____

For the success of this recipe, it's important that you use the chunky fresh refrigerated salsa found most often in the produce department of supermarkets. A jarred salsa will not produce the same flavor or texture.

Heat oil in a large skillet over medium heat; add onions and garlic. Cook and stir for 4 to 5 minutes or until onion is translucent and soft. Stir in beans soup mix, water, chilies, and salsa. Bring to a boil over medium heat, stirring occasionally. Reduce heat to low, and simmer beans, uncovered, for 10 minutes, stirring occasionally, or until beans are hot and have begun to soften.

Mash beans with a potato masher or the back of a heavy spoon until beans are soft but some beans still remain whole. Season with cayenne to taste.

# Spicy Black Beans

Prep time: less than 15 minutes    •    Cooking time: 15 minutes    •    Makes 6 servings

2 TB. vegetable oil

1 onion, diced

1 small jalapeño or serrano chili, seeds and ribs removed, and finely chopped

3 garlic cloves, minced

2 TB. chili powder

1 TB. ground cumin

1 envelope vegetable soup mix

1 cup water

1 (14½-oz.) can diced tomatoes, juice reserved

3 (15-oz.) cans black beans, drained and rinsed

¼ cup chopped fresh cilantro

Freshly ground black pepper to taste

### Mix Mastery

If you want a dish that's less hot, omit the chili pepper. The chili powder and cumin will still deliver a good flavor but a less spicy one.

Heat oil in a large skillet over medium heat; add onion, jalapeño, and garlic. Cook and stir for 3 minutes or until onion is translucent. Reduce heat to low; add chili powder and cumin. Cook and stir for 1 minute.

Add soup mix, water, and tomatoes and their juice to the skillet. Stir well. Add beans and bring to a boil over medium heat. Reduce heat to low, cover, and simmer beans for 15 minutes, stirring occasionally. Stir in cilantro, and season with black pepper to taste.

# Chapter 16

# Vibrant Vegetarian Entrées

## In This Chapter

- ◆ Vegetarian pastas
- ◆ Vegetable and bean stews
- ◆ Egg dishes with vegetables

Vegetarian food is part of all cultures, and the options are as versatile as they are vibrantly flavored and vividly colored. In this chapter, you'll find many recipes for vegetarian entrées.

Many people who eat meat some nights are becoming part of the eating segment known as the "occasional vegetarian" as a way of controlling cholesterol and adding fiber to their diet. Vegetarian food is essentially healthful, although not fat-free when foods such as cheese are part of a dish.

## Star or Side Kick

The vegetarian recipes in this chapter were created to be served as entrées, but there's no reason why any one of them can't work double duty and be the starring side dish that accompanies simple grilled or baked foods.

All these recipes are "saucy foods," so you would not want to serve them with foods made with other sauces. However, they'll become the stars when placed next to something simple. If you're serving these dishes on the side, they will make 10 to 12 servings rather than 6.

# Completing Proteins

Beans are paired with rice and other grains around the world for more than the compatibility of flavor and texture. What generations before us knew instinctively, and we now know scientifically, is that the protein in beans is "incomplete." This means that to deliver their best nutritional content, beans need to be paired with carbohydrate-rich grains such as rice.

When the beans and grains are eaten together, they supply a quality of protein that's as good as that from eggs or beef. If you're serving a bean dish as a vegetarian entrée, plop them on top of some rice or another grain.

## The Least You Need to Know

- ◆ Vegetarian dishes are not low in fat if they contain a large amount of cheese.
- ◆ When paired with rice or other grains, beans and other legumes create a complete protein. (Beans alone contain protein, but it is incomplete.)
- ◆ Quiche are egg custards baked in piecrust shells.
- ◆ Strata are savory bread puddings.

# Spinach Lasagna

Prep time: less than 20 minutes    •    Cooking time: 1 hour    •    Makes 6 servings

12 lasagna noodles

2 TB. butter

½ onion, finely chopped

2 garlic cloves, minced

1 (10-oz.) box frozen leaf spinach, thawed and drained

1 envelope leek soup mix

½ cup milk

1 tsp. Italian seasoning

1 egg, lightly beaten

1 (15-oz.) container ricotta cheese

½ cup grated Parmesan cheese

Freshly ground black pepper to taste

2 cups prepared spaghetti sauce

1 cup grated mozzarella cheese

Preheat the oven to 350°F, and spray a 9×13-inch pan with vegetable oil spray.

Bring a large pot of salted water to a boil. Boil lasagna noodles according to package directions or until they are *al dente* and drain.

Heat butter in a medium saucepan over medium heat; add onion and garlic. Cook and stir for 3 minutes or until onion is translucent. Add spinach, soup mix, and milk. Reduce heat to low and bring to a boil, stirring occasionally. Simmer uncovered for 5 minutes. Remove the skillet from heat, and allow to cool for 5 minutes. Stir in Italian seasoning, egg, ricotta, and Parmesan. Stir well and season with black pepper.

Spread ⅔ cup spaghetti sauce in the bottom of the pre-pared pan, and top with half of lasagna noodles. Layer with half of spinach mixture, and top with another ⅔ cup sauce. Top with another layer of noodles, spinach, and sauce. Sprinkle mozzarella on top.

Bake for 1 hour or until cheese mixture is bubbly and cheese on top has browned.

### Ellen on Edibles

*Al dente* literally means "to the tooth" in Italian, and it describes the way pasta should be perfectly cooked. Pasta should be cooked through and not have a raw flour taste, but it should still be resilient to the bite. The best way to achieve this is to time the minimal amount of cooking time and then taste the pasta every 30 seconds.

# Pasta Primavera

Prep time: less than 20 minutes • Cooking time: 15 minutes • Makes 6 servings

½ lb. thin asparagus, trimmed and cut into 1-inch pieces

¼ lb. green beans, trimmed and cut into 1-inch pieces

1 cup broccoli florets

2 TB. butter

2 scallions, trimmed and thinly sliced

3 garlic cloves, minced

½ red bell pepper, seeds and ribs removed, and finely sliced

1 envelope leek soup mix

1½ cups whole milk

½ cup grated Parmesan cheese

¼ cup chopped fresh parsley

¼ cup chopped fresh basil or 1 TB. dried

1 (14½-oz.) can diced tomatoes, drained

1 lb. thin spaghetti or linguine, cooked according to package directions

Red pepper flakes to taste

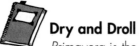

### Dry and Droll

*Primavera* is the Italian word for "springtime," and although this dish sounds quintessentially Italian, it was born and bred in New York. Restaurateur Sirio Maccioni created it in the mid-1970s for his famed Le Cirque restaurant, and food writers popularized the dish nationally.

Bring a large pot of water to a boil. Prepare a bowl of ice water. Add asparagus, green beans, and broccoli to the boiling water. Boil for 2 minutes, drain, and plunge vegetables into ice water for 2 minutes to stop the cooking action. Drain again and set aside.

Heat butter in a medium saucepan over medium heat; add scallions, garlic, and red bell pepper. Cook and stir for 3 minutes or until scallions are soft. Stir soup mix and milk into pan. Bring to a boil over medium heat, stirring frequently. Reduce heat to low, and simmer for 5 minutes, stirring frequently. Stir in cheese, parsley, basil, and tomatoes. Stir until cheese melts.

Add vegetables and cook for 3 minutes or until hot. Toss sauce with pasta, and season with red pepper flakes to taste.

# Southwestern Baked Pasta

Prep time: less than 15 minutes    •    Cooking time: 25 minutes    •    Makes 6 servings

1 envelope white sauce mix

Milk as specified on mix package

2 cups (½ lb.) grated Monterey Jack or *Mexican blended cheese*

⅔ cup refrigerated tomato salsa from the produce aisle of the supermarket

1 (10-oz.) box frozen corn, thawed and drained

1 (15-oz.) can red kidney beans, rinsed and drained

¼ cup chopped pimiento

5 cups cooked small pasta, such as macaroni, small shells, or twists

Freshly ground black pepper to taste

1 cup crushed tortilla chips

Preheat the oven to 350°F, and spray a 9×13-inch pan with vegetable oil spray. Combine sauce mix and milk in a medium saucepan, and bring to a boil over medium heat, stirring frequently. Reduce heat to low, and simmer sauce for 3 minutes. Stir in cheese and salsa. Cook and stir for 2 minutes, or until cheese is melted.

Place corn, beans, pimiento, and pasta into the prepared baking pan. Pour sauce over mixture, and stir to coat. Season with black pepper, and spread mixture in an even layer. Sprinkle tortilla chips over top.

Bake for 15 minutes or until hot and bubbly.

**Ellen on Edibles**

Many companies now produce a grated **Mexican blended cheese** that is a combination of Monterey Jack, cheddar, and asagio. This adds a more complex flavor to Mexican dishes than just using Monterey Jack.

# Pasta with Mushroom Sauce

Prep time: less than 15 minutes   •   Cooking time: 15 minutes   •   Makes 6 servings

2 TB. olive oil

1 TB. butter

½ lb. crimini or shiitake mushrooms, rinsed, stemmed, and sliced

2 garlic cloves, minced

1 shallot, minced

1 envelope wild mushroom and chive soup mix

½ cup water

½ cup dry white wine

½ cup heavy cream

1 (14½-oz.) can diced tomatoes, drained

1 tsp. Italian seasoning

1 lb. linguine or spaghetti, cooked according to package directions

Freshly ground black pepper to taste

Grated Parmesan cheese

> **Mix Mastery**
>
> The cream smoothes out the flavors in the sauce, but if you want to create a sauce without cream, increase the amount of water to 1 cup. Do not increase the amount of wine, though, or the flavor of the sauce will become too strong.

Heat oil and butter in a medium saucepan over medium heat; add mushrooms, garlic, and shallot. Cook and stir for 3 minutes or until mushrooms begin to soften and shallot is translucent. Stir in soup mix, water, wine, cream, tomatoes, and Italian seasoning.

Bring mixture to a boil over medium heat, stirring frequently. Reduce heat to low, and simmer sauce for 10 minutes, stirring occasionally. Toss sauce with cooked pasta, and season with black pepper to taste. Pass grated Parmesan separately.

# Herbed Macaroni and Cheese

Prep time: less than 15 minutes   •   Cooking time: 50 minutes   •   Makes 6 servings

| | |
|---|---|
| 2 TB. butter | 1 tsp. Worcestershire sauce |
| 2 shallots, minced | ½ tsp. dried thyme |
| 1 envelope leek soup mix | 2 TB. chopped fresh parsley |
| 1½ cups whole milk | 1 lb. macaroni or other small pasta, cooked according to package directions |
| 2 cups shredded mild or sharp cheddar cheese | Freshly ground black pepper to taste |

Preheat the oven to 350°F, and spray a 3-quart baking pan with vegetable oil spray.

Heat butter in a medium saucepan over medium heat; add shallots. Cook and stir for 3 minutes or until shallots are translucent. Stir soup mix and milk into pan. Bring to a boil, stirring frequently. Reduce heat to low, and simmer sauce for 5 minutes, stirring often. Add cheese, and stir until cheese melts.

Stir Worcestershire, thyme, and parsley into sauce. Place macaroni in the prepared baking pan, and toss with sauce until evenly coated. Season with black pepper to taste, and bake for 30 to 40 minutes or until bubbly and top is browned.

 **Mix Mastery**

This is a classic "mac and cheese" recipe, but you can vary the cheese and totally transform the dish. Instead of the cheddar, use a combination of half crumbled blue cheese and half mozzarella. Or make the dish spicy by using a pepper jack.

# Penne alla Vodka

Prep time: less than 15 minutes  •  Cooking time: 10 minutes  •  Makes 6 servings

3 TB. olive oil

4 garlic cloves, minced

1 (28-oz.) can crushed tomatoes in tomato purée

1 envelope roasted garlic herb soup mix

½ cup heavy cream

¼ cup vodka

3 TB. chopped fresh parsley

1 lb. penne or similar size pasta, cooked according to package directions

Red pepper flakes to taste

Grated Parmesan cheese to taste

**Mix with Care** _____

Using the right tomatoes is the key to the success of this simple dish. Make sure you are using crushed tomatoes that are packed in a thick purée and not diced tomatoes in water.

Heat oil in a medium saucepan over medium heat; add garlic. Cook and stir for 2 minutes. Add tomatoes with their purée, and stir in soup mix, cream, and vodka. Bring to a boil, and reduce heat to low. Simmer sauce for 5 minutes and then add parsley.

Toss pasta with sauce, and season with red pepper flakes to taste. Pass grated Parmesan separately.

# Cold Tortellini Salad

Prep time: less than 15 minutes  •  Cooking time: 10 minutes  •  Makes 6 servings

⅔ cup mayonnaise

¼ cup white wine vinegar

1 envelope vegetable soup mix

1½ lb. cheese tortellini

2 TB. olive oil

½ cup sliced pimiento-stuffed green olives

4 scallions, trimmed and thinly sliced

2 tomatoes, cored, seeded, and cut into ½-inch dice

1 (15-oz.) can chickpeas, drained and rinsed

¼ cup chopped fresh basil or 1 TB. dried

2 TB. chopped fresh parsley

Freshly ground black pepper to taste

Combine mayonnaise, vinegar, and soup mix in a mixing bowl. Stir well and refrigerate for at least 2 hours to blend flavors. Cook tortellini according to package directions. Drain, toss with oil, and refrigerate covered with plastic wrap until chilled.

When tortellini is chilled, add olives, scallions, tomatoes, chickpeas, basil, and parsley. Add dressing and toss. Season with black pepper to taste.

# Vegetarian Chili

Prep time: less than 20 minutes     •     Cooking time: 35 minutes     •     Makes 6 servings

2 TB. olive oil

1 large onion, diced

4 garlic cloves, minced

1 red bell pepper, seeds and ribs removed, and cut into ¾-inch dice

4 to 6 TB. chili powder

1 TB. ground cumin

2 medium zucchini, trimmed and cut into ¾-inch dice

1 (28-oz.) can diced tomatoes, juice reserved

1 envelope tomato with basil soup mix

1½ cups water

1 (4-oz.) can chopped green chilies

1 (15-oz.) can red kidney beans, rinsed and drained

1 (10-oz.) box frozen corn kernels, thawed

Freshly ground black pepper to taste

Heat oil in a large saucepan over medium heat; add onion, garlic, and bell pepper. Cook and stir for 3 minutes or until onion is translucent. Stir in chili powder and cumin. Cook and stir for 1 minute.

Add zucchini, tomatoes and their juice, soup mix, water, chilies, and beans. Stir well and bring to a boil over medium heat. Reduce heat to low, and simmer uncovered for 25 to 35 minutes or until vegetables are soft, stirring occasionally. Add corn and cook for an additional 5 minutes. Season with black pepper to taste.

 **Mix Mastery**

You can personalize this dish in many ways. Add carrot and celery in place of or in addition to the bell pepper, or substitute yellow squash for the zucchini. You can also use any type of canned bean because they are all already cooked.

# Stewed Red Beans and Rice

Prep time: less than 15 minutes • Cooking time: 15 minutes • Makes 6 servings

3 TB. olive oil

2 onions, chopped

1 celery stalk, trimmed and chopped

4 garlic cloves, minced

½ green bell pepper, seeds and ribs removed, and chopped

1 envelope tomato with basil soup mix

1½ cups water

3 (15-oz.) cans red kidney beans, rinsed and drained

2 tsp. dried thyme

1 bay leaf

Hot pepper sauce to taste

3 cups cooked white rice

**Dry and Droll** _____

Jazz great Louis Armstrong, a great fan of the cooking of his native Louisiana, reportedly signed his letters "Red beans and ricely yours."

Heat oil in a large saucepan over medium heat; add onions, celery, garlic, and green bell pepper. Cook and stir for 3 minutes or until onion is translucent. Add soup mix and water, and bring to a boil, stirring frequently.

Add kidney beans, thyme, and bay leaf. Bring to a boil, and reduce heat to low. Simmer beans uncovered for 10 minutes, stirring frequently. Remove and discard bay leaf, and season with hot pepper sauce to taste. Serve over rice.

# Mexican Mixed Bean Stew

Prep time: less than 15 minutes   •   Cooking time: 20 minutes   •   Makes 6 servings

3 TB. olive oil

1 onion, diced

3 garlic cloves, minced

½ red bell pepper, seeds and ribs removed, and finely chopped

1 TB. chili powder

2 tsp. ground cumin

½ envelope savory herb with garlic soup mix

1 (4-oz.) can chopped green chilies

1 (8-oz.) can tomato sauce

1 cup water

2 medium zucchini, trimmed and cut into ½-inch dice

1 (15-oz.) can red kidney beans, drained and rinsed

1 (15-oz.) can chickpeas, drained and rinsed

Freshly ground black pepper to taste

3 cups cooked brown or white rice

Heat oil in a large saucepan over medium heat; add onion, garlic, and red bell pepper. Cook and stir for 3 minutes or until onion is translucent. Stir in chili powder and cumin. Cook for 1 minute, stirring constantly. Stir in soup mix, chilies, tomato sauce, water, zucchini, kidney beans, and chickpeas.

Bring to a boil, and reduce heat to low. Simmer uncovered for 10 to 15 minutes or until zucchini is tender and sauce has thickened. Season with black pepper to taste, and serve over rice.

### Mix with Care

Many small cans of chilies line the supermarket shelves, and right next to the mild chopped chilies are chopped hot peppers. Make sure you buy the right can. A whole can of hot peppers would make anyone who ate this dish breathe fire.

# Hearty Lentil Stew

Prep time: less than 15 minutes • Cooking time: 50 minutes • Makes 6 servings

2 TB. vegetable oil

1 onion, diced

4 garlic cloves, minced

2 TB. minced fresh ginger

2 TB. ground cumin

1 TB. prepared mustard

1 lb. *lentils*, rinsed and picked over

1 envelope roasted garlic herb soup mix

6 cups water

2 large tomatoes, cored, seeded, and diced

2 medium zucchini, trimmed and cut into ½-inch thick slices

Freshly ground black pepper to taste

3 TB. chopped fresh cilantro

### Ellen on Edibles

**Lentils** are tiny lens-shape pulses and one of the oldest foods in the world. We commonly find brownish gray lentils, but they also come in bright red, green, and yellow. You'll find the more colorful species at Indian and other Asian food stores.

Heat oil in a large saucepan over medium heat; add onion, garlic, and ginger. Cook and stir for 3 minutes or until onion is translucent.

Add cumin, mustard, lentils, soup mix, water, tomatoes, and zucchini. Stir well and bring to a boil over medium heat. Reduce heat to low, cover, and simmer, stirring occasionally for 40 to 50 minutes or until lentils are tender. Season with black pepper to taste, and stir in cilantro.

# Broccoli and Cheese Quiche

Prep time: less than 15 minutes  •  Cooking time: 50 minutes  •  Makes 6 servings

1 (10-oz.) box frozen chopped broccoli

3 eggs

1 egg yolk

1½ cups whole milk

1 envelope spring vegetable soup mix

1 cup grated Swiss cheese

Freshly ground black pepper to taste

1 (9-inch) frozen deep-dish piecrust, partially baked according to package directions

Cook broccoli according to package directions. Drain and set aside to cool.

Preheat the oven to 375°F.

Combine eggs, egg yolk, milk, and soup mix in mixing bowl. Whisk well. Add cheese and broccoli. Season with black pepper to taste. Pour mixture into piecrust. Bake for 40 to 50 minutes or until a toothpick inserted in the center of quiche comes out clean. Serve hot or at room temperature.

 **Mix Mastery**

To avoid the house smelling like broccoli (or cauliflower or Brussels sprouts) for a week, add a piece of stale bread to the water in which it's boiling.

# Spinach Quiche

Prep time: less than 15 minutes  •  Cooking time: 50 minutes  •  Makes 6 servings

1 (10-oz.) box frozen chopped spinach, thawed and drained

3 eggs

1 egg yolk

1½ cups whole milk

1 envelope leek soup mix

1 cup grated cheddar cheese

¼ cup chopped pimientos

Freshly ground black pepper to taste

1 (9-inch) frozen deep-dish piecrust, partially baked according to package directions

Preheat the oven to 375°F. Place spinach in a strainer, and press with the back of a spoon to extract as much liquid as possible.

Combine eggs, egg yolk, milk, and soup mix in a mixing bowl. Whisk well. Add spinach, cheese, and pimientos. Season with black pepper to taste. Pour mixture into piecrust. Bake for 40 to 50 minutes or until a toothpick inserted in the center of quiche comes out clean. Serve hot or at room temperature.

# Mushroom Strata

Prep time: less than 20 minutes, • Cooking time: 60 minutes • Makes 6 servings
plus 4 hours to soak prior to baking

3 TB. butter

2 TB. olive oil

1 onion, diced

2 garlic cloves, minced

½ lb. white mushrooms, rinsed, stemmed, and thinly sliced

½ lb. shiitake mushrooms, rinsed, stemmed, and thinly sliced

5 eggs, lightly beaten

1 envelope wild mushroom and chive soup mix

2 cups half-and-half

½ to ¾ loaf French or Italian bread, cut into ¾-inch cubes (8 cups cubes)

1 cup grated Gruyère or Swiss cheese

Freshly ground black pepper to taste

Heat butter and oil in a large skillet over medium heat; add onion, garlic, white mushrooms, and shiitake mushrooms. Cook and stir for 5 minutes or until mushrooms are soft. Set aside to cool.

### Ellen on Edibles

**Strata** sounds Italian, but the derivation of the dish is unknown. It's just a fancy name for a savory bread pudding. Sometimes the bread is sliced rather than cubed, but the constants are an egg custard and some sort of cheese.

Combine eggs, soup mix, and half-and-half in a large mixing bowl. Add bread cubes, cheese, and mushroom mixture. Season with black pepper to taste. Stir well and push down bread cubes so they will absorb liquid. Cover bowl and refrigerate for at least 4 hours or up to 24 hours. Stir occasionally so bread absorbs liquid evenly.

Preheat the oven to 350°F, and spray a 9×13-inch pan with vegetable oil spray. Transfer bread mixture to pan, and spread evenly. Bake strata for 50 to 60 minutes or until top is golden brown and an instant-read thermometer registers 165°F when placed in the center of strata.

# Stuffed Zucchini

Prep time: less than 30 minutes    •    Cooking time: 25 minutes    •    Makes 6 servings

| | |
|---|---|
| 6 medium zucchini | 1¼ cups whole milk |
| 2 TB. butter | ½ tsp. dried thyme |
| 2 shallots, minced | ½ cup Italian-style breadcrumbs |
| ½ lb. fresh spinach, rinsed and stemmed | Freshly ground black pepper to taste |
| 1 envelope cream of spinach soup mix | |

Bring a large pot of salted water to a boil, and preheat the oven to 375°F. Line a baking sheet with aluminum foil.

Trim ends off zucchini, and cut them in half lengthwise. Boil zucchini halves for 3 minutes and drain. Scrap pulp out of zucchini, and reserve, leaving a shell that is about ½-inch thick. Chop pulp and set aside.

Place butter in a large saucepan over medium heat; add shallots. Cook and stir for 3 minutes or until shallots are translucent. Raise heat to medium-high and add spinach. Turn with spatula until spinach wilts, about 2 minutes. Stir soup mix, milk, and thyme into the pan, and bring to a boil, stirring frequently. Reduce heat to low, and simmer for 5 minutes.

Remove the pan from heat, and stir in zucchini pulp and breadcrumbs. Season with black pepper to taste. Place zucchini shells skin side down on the prepared baking sheet, and divide stuffing mixture between shells.

Bake for 15 to 20 minutes or until zucchini is tender.

### Dry and Droll
Zucchini is a nutritional treasure trove. It's very low in calories and sodium and is an excellent source of vitamins A and C, as well as potassium.

# Chapter 17

# Terrific Tubers and Glorious Grains

## In This Chapter

- ◆ Creamy and crisp potatoes
- ◆ Rice to draw raves
- ◆ Great ways with grains

Potatoes, sweet potatoes, and grains are all complex carbohydrates that are increasingly important in maintaining a healthy body. These foods are also versatile, as you'll see when cooking the recipes in this chapter.

And it's such a bonus that the foods that are good for us are also so delicious.

## Super Spuds

Potatoes, sweet potatoes, and yams are all tubers. Tubers are the elongated starchy roots spawned by some plants underground. Although these tubers are edible, flowers such as dahlias also grow from tubers. Potatoes and their cousin tubers, sweet potatoes and yams, are excellent sources of potassium as well as fiber.

Potatoes are like a blank canvas that needs some paint to create a masterpiece. In this case, soup mixes as well as other ingredients provide the hues. Because potatoes are inherently bland, the sodium in a soup mix adds just the right amount of salt along with its flavors.

If you are using a soup mix to coat potatoes that are cut in wedges or slices to bake crisp, the ones that work best are those mixes that do not have many large pieces of dehydrated vegetables. Small bits of onion absorb moisture from the potato, but large pieces of vegetables in a vegetable soup do not.

# Glorious Grains

All grains, including rice, are the fruit produced by grasses, and the less processed the grain, the more fiber it adds to our diets. For example, brown rice has only the inedible husk removed, and the bran coating is extremely high in fiber. It's also what gives brown rice its chewy texture and nutlike flavor.

Although corn is a grain, we treat it in different ways depending on its form. You can find recipes for corn kernels in Chapter 15; I have included recipes for cornmeal in this chapter.

## The Least You Need to Know

- Potatoes, sweet potatoes, and yams are all tubers.
- Grains are the fruit produced by grasses.
- Red-skinned potatoes do not need to be peeled; however, russet potatoes should be peeled unless they are baked.
- Brown rice takes longer to cook than white rice.

# Roasted Garlic Mashed Potatoes

Prep time: less than 15 minutes    •    Cooking time: 20 minutes    •    Makes 6 servings

3 lb. red-skinned potatoes, scrubbed and cut into 1-inch pieces

Salt

1 envelope roasted garlic herb soup mix

½ to ⅔ cup half-and-half

4 TB. butter, cut into small pieces

Freshly ground black pepper to taste

Place potatoes in a saucepan, with enough cold water to cover. Salt water and bring to a boil over high heat. Reduce heat to medium, and boil potatoes for 15 to 20 minutes or until cubes are very soft when pierced with tip of a knife. Drain potatoes in a colander, and shake it a few times to remove excess water. Return potatoes to the pot.

While potatoes are boiling, combine soup mix, half-and-half, and butter in a small saucepan. Stir well and bring to a boil over medium heat, stirring frequently. Reduce heat to low, and simmer mixture for 5 minutes.

Pour mixture over hot potatoes, and mash them with a potato masher or with an electric mixer on low speed until light and fluffy. Do not overmix, or potatoes will become gluey. Season with black pepper to taste.

## Mix Mastery

I've used red-skinned potatoes in this recipe because I like the way the bits of skin look in the dish, the dish is faster to make because the potatoes do not need peeling, and the skins add more fiber. If you want to use russet potatoes, go ahead—but peel them.

# Potato and Leek Purée

Prep time: less than 15 minutes   •   Cooking time: 25 minutes   •   Makes 6 servings

5 large Russet potatoes, peeled and cut into 1-inch pieces

Salt

4 cups finely chopped leeks, white parts only, washed well and drained well

6 TB. (¾ stick) butter

2 garlic cloves, minced

1 envelope leek soup mix

1 cup milk or half-and-half, heated until just below a simmer

Freshly ground black pepper to taste

Place potatoes in a saucepan, with enough cold water to cover. Salt water and bring to a boil over high heat. Reduce heat to medium, and boil potatoes for 15 to 20 minutes or until cubes are very soft when pierced with the tip of a knife. Drain potatoes in a colander, and shake it a few times to remove excess water. Return potatoes to the pot.

 **Mix with Care**

Do not purée potatoes in a food processor because they become gluey. If you want a smoother texture and don't have a ricer or food mill, you can mash them with a potato masher and then beat the dish with an electric mixer set at low speed very briefly.

While potatoes are cooking, bring another saucepan of water to a boil over high heat. Add leeks, boil for 5 minutes, and drain well. Melt butter in a skillet over medium heat; add garlic and leeks. Cook over low heat, stirring frequently, for 10 minutes or until leeks are soft. Scrape mixture into a food processor fitted with a steel blade, add soup mix and hot milk, and purée until smooth.

Put potatoes through a food mill or ricer, or mash them by hand. Do not overmix or potatoes will become gluey. Stir leek mixture into potatoes, and season with black pepper to taste.

# Cheesy Puffed Potatoes

Prep time: less than 20 minutes   •   Cooking time: 1 hour   •   Makes 6 servings

4 to 6 large russet potatoes, peeled and cut into 1-inch chunks

1 envelope golden onion soup mix

1 cup half-and-half

4 TB. butter

1 cup grated cheddar cheese

3 eggs, lightly beaten

Freshly ground black pepper to taste

Preheat the oven to 375°F, and spray a 9×13-inch baking dish with vegetable oil spray.

Place potatoes in a large saucepan, with enough water to cover. Bring to a boil over high heat. Reduce heat to medium, and boil potatoes for 15 to 20 minutes or until cubes are very tender when pierced with the tip of a knife. Drain potatoes in a colander, shaking them a few times to remove excess water. Return potatoes to pot.

While potatoes are boiling, combine soup mix, half-and-half, butter, and ½ cup cheese in a small saucepan. Stir well and bring to a boil over medium heat, stirring frequently. Reduce heat to low, and simmer for 5 minutes.

Pour liquid over potatoes, and mash well using a potato masher or an electric mixer on low speed. Do not over-mix or potatoes will become gluey. Stir in eggs, and beat well again. Season with black pepper to taste, and spread mixture into the prepared pan. Sprinkle with remaining ½ cup cheese.

Bake for 30 to 40 minutes or until potatoes have puffed and top is browned.

 **Dry and Droll**

The ancient Incas first started cultivating potatoes thousands of years ago, and the first conquistadors exported the tubers to Europe. Potatoes were not popular, however, until Sir Walter Raleigh planted them on his estate in Ireland in the eighteenth century.

# Southwest Potato Gratin

Prep time: less than 15 minutes • Cooking time: 1½ hours • Makes 6 servings

3 lb. red-skinned potatoes, scrubbed

1 envelope leek soup mix

1½ cups whole milk

1 (4-oz.) can chopped green chilies

2 garlic cloves, minced

1½ cups grated Monterey Jack or Mexican blend cheese

Freshly ground black pepper to taste

Preheat the oven to 375°F, and spray the inside of a baking dish with vegetable oil spray. Cover a baking sheet with aluminum foil. Thinly slice potatoes and set aside.

**Mix Mastery**

Consider this a basic recipe for au gratin potatoes. You can omit the chilies and use cheddar cheese in place of the Monterey Jack. Another variation is to use a smoked gouda or smoked Gruyère to add that flavor nuance.

Combine soup mix, milk, chilies, and garlic in a small saucepan. Bring to a boil over medium heat, stirring occasionally. Reduce heat to low, and simmer for 3 minutes. Add 1 cup cheese, and stir until cheese is melted. Season sauce with black pepper to taste.

Arrange ½ potato slices in a casserole and top with ½ sauce. Repeat with remaining potatoes and sauce. Top with remaining ½ cup cheese.

Place the casserole on the prepared baking sheet. Bake for 1¼ to 1½ hours or until potatoes are soft and the top layer is browned.

# Oven-Fried Potatoes

Prep time: less than 15 minutes • Cooking time: 1 hour • Makes 6 servings

½ cup vegetable oil

1 envelope savory herb with garlic soup mix

Freshly ground black pepper to taste

6 russet potatoes, scrubbed and cut into ½-inch wedges

Preheat the oven to 400°F, and line a roasting pan with aluminum foil.

Combine oil, soup mix, and black pepper to taste in a mixing bowl. Add potato wedges and toss to coat evenly. Transfer potatoes to the prepared roasting pan. Bake for 45 minutes to 1 hour or until potatoes are crisp. Turn with metal spatula halfway through baking time.

# Twice-Baked Potatoes

Prep time: less than 15 minutes  •  Cooking time: 1½ hours  •  Makes 6 servings

6 russet potatoes, scrubbed well

2 TB. vegetable oil

1 envelope leek soup mix

¾ cup half-and-half

1 (3-oz.) package cream cheese, softened

1 cup grated Gruyère or Swiss cheese

Freshly ground black pepper to taste

Preheat the oven to 425°F, and line a baking pan with aluminum foil. Rub potatoes with vegetable oil, and prick them all over with a meat fork. Bake potatoes on the middle rack of the oven for 50 to 65 minutes or until they are very tender when pierced with the tip of a knife. Reduce the oven temperature to 375°F.

While potatoes are baking, combine soup mix, half-and-half, cream cheese, and ½ cup cheese in a small saucepan. Stir well and bring to a boil over medium heat. Reduce heat to low, and simmer for 5 minutes, stirring frequently.

Remove potatoes from the oven, and slice in half lengthwise. Scoop out the pulp, leaving a ¼-inch shell next to the skin. Mash potatoes with the cheese mixture until light and fluffy using a potato masher or an electric mixer on low speed. Do not overmix or potatoes will become gluey. Season with black pepper to taste.

Mound mashed potatoes into potato shells, and sprinkle with remaining ½ cup cheese. Place potatoes on the prepared baking sheet, and bake for 15 to 20 minutes or until hot and browned.

**Variations:** You can add ½ cup crumbled cooked bacon, 1 cup cheddar cheese instead of the cheeses listed, or ½ cup finely chopped tomato to this master recipe to vary the results.

### Mix Mastery
Mashed potatoes should be prepared on the day they're served, but there's no reason why these potatoes can't have their second baking a day or two later. Add about 10 minutes to the baking time if you refrigerate the potatoes before browning them.

# Twice-Baked Yams with Tomatillo Sauce

Prep time: less than 15 minutes  •  Cooking time: 1¼ hours  •  Makes 6 servings

| | |
|---|---|
| 6 (8-oz.) yams or sweet potatoes, scrubbed | ¾ cup sour cream |
| 2 TB. vegetable oil | ¼ cup green *tomatillo* salsa |
| ½ envelope roasted garlic herb soup mix | Freshly ground black pepper to taste |
| ¼ cup boiling water | ¾ cup grated Monterey Jack cheese |

Preheat the oven to 400°F, and line a baking pan with aluminum foil. Rub yams or sweet potatoes with oil, and prick them all over with a meat fork. Place potatoes in the prepared pan, and bake for 30 minutes. Turn potatoes with tongs, and bake for an additional 30 minutes or until soft when pierced with a meat fork.

### Ellen on Edibles

The **tomatillo** is a small, round, green fruit that resembles the tomato, but it is actually botanically closer to the gooseberry. They are covered with a papery husk and used in both Mexican and Southwestern cooking. They are tart and acidic and are never eaten raw. Bottled tomatillo salsa is available in most supermarkets.

While potatoes are baking, place soup mix in a small mixing bowl and pour boiling water over it. Stir well and let sit for 10 minutes. Stir in sour cream and salsa.

Cut potatoes in half lengthwise, and scrape out pulp, leaving a ¼-inch shell next to skin. Mash pulp with sour cream mixture until light and fluffy using a potato masher or an electric mixer on low speed. Do not overmix or potatoes will become gluey. Season with black pepper to taste. Mound mashed potatoes into potato shells, and sprinkle each with cheese. Bake for 10 to 15 minutes or until potatoes are hot and cheese is browned.

# Hash-Brown Potato Salad with Bacon

Prep time: less than 20 minutes   •   Cooking time: 30 minutes   •   Makes 6 servings

1½ lb. red-skinned potatoes, quartered length-wise and cut crosswise into 1-inch slices

¼ lb. bacon, cut into ½-inch slices

2 TB. vegetable oil

1 TB. mustard seeds

1 TB. chopped fresh rosemary or 1 tsp. dried

3 TB. cider vinegar

½ red onion, finely chopped

1 celery stalk, trimmed and thinly sliced

2 TB. chopped fresh parsley

½ envelope savory herb with garlic soup mix

⅓ cup mayonnaise or to taste

Freshly ground black pepper to taste

Steam potatoes in a steamer set over boiling water, covered, for 6 to 8 minutes or until they are barely tender. Remove potatoes from the steamer and set aside.

Cook bacon in a large skillet over medium-high heat until crisp. Remove bacon from the pan with a slotted spoon, reserving the grease. Drain bacon on paper towels. Discard all but 2 tablespoons grease from the pan.

Add oil to the skillet, heat over medium heat, and fry mustard seeds, partially covered, for 10 seconds or until they stop popping. Add potatoes and rosemary, and cook, turning potatoes carefully, for 10 minutes. Add 2 tablespoons vinegar, and cook potatoes, turning carefully, for 5 minutes or until they are crusty and golden.

Transfer potatoes to a large bowl, and let them cool. Add onion and celery. Add bacon and parsley. Stir soup mix and remaining 1 tablespoon vinegar into mayonnaise; add it to salad and toss gently. Season with black pepper to taste. Toss salad and serve at room temperature.

 **Mix Mastery**

To prevent uncooked, peeled potatoes from browning, drop them into cold water or just wrap them in several layers of damp paper towels.

# Wild Mushroom Polenta

Prep time: less than 30 minutes, • Cooking time: 25 minutes • Makes 6 to 8 servings
plus 4 hours for chilling

| | |
|---|---|
| 12 TB. butter, plus more for greasing | 1 envelope wild mushroom and chive soup mix |
| 1 medium onion, chopped | |
| 3 garlic cloves, minced | 2 cups water |
| ½ lb. fresh shiitake mushrooms, stemmed and sliced | 1 cup yellow cornmeal |
| | Freshly ground black pepper to taste |

Butter a 9×5-inch loaf pan. Heat 4 tablespoons butter in a skillet over medium heat; add onions and garlic. Cook and stir for 3 minutes or until onion is translucent. Add mushrooms; cook and stir for 5 minutes or until mushrooms are soft and have released their liquid. Set aside.

Bring soup mix and 1½ cups water to a boil in a heavy saucepan. Moisten cornmeal with remaining ½ cup water. Slowly add cornmeal to boiling water, whisking constantly until smooth. Bring mixture back to a simmer, and cook for 15 minutes, stirring constantly with a wooden spoon. Mixture will become very thick. Stir in mushrooms. Season with black pepper to taste.

### Dry and Droll

*Polenta* is the Italian term for a mixture of cornmeal mush, but the dish arrived in Italy from the New World. Cornmeal was a staple of the Native American diet, and variations on polenta were made on this continent hundreds of years before corn was exported to Italy in the sixteenth century.

Pour polenta into the prepared loaf pan. Cool it to room temperature, then cover tightly and refrigerate for at least 4 hours, preferably overnight.

To serve, run a sharp knife around the sides of the loaf pan and unmold polenta onto a cutting board. Slice into ¾-inch-thick slices. Heat remaining 8 tablespoons butter in a large skillet over medium heat. Add as many polenta slices as will fit into the skillet in a single layer. Fry for 3 to 4 minutes or until bottom is brown. Carefully turn slices with a spatula and fry other side. Continue until all slices are fried. Cut each slice in half diagonally and serve immediately.

# Risotto with Sun-Dried Tomatoes

Prep time: less than 30 minutes   •   Cooking time: 40 minutes   •   Makes 6 servings

2 oz. (about 20) sun-dried tomatoes (not packed in oil)

6 to 7 cups water, heated to just below simmer

4 TB. butter

2 garlic cloves, minced

1 medium onion, diced

2 cups arborio rice

¾ cup white wine

1 envelope roasted garlic herb soup mix

¾ cup grated Parmesan cheese

Freshly ground black pepper to taste

Place sun-dried tomatoes in a pan with water, and boil for 1 minute. Remove with a slotted spoon, and reserve tomato soaking liquid. Chop tomatoes finely. Set aside.

Melt butter in a heavy saucepan over medium heat; add garlic and onion. Cook and stir for 3 minutes or until onion is translucent. Add rice and stir to coat with butter. Raise heat to high, add wine, and cook for 3 minutes, stirring constantly, until wine has almost evaporated. Reduce heat to medium and stir in soup mix and reserved sun-dried tomatoes. Ladle ½ cup tomato soaking water over rice. Wait for rice to absorb water while stirring almost constantly. Repeat with another ½ cup liquid, continually stirring, and wait until rice absorbs it. Continue adding liquid, ½ cup at a time, for 12 to 15 minutes until at least 5 cups water have been added. The consistency should be creamy, and rice should still be slightly resilient. Add more water, if necessary.

Add cheese, season with black pepper to taste, and allow to sit for 3 minutes before serving.

### Dry and Droll

Risotto (pronounced *ree-SOH-tow*) hails from Milan and was supposedly invented in the late-sixteenth century by a stained-glass maker who was cooking for his boss's daughter's wedding. Traditional *risotto alla Milanese* is made with saffron, which was the dye used to make yellow stained glass.

# Risotto with Wild Mushrooms

Prep time: less than 30 minutes • Cooking time: 40 minutes • Makes 6 servings

½ lb. fresh wild mushrooms (some combination of shiitake, oyster, chanterelles, porcini, etc.)

¼ lb. butter

2 garlic cloves, minced

1 medium onion, diced

2 cups arborio rice

¾ cup white wine

1 envelope wild mushroom and chive soup mix

6 to 7 cups water, heated to just below simmer

¾ cup grated Parmesan cheese

Freshly ground black pepper to taste

Clean mushrooms, discarding stems. Slice, if large. Heat 3 tablespoons butter in a skillet over medium-high heat; add mushrooms and garlic. Cook and stir for 5 minutes or until mushrooms are soft. Set aside.

Place remaining butter in a heavy saucepan and melt over low heat; add onion. Cook and stir for 3 minutes or until onion is translucent. Add rice and stir to coat with butter. Raise heat to high, add wine, and cook for 3 minutes, stirring constantly, until wine has almost evaporated. Reduce heat to medium, and stir in soup mix.

Ladle ½ cup hot water over rice. Wait for rice to absorb water while stirring almost constantly. Repeat with another ½ cup water, continually stirring, and wait until rice absorbs it. Continue adding water, ½ cup at a time, and stirring for 12 to 15 minutes or until at least 5 cups water have been added. The consistency should be creamy, and rice should still be slightly resilient. Add more water, if necessary. Add sautéed mushrooms and cheese. Season with black pepper to taste, and allow to sit for 3 minutes before serving.

### Mix Mastery

Contrary to popular opinion, risotto can be started a day in advance and this will save about 35 minutes of time on the day you want to serve it. Refrigerate the sautéed mushrooms. Prepare the rice, and when all but 1 cup water has been added, remove the pan from the heat and spread the rice onto a baking sheet. Cover the sheet with plastic wrap, and refrigerate until cold. The next day, return the rice to a saucepan, stir in the mushrooms, and add the remaining water.

# Confetti Rice

Prep time: less than 15 minutes  •  Cooking time: 40 minutes  •  Makes 6 servings

2 TB. butter

½ onion, diced

1 cup uncooked brown rice

1 envelope vegetable soup mix

2½ cups water

½ tsp. dried thyme

Freshly ground black pepper to taste

Heat butter in a medium saucepan over medium heat; add onion. Cook and stir for 2 minutes. Add rice. Cook and stir for 2 minutes or until onion is translucent. Add soup mix, water, and thyme. Bring to a boil over medium-high heat, stirring occasionally.

Reduce heat to low, cover pan, and simmer rice for 35 to 40 minutes or until water is absorbed. Season with black pepper to taste.

**Mix with Care**

Brown rice takes much longer to soften than white rice, which has been milled to remove the bran coating. If you're using white rice for this recipe, reduce the water to 2 cups and the rice will cook in 20 to 25 minutes.

# Spanish Rice

Prep time: less than 15 minutes  •  Cooking time: 25 minutes  •  Makes 6 servings

2 TB. olive oil

1 onion, diced

2 garlic cloves, minced

1 cup uncooked converted long-grain white rice

1 envelope golden onion soup mix

1½ cups water

1 (14-oz.) can diced tomatoes, drained

1 cup frozen peas, thawed

¼ cup sliced pimiento-stuffed green olives

Freshly ground black pepper to taste

Heat oil in a medium skillet over medium heat; add onion and garlic. Cook and stir for 3 minutes or until onion is translucent. Add rice; cook and stir for 2 minutes or until grains are opaque.

Stir in soup mix, water, tomatoes, and peas. Stir well and bring to a boil. Reduce heat to low, cover the pan, and cook rice for 20 minutes or until liquid is absorbed and rice is soft. Stir in olives, and season with black pepper to taste.

# Braised Wild Rice with Pine Nuts

Prep time: less than 15 minutes • Cooking time: 1½ hours • Makes 6 servings

¾ cup wild rice

2 TB. butter

1 onion, diced

1 envelope vegetable soup mix

2½ cups water

1 TB. fresh thyme leaves or 1 tsp. dried

1 bay leaf

Freshly ground black pepper to taste

⅓ cup pine nuts, toasted in a 325°F oven for 7 to 10 minutes or until lightly browned

Place wild rice in a strainer, and rinse under cold running water for about 2 minutes until water runs clear. Shake the strainer to remove as much excess water as possible.

Melt butter in a saucepan over medium heat; add onion and wild rice. Cook and stir for 3 minutes or until onion is translucent. Add soup mix, water, thyme, and bay leaf.

Bring to a boil, then reduce heat to low and cook rice, covered, for 1 to 1½ hours or until rice is very fluffy and tender and has absorbed liquid. Stir occasionally, adding more water if rice becomes dry before it is fluffy and tender. Remove and discard bay leaf, season with black pepper to taste, and garnish with toasted pine nuts.

### Dry and Droll

Wild rice, native to the Chippewa Indian lands in the lake country of Minnesota, is America's only native species and is a distant cousin of Asian rice. It is really an aquatic grass, *Zizania aquatica*, and was named wild rice because of the visual similarity to familiar rice fields. It contains more protein than most rice and is processed by fermenting it first to develop the characteristic nutty flavor. It is then roasted, which accounts for the brown color.

# Toasted Barley "Risotto"

Prep time: less than 30 minutes   •   Cooking time: 1 hour   •   Makes 6 servings

1½ cups pearl barley

3 TB. butter

1 onion, chopped

3 garlic cloves, minced

1 envelope roasted garlic herb soup mix

6 cups water

1 (14-oz.) can diced tomatoes, juice reserved

½ cup grated Parmesan cheese

3 TB. chopped fresh parsley

Freshly ground black pepper to taste

Stir barley in a large saucepan over medium heat for 5 minutes or until lightly toasted. Scrape barley into mixing bowl, and return saucepan to stove. Heat butter; add onion and garlic. Cook and stir for 3 minutes or until onion is translucent. Add barley and stir to coat grains.

Stir in soup mix and 2 cups water, and bring to a boil. Reduce heat to medium-low and cook for 7 minutes, stirring frequently, until liquid is almost absorbed. Add 2 cups more water and repeat procedure. Add remaining water, tomatoes and their juice, and cook for 20 to 30 minutes or until barley is tender and creamy. Add cheese and parsley. Cook until cheese is melted. Season with black pepper to taste.

### Dry and Droll

Barley is one of the oldest grains known to man, dating back to the Stone Age. Even if you think you haven't eaten barley, there's a good chance you've enjoyed it in other forms. Barley is malted to make both beer and whiskey.

# Cornbread Stuffing

Prep time: less than 15 minutes • Cooking time: 1 hour • Makes 6 to 8 servings (enough for a 12-pound turkey)

| | |
|---|---|
| 1 loaf cornbread, crumbled (6 cups) | 1 envelope golden onion soup mix |
| ¼ lb. butter | 1 TB. dried sage |
| 1 onion, diced | 1 tsp. dried thyme |
| 2 celery stalks, trimmed and thinly sliced | ½ cup dried currants |
| 1½ cups apple juice | Freshly ground black pepper to taste |

Preheat the oven to 375°F, line a roasting pan with aluminum foil, and spray a large casserole with vegetable oil spray. Place cornbread in pan, and bake for 8 to 10 minutes or until dry and lightly browned. Remove from oven and set aside. Reduce oven temperature to 350°F.

Melt butter in a large skillet over medium heat; add onion and celery. Cook and stir for 3 minutes or until onion is translucent. Add apple juice, soup mix, sage, thyme, and currants. Stir well. Bring to a boil, reduce heat to low, and simmer, uncovered, for 5 minutes.

### Mix with Care

Never place stuffing inside of poultry until just before it is ready to go into the oven, because naturally occurring bacteria from the poultry could contaminate the stuffing. Also, take out all stuffing from the bird as soon as it comes out of the oven, and refrigerate any leftovers separately.

Add cornbread crumbs, tossing to moisten them evenly. Season with black pepper to taste, and transfer stuffing to a casserole dish. Cover the casserole with aluminum foil, and bake stuffing for 30 minutes. Remove foil and continue to bake for an additional 15 to 20 minutes or until top is brown.

Alternatively, loosely pack cavity of turkey or roasting chicken with mixture and bake until internal temperature of stuffing registers 165°F on an instant-read thermometer.

# Herbed Wild Mushroom Sausage Stuffing

Prep time: less than 30 minutes   •   Cooking time: 1 hour   •   Makes 6 to 8 servings (enough for a 12-pound turkey)

1 loaf stale French or Italian bread, cut into ½-inch cubes

¼ lb. butter

2 onions, diced

3 celery stalks, trimmed and sliced

4 garlic cloves, minced

½ lb. fresh shiitake mushrooms, stemmed and sliced

¾ lb. bulk pork sausage

1 envelope wild mushroom and chive soup mix

2 cups water

1 TB. dried sage

1 tsp. dried thyme

Freshly ground black pepper to taste

Preheat the oven to 375°F, line a roasting pan with aluminum foil, and spray a large casserole with vegetable oil spray. Place bread cubes in roasting pan, and bake for 8 to 10 minutes or until dry and lightly browned. Remove bread from oven and place in a large mixing bowl. Reduce oven temperature to 350°F.

Melt butter in a large skillet over medium heat; add onion, celery, and garlic. Cook and stir for 3 minutes or until onion is translucent. Raise heat to medium-high; add mushrooms. Cook and stir for 3 minutes or until mushrooms begin to soften. Scrape mixture into the mixing bowl with bread.

Return the pan to heat, add sausage, and cook, breaking up lumps with a fork, for 3 minutes or until browned. Add soup mix, water, sage, and thyme. Stir well and bring to a boil. Simmer for 5 minutes, stirring occasionally. Pour liquid over bread and vegetables, and toss well to moisten evenly.

Season with black pepper to taste, and transfer stuffing to the prepared casserole dish. Cover with aluminum foil, and bake stuffing for 30 minutes. Remove foil and continue to bake for an additional 15 to 20 minutes or until top is browned.

Alternatively, loosely pack cavity of turkey or roasting chicken with mixture, and bake until internal temperature of stuffing registers 165°F on an instant-read thermometer.

### Dry and Droll

*Stuffing,* a noun made from the verb *to stuff,* first appeared in print in the sixteenth century, but the proper Victorians in the late-nineteenth century found the word offensive and instead used the term *dressing* for the mixture.

# Part 7

## Sweet Sensations

What would a book devoted to mixes be without desserts based on tried-and-true cake mixes? That's what you'll find in this part.

The first chapter contains improvisations that are all cakes. Some are classical bundt cakes, sheet cakes, and layer cakes, and then there are a few surprises. The part also includes a chapter of cookie recipes made with cake mixes and concludes with recipes for some off-beat baked goods, such as English trifle and Italian cassata.

# Chapter 18

# Cakes for All Occasions

## In This Chapter

- ◆ Homey bundt cakes
- ◆ Rich layer cakes
- ◆ Special occasion cakes

Cakes make any day seem as festive as a birthday, and you can achieve a huge range of sizes, flavors, and presentations for cakes. Some of these recipes are family fare that can be enjoyed for days, while others are elegant and intended for entertaining.

What unites the recipes in this chapter is that they all have a foolproof, always-reliable cake mix as the foundation for the cake. But unless you tell, no one will ever guess that these cakes started out in a box.

## Picking Your Pan

It's always best to use the pan specified in a recipe, but sometimes that's either not feasible because you don't own that size pan or you want a different format. For example, if you're taking a cake on a picnic, it's best to use a 9×13-inch baking pan rather than trying to juggle a multi-layer cake across sand dunes.

**Dry and Droll**

Duncan Hines could be dubbed the country's first national food critic. He was a traveling salesman with a passion for food, who would send out restaurant lists instead of Christmas cards. In 1936, he published *Adventures in Good Eating,* which described the food and ambiance of thousands of restaurants. He then went on to pen a few cookbooks as well as update his dining guides, and in 1948, he co-founded a line of food products under the Duncan Hines name. The baking mix line was purchased a few years later by Procter & Gamble, which sold it in 1998 to St. Louis–based Aurora Foods.

The important thing is to know the volume of the pan you're using to make sure it's large enough for the recipe and to adjust the baking time. The larger the pan, the longer the cake will take to bake.

The following chart should help you calculate. The baking times are estimates because additions to the mix can affect the time.

## Baking Times Based on Pan Size

| Pan Size | Volume | Baking Time |
| --- | --- | --- |
| 8 inches round×1½ inches | 4 cups | 25 to 35 minutes |
| 9 inches round×1½ inches | 6 cups | 30 to 35 minutes |
| 8×8×2 inches | 6 cups | 35 to 40 minutes |
| 9×9×2 inches | 10 cups | 40 to 45 minutes |
| 9×13×2 inches | 14 cups | 30 to 50 minutes |
| Bundt pan or 10-inch tube pan | 12 cups | 45 to 55 minutes |
| Muffin or cupcake pans | ⅔ cup | 18 to 22 minutes |

**Mix Mastery**

Your eye is not a great judge of whether or not batter is divided evenly between pans. That's when a kitchen scale comes in handy. Place what you think are equivalent amounts in the pans and weigh them. You can transfer batter from one pan to the other before smoothing the top.

## The Least You Need to Know

◆ It's best to use the size pan specified in a recipe, but you can substitute and change the baking time.

◆ A cake is done when a toothpick or cake tester inserted into the center comes out clean.

◆ Cakes should be baked in the center of the oven.

# Mexican Chocolate Cake

Prep time: less than 15 minutes  •  Cooking time: 55 minutes  •  Makes 12 servings

**For cake:**

1 box devil's food cake mix

1 (4-serving) box chocolate instant pudding mix

4 eggs

1 cup sour cream

¼ lb. butter, melted

⅓ cup rum

2 tsp. ground cinnamon

1 cup semisweet chocolate chips

1 cup slivered almonds, toasted in a 350°F oven for 5 to 7 minutes or until lightly browned

**For glaze:**

1½ cups semisweet chocolate chips

4 TB. butter

½ tsp. ground cinnamon

For cake, preheat the oven to 350°F. Grease a 12-cup bundt pan or 10-inch tube pan with butter, and dust with flour. Tap to remove excess flour, and set the pan aside.

Combine cake mix, pudding mix, eggs, sour cream, melted butter, rum, and cinnamon in a large mixing bowl. Beat with an electric mixer on low speed for 1 minute to combine. Scrape down the sides of the bowl with a rubber spatula, and beat for 2 minutes at medium speed or until batter is thick and fluffy. Scrape the bowl as necessary.

Fold chocolate chips and almonds into batter. Spoon batter into the prepared pan, smooth top of batter, and tap the pan on the countertop to remove any air pockets. Bake cake in the center of the oven for 45 to 55 minutes or until a toothpick or cake tester inserted into the center comes out clean.

Cool cake in the pan on a wire rack for 20 minutes. Then invert cake onto the rack and cool completely.

For glaze, combine chocolate chips, butter, and cinnamon in a microwave-safe bowl. Microwave on high (100 percent) for 30 seconds. Stir and repeat until chocolate is melted and mixture is smooth. Pour hot glaze on top of cooled cake, and allow it to run down the sides.

**Mix with Care**

Many sizes of chocolate chips are on the market today, but for cake recipes you should use the standard size or mini size. The larger pieces have a tendency to sink to the bottom of the batter rather than remain dispersed.

# Lemon Blueberry Cake

Prep time: less than 15 minutes • Cooking time: 55 minutes • Makes 12 servings

**For cake:**

1 box white cake mix

1 (4-serving) box lemon instant pudding mix

4 eggs

1 cup sour cream

¼ lb. butter, melted

⅓ cup lemon juice

2 tsp. grated lemon zest

1 pint fresh blueberries, rinsed and picked over

**For glaze:**

1 cup confectioners' sugar

2 TB. lemon juice

Preheat the oven to 350°F. Grease a 12-cup bundt pan or 10-inch tube pan with butter, and dust with flour. Tap to remove excess flour, and set the pan aside.

Combine cake mix, pudding mix, eggs, sour cream, melted butter, lemon juice, and lemon zest in a large mixing bowl. Beat with an electric mixer on low speed for 1 minute to combine.

**Dry and Droll**

Betty Crocker is looking pretty good for a woman who came onto the scene as an adult in 1921. She was named in honor of a retired director of General Mills, and the company's female employees had a contest to see who could create the most distinctive signature for Betty.

Scrape down the sides of the bowl with a rubber spatula, and beat for 2 minutes on medium speed or until batter is thick and fluffy. Scrape the bowl as necessary.

*Fold* blueberries into batter. Spoon batter into the prepared pan, smooth top of batter, and tap the pan on the countertop to remove any air pockets. Bake cake in the center of the oven for 45 to 55 minutes or until a toothpick or cake tester inserted into the center comes out clean.

Cool cake in the pan on a wire rack for 20 minutes. While cake is cooling, prepare glaze. Combine confectioners' sugar and lemon juice in a small bowl, and stir to blend thoroughly. Invert cake onto the rack, and spread top with glaze. Cool completely.

**Ellen on Edibles**

To **fold** is a process of combining ingredients. Place a heavier ingredient—in this case, blueberries—on top of a lighter one. Using a rubber spatula, cut down into the center of the bowl and pull the spatula toward you along the side of the bowl. Then turn the bowl a quarter-turn and repeat the process as many times as it takes to incorporate the ingredient evenly.

# Double Cranberry Cake

Prep time: less than 15 minutes    •    Cooking time: 55 minutes    •    Makes 12 servings

**For cake:**

1 box yellow cake mix with pudding

½ cup sour cream

½ cup orange juice

¼ lb. butter, melted

4 eggs

1 TB. grated orange zest

1½ cups fresh or frozen whole cranberries

1 cup dried cranberries

**For glaze:**

1 cup confectioners' sugar

¼ cup orange juice

1 TB. grated orange zest

Preheat the oven to 350°F. Grease a 12-cup bundt pan or 10-inch tube pan with butter, and dust with flour. Tap to remove excess flour, and set the pan aside.

Combine cake mix, sour cream, orange juice, butter, eggs, and orange zest in a large mixing bowl. Beat with an electric mixer on low speed for 1 minute to combine. Scrape down the sides of the bowl with a rubber spatula, and beat on medium speed for 2 minutes or until batter is thick and fluffy. Scrape the bowl as necessary.

Fold cranberries and dried cranberries into batter. Spoon batter into the prepared pan, smooth top of batter, and tap the pan on the countertop to remove any air pockets. Bake cake in the center of the oven for 45 to 55 minutes or until a toothpick or cake tester inserted into the center comes out clean.

While cake is baking, prepare glaze. Combine confectioners' sugar, orange juice, and orange zest in a small bowl. Stir well.

Cool cake in the pan on a wire rack for 20 minutes. Invert cake onto the rack, and spread top with glaze, letting it drip down the sides. Cool completely.

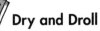 **Dry and Droll**

Perhaps no food is as closely associated with New England's tribes of Native Americans as the cranberry. The Native Americans pounded them with animal fat and dried the mixture to produce pemmican, which they ate for protein.

# Rum Raisin Banana Cake with Caramel Frosting

Prep time: less than 15 minutes   •   Cooking time: 40 minutes   •   Makes 12 servings

**For cake:**

1 box yellow cake mix

1 (4-serving) box vanilla instant pudding mix

¼ lb. butter, melted

4 eggs

1½ cups (3 or 4) large ripe bananas, mashed

⅓ cup rum

1 tsp. ground cinnamon

1 tsp. pure vanilla extract

1 cup raisins

**For frosting:**

¼ lb. butter

1 cup firmly packed dark brown sugar

¼ cup whole milk

2 cups confectioners' sugar

1 tsp. pure vanilla extract

Preheat the oven to 350°F. Grease a 9×13-inch baking pan with butter, and dust with flour. Tap to remove excess flour, and set the pan aside.

Combine cake mix, pudding mix, butter, eggs, bananas, rum, cinnamon, and vanilla in a large mixing bowl. Beat with an electric mixer on low speed for 1 minute to combine. Scrape down the sides of the bowl with a rubber spatula, and beat on medium speed for 2 minutes or until batter is thick and fluffy. Scrape the bowl as necessary.

Fold raisins into batter. Spoon batter into the prepared pan, smooth top of batter, and tap the pan on the countertop to remove any air pockets. Bake cake in the center of the oven for 35 to 40 minutes or until a toothpick or cake tester inserted into the center comes out clean.

 **Mix Mastery**

> If you have bananas that are too ripe to eat and are perfect for a cake, you don't have to bake them right at that second. Freeze the bananas right in the skins, then defrost and mash them at a later time.

While cake is baking, make frosting. Combine butter, brown sugar, and milk in a medium saucepan over medium heat. Cook, stirring, until mixture comes to a boil. Reduce heat to low and simmer for 1 minute. Cool to room temperature. Stir in confectioners' sugar and vanilla, and continue stirring until creamy.

Cool cake in the pan on a wire rack for 20 minutes. Invert cake on the rack, spread with frosting, and cool completely.

# Apple Cake with Cinnamon Frosting

Prep time: less than 20 minutes • Cooking time: 40 minutes • Makes 12 servings

**For cake:**

1 box white cake mix

3 eggs

1 cup whole milk

¼ lb. butter, melted

1 tsp. pure vanilla extract

1 tsp. ground cinnamon

4 cups (4 to 5 apples) peeled, cored, and thinly sliced apples

**For frosting:**

¼ lb. butter, softened

4 cups confectioners' sugar

⅓ cup half-and-half

½ tsp. pure vanilla extract

1 tsp. ground cinnamon

Preheat the oven to 350°F. Grease a 9×13-inch baking pan with butter, and dust with flour. Tap to remove excess flour, and set the pan aside.

Combine cake mix, eggs, milk, butter, vanilla, and cinnamon in a large mixing bowl. Beat with an electric mixer on low speed for 1 minute to combine. Scrape down the sides of the bowl with a rubber spatula, and beat on medium speed for 2 minutes or until batter is thick and fluffy. Scrape the bowl as necessary.

Fold apples into batter. Spoon batter into the prepared pan, smooth top of batter, and tap the pan on the countertop to remove any air pockets. Bake cake in the center of the oven for 35 to 40 minutes or until a toothpick or cake tester inserted into the center comes out clean. While cake is baking, prepare frosting. Combine butter and ½ confectioners' sugar in a large mixing bowl. Beat with an electric mixer on low speed to combine. Scrape down the sides of the bowl. Beat on medium speed for 1 minute. Add half-and-half, vanilla, and cinnamon. Add remaining confectioners' sugar, and beat until light and fluffy.

Remove cake from the oven, and cool on a wire rack in the pan for 20 minutes. Invert cake on rack, spread with frosting and cool completely.

 **Mix Mastery**

These recipes specify butter (or you could also use solid shortening) to grease the pans, which are then floured. If you're an ardent baker, you might want to invest in a product found in most supermarkets that saves the flouring step. It's an aerosol can that contains a mixture of fat and flour so you can complete this preliminary task in one step.

# Carrot Cake with Cream Cheese Frosting

Prep time: less than 20 minutes • Cooking time: 35 minutes • Makes 12 servings

**For cake:**

2 firmly packed cups grated carrot (4 to 5 carrots)

1 box yellow cake mix

1 (4-serving) box vanilla instant pudding mix

1 (8-oz.) can crushed pineapple in pineapple juice

4 eggs

½ cup vegetable oil

½ cup orange juice

2 tsp. ground cinnamon

1 tsp. ground ginger

¾ cup sweetened coconut

¾ cup raisins

¾ cup chopped walnuts or pecans, toasted in a 350°F oven for 5 minutes or until lightly browned

**For frosting:**

6 cups (1½ lb.) confectioners' sugar

3 (8-oz.) pkg. cream cheese, softened

6 TB. butter, softened

2 tsp. pure vanilla extract

Preheat the oven to 350°F. Grease 2 (9-inch) round layer pans with butter, and dust with flour. Tap to remove excess flour, and set the pans aside.

Combine carrots, cake mix, pudding mix, pineapple with its juice, eggs, oil, orange juice, cinnamon, and ginger in a large mixing bowl. Beat with an electric mixer on low speed for 1 minute to combine. Scrape down the sides of the bowl with a rubber spatula, and beat for 2 minutes on medium speed until batter is thick and fluffy. Scrape the bowl as necessary.

Fold coconut, raisins, and nuts into batter. Divide batter between the 2 pans and smooth top with a spatula. Tap the pans down on the countertop to remove any air pockets.

Bake cake in the center of the oven for 30 to 35 minutes or until lightly browned and a toothpick or cake tester inserted in the center comes out clean.

Cool cakes on a wire rack for 10 minutes. Invert cakes onto the wire rack and cool completely.

While cakes are cooling, prepare frosting. Combine confectioners' sugar, cream cheese, butter, and vanilla in a large mixing bowl. Beat with an electric mixer on low speed to combine. Scrape down the sides of the bowl, and beat on high speed for 2 to 3 minutes or until light and fluffy.

Place one cake layer on overlapping sheets of plastic wrap or wax paper. Spread ⅓ frosting on top of layer. Top with second layer, and frost sides and top of cake with remaining frosting.

Refrigerate cake, lightly covered with wax paper, for at least 30 minutes or until frosting is set. Pull out the sheets of wax paper from under cake, remove the top layer of wax paper, and serve.

# Mocha Fudge Cake

Prep time: less than 30 minutes    •    Cooking time: 35 minutes    •    Makes 12 servings

**For cake:**

1 box devil's food cake mix

3 eggs

1 cup whole milk

1 TB. instant coffee powder

½ cup sour cream

5 TB. butter, melted

1 tsp. pure vanilla extract

**For filling:**

½ lb. semisweet chocolate, chopped

1 cup heavy cream

**For glaze:**

4 oz. semisweet chocolate

2 TB. brewed coffee

3 TB. butter, softened

Preheat the oven to 350°F. Grease 2 (9-inch) round layer pans with butter, and dust with flour. Tap to remove excess flour, and set the pans aside.

Combine cake mix, eggs, milk, coffee powder, sour cream, butter, and vanilla in a large mixing bowl. Beat with an electric mixer on low speed for 1 minute to combine. Scrape down the sides of the bowl with a rubber spatula, and beat for 2 minutes on medium speed or until batter is thick and fluffy. Scrape the bowl as necessary. Divide batter between the 2 pans, and even the top with a spatula. Tap the pans down on the countertop to remove any air pockets.

Bake cake in the center of the oven for 30 to 35 minutes or until lightly browned and a toothpick or cake tester inserted in the center comes out clean.

While cakes are baking, prepare filling. Combine chocolate and cream in a small saucepan over medium heat. Heat, stirring constantly, until chocolate is melted and mixture is glossy. Set aside to cool to spreading consistency.

Cool cakes on a wire rack for 10 minutes. Invert cakes onto the rack and cool completely. While cakes are cooling, prepare glaze.

Combine chocolate, coffee, and butter in a small saucepan and heat over low heat, stirring constantly, until chocolate has melted and mixture is glossy.

To assemble, place one cake layer top side down on a serving platter. Spread filling on layer. Top with second layer. Pour hot glaze over top of cake and let it run down the sides. Refrigerate for at least 30 minutes to set glaze.

**Mix with Care**

Melt chocolate either on the stove or in a microwave oven, but melt it slowly so it doesn't scorch. On the stove, melt it in the top of a double boiler set over simmering water. In the microwave, melt it on medium (50 percent) power in 30-second intervals. Also, never cover a pan in which you're melting chocolate.

# Black Forest Torte

Prep time: less than 30 minutes • Cooking time: 30 minutes • Makes 12 servings

**For cake:**

1 box devil's food cake mix

¼ cup unsweetened cocoa powder

4 eggs

1 cup sour cream

¼ lb. butter, melted

1 tsp. pure vanilla extract

**For filling:**

¼ cup granulated sugar

3 TB. cornstarch

2 (14-oz.) cans sour cherries in syrup, drained, juice reserved

⅓ cup cherry liqueur

**For cream topping:**

3 cups whipping cream, well chilled

½ cup confectioners' sugar

½ tsp. pure vanilla extract

Preheat the oven to 350°F. Grease 3 (8-inch) round layer pans with butter, and dust with flour. Tap to remove excess flour, and set the pans aside. Chill a mixing bowl and set aside.

Combine cake mix, cocoa powder, eggs, sour cream, butter, and vanilla in a large mixing bowl. Beat with an electric mixer on low speed for 1 minute to combine. Scrape down the sides of the bowl with a rubber spatula, and beat for 2 minutes on medium speed or until batter is thick and fluffy. Scrape the bowl as necessary.

Divide batter between the 3 pans, and smooth the top with a spatula. Tap the pans down on the countertop to remove any air pockets. Bake cake in the center of the oven for 25 to 30 minutes or until lightly browned and a toothpick or cake tester inserted in the center comes out clean.

While cakes are baking, prepare filling. Combine sugar, cornstarch, 1 cup reserved cherry juice, and cherry liqueur in a saucepan. Stir well and bring to a boil over medium heat, stirring occasionally. When mixture is bubbly and thickened, stir in cherries, and chill for at least 30 minutes, or until thick and cold.

Cook cakes on wire racks for 10 minutes. Then invert onto the racks to cool completely.

After cakes are cool, make cream topping. Place cream in the chilled mixing bowl. Beat on medium speed with an electric mixer until slightly thickened. Add confectioners' sugar and vanilla. Beat on high speed, scraping down the sides of the bowl as necessary, until stiff peaks form.

To assemble torte, place 1 cake layer top side down on a serving platter. Cover with ½ cherry filling. Spread ¼ whipped cream on top of cherry filling. Top with second cake layer, and spread with remaining cherry filling and ¼ whipped cream. Top with third layer, and spread remaining whipped cream on tops and sides of torte. Chill for at least 2 hours before serving.

# Lemon Poppy Seed Torte

Prep time: less than 30 minutes  •  Cooking time: 35 minutes  •  Makes 12 servings

**For cake:**

1 box lemon cake mix

3 eggs

1 cup whole milk

⅓ cup lemon juice

1 TB. grated lemon zest

6 TB. butter, melted

¼ cup poppy seeds

**For filling and frosting:**

6 cups (1½ lb.) confectioners' sugar

3 (8-oz.) pkg. cream cheese, softened

6 TB. butter, softened

2 tsp. pure vanilla extract

Preheat the oven to 350°F. Grease 2 (9-inch) round layer pans with butter, and dust with flour. Tap to remove excess flour, and set the pans aside.

Combine cake mix, eggs, milk, lemon juice, lemon zest, butter, and poppy seeds in a large mixing bowl. Beat with an electric mixer on low speed for 1 minute to combine. Scrape down the sides of the bowl with a rubber spatula, and beat for 2 minutes on medium speed, or until batter is thick and fluffy. Scrape the bowl as necessary. Divide batter between the 2 pans, and smooth the top of batter with a spatula. Tap the pans down on the countertop to remove any air pockets.

Bake cake in the center of the oven for 30 to 35 minutes or until lightly browned and a toothpick or cake tester inserted in the center comes out clean. While cake is baking, make frosting. Combine confectioners' sugar, cream cheese, butter, and vanilla in a large mixing bowl. Beat on low speed with an electric mixer to combine. Scrape down the sides of the bowl, and beat on high speed for 2 to 3 minutes or until light and fluffy.

Cool cakes on wire racks for 10 minutes. Then invert onto the wire racks to cool completely.

Place 1 layer on overlapping sheets of plastic wrap or wax paper. Spread with ¼ frosting. Place second layer on top, and frost sides and top of cake with remaining frosting.

Refrigerate cake for at least 30 minutes, lightly covered with wax paper, until frosting is set. Pull out sheets of wax paper from under cake, remove the top layer of wax paper, and serve.

 **Mix Mastery**

The combination of lemon and poppy seeds is also great when made as a homey bundt cake. Make the batter the same way and bake the cake for 40 to 50 minutes.

# Chocolate Almond Cheesecake

Prep time: less than 15 minutes • Cooking time: 45 minutes • Makes 12 servings

**For crust:**

1 box chocolate cake mix

4 TB. butter, melted

1 egg

3 TB. unsweetened cocoa powder

½ tsp. pure vanilla extract

**For topping:**

2 (8-oz.) pkg. cream cheese, softened

3 eggs

½ cup sour cream

1 (14-oz.) can sweetened condensed milk

2 tsp. pure almond extract

¼ cup unsweetened cocoa powder

1 cup blanched slivered almonds, toasted in a 350°F oven for 5 to 7 minutes or until lightly browned

Preheat the oven to 350°F, and lightly grease a 9×13-inch baking pan with butter and set aside.

Measure out ½ cup cake mix and set aside. Combine remaining cake mix with butter, egg, cocoa powder, and vanilla in a large mixing bowl. Beat with an electric mixer on low speed for 2 minutes, scraping down the sides of the bowl with a rubber spatula as necessary. Pat mixture into bottom and 1½ inches up the sides of the pan.

### Mix with Care

Be careful not to overbake cheesecakes or they will crack when cooled. You can tell the topping is cooked when it's shiny and doesn't jiggle when you gently shake the pan.

For topping, combine reserved ½ cup cake mix, cream cheese, eggs, sour cream, sweetened condensed milk, almond extract, and cocoa powder in a mixing bowl. Beat on medium speed for 3 to 5 minutes, scraping down the sides of the bowl as necessary, until topping is thick. Fold in almonds, and scrape topping over crust.

Bake cheesecake in the center of the oven for 40 to 45 minutes or until top is set. Cool on a wire rack for 1 hour, or until room temperature and then chill, lightly covered with plastic wrap, until cold.

# Maui Upside-Down Cake

Prep time: less than 20 minutes   •   Cooking time: 50 minutes   •   Makes 10 to 12 servings

**For topping:**

4 TB. butter

¾ cup firmly packed dark brown sugar

½ tsp. ground cinnamon

1 small (3-lb.) ripe pineapple, peeled, halved lengthwise, cored, and cut into ¾-inch slices

1½ cups (7-oz. jar) macadamia nuts

**For cake:**

1 yellow cake mix

½ cup firmly packed dark brown sugar

¼ lb. butter, melted

2 eggs

¾ cup milk

¼ cup rum

1 tsp. pure vanilla extract

Preheat the oven to 350°F, and grease a 10-inch cast-iron skillet or other 10-inch ovenproof skillet with butter. Place the skillet over medium heat and add butter, brown sugar, and cinnamon. Cook, stirring, for 2 minutes. Spread mixture to make even layer in the skillet and then arrange as many pineapple slices as will fit into it. Place macadamia nuts between pineapple slices, and sprinkle any additional nuts on top of slices; they will bake into cake.

Combine cake mix, brown sugar, butter, eggs, milk, rum, and vanilla in a large mixing bowl. Beat with an electric mixer on low speed for 1 minute to combine. Scrape down the sides of the bowl with a rubber spatula, and beat on medium speed for 2 minutes, until batter is thick and fluffy. Scrape the bowl as necessary.

Spoon batter into the skillet over the pineapple layer, and smooth the top. Bake cake in the center of the oven for 45 to 50 minutes or until a toothpick or cake tester inserted in the center of cake comes out clean.

Remove cake from the oven and run a spatula around the inner edge of the skillet to free cake. Hold a platter over the skillet with one hand and invert cake onto the platter. Lift off the skillet and spoon any remaining juices over top of cake. Serve warm.

**Mix with Care** _____

If you don't have a cast-iron skillet, you can use any 10-inch skillet for this cake as long as the sides are at least 2 inches high. However, if your skillet has a plastic handle, wrap the handle with layers of aluminum foil to protect it while in the oven.

# Chocolate Peanut Butter Mousse Roulade

Prep time: less than 30 minutes • Cooking time: 25 minutes • Makes 10 to 12 servings

**For cake:**

1 box deep chocolate cake mix

¼ lb. butter, melted

1 cup buttermilk

4 eggs

¼ cup unsweetened cocoa powder

Confectioners' sugar for dusting

**For mousse:**

1 cup creamy peanut butter

¾ cup granulated sugar

1 (8-oz.) package cream cheese, softened

1 TB. butter, melted

1 tsp. pure vanilla extract

1 cup heavy cream

**For topping:**

½ lb. bittersweet chocolate, chopped

1 cup heavy cream

Preheat the oven to 350°F. Grease the bottom only of an 11×15-inch jelly roll pan with butter. Cut a sheet of parchment paper to fit the bottom of the pan, so it extends a few inches up the sides of the pan, and grease the parchment paper.

Combine cake mix, butter, buttermilk, eggs, and cocoa powder in a large mixing bowl. Beat with an electric mixer on low speed for 1 minute to combine. Scrape down the sides of the bowl with a rubber spatula, and beat on medium speed for 2 minutes, until batter is thick and fluffy. Scrape the bowl as necessary.

Scrape batter into the prepared pan and smooth top. Bake in the center of the oven for 20 to 25 minutes or until a toothpick or cake tester inserted in the center comes out clean.

While cake is baking, sprinkle confectioners' sugar on 20-inch sheet of parchment paper. When cake is done, invert it onto the fresh sheet of parchment paper, and discard the parchment on which the cake was baked. Using the sugared parchment as a guide, roll up the hot cake lengthwise. Place roll on the counter seam side down, and cover cake with a clean kitchen towel.

Next, make mousse. Beat peanut butter and sugar with an electric mixer on medium speed for 2 minutes, until light and fluffy. Add cream cheese, butter, and vanilla and beat well.

In another mixing bowl, whip cream until medium-soft peaks form, then fold it into peanut butter mixture until thoroughly combined. Refrigerate for 30 minutes or until slightly firm.

While mousse is chilling, make topping. Combine chocolate and cream in a small saucepan over low heat. Heat mixture, stirring frequently, until chocolate is melted and mixture is glossy. Set aside.

Remove mousse from the refrigerator. Beat with an electric mixer on low speed for at least 5 to 7 minutes or until mousse is light and fluffy. Return mousse to refrigerator.

To assemble, carefully unroll cake enough to fill it with mousse. Roll it again and place it on a serving platter seam side down. Trim off ends to make roll even. Spread roll with topping. Chill roll, lightly covered with plastic wrap, for at least 2 hours to set topping.

**Ellen on Edibles**

*Roulade* is a French term for a rolled food that has contrasting flavors and textures. It's used for many rolled desserts, but it can also be used to describe chicken breasts or meat that is pounded thin and rolled around a filling.

# Chapter 19

# Contents for the Cookie Jar

## In This Chapter

- ◆ Rich bar cookies
- ◆ Homey drop cookies
- ◆ Crisp biscotti and gingerbread

You would assume that cake mixes make cakes, but you might not realize that the same ingredients also form the basis for cookies. Cookies also require flour, sugar, and a leavening agent. The difference is that cookies need a firmer dough than a cake batter so they will hold their shape and have a harder texture when baked.

In this chapter, you'll find recipes for rich cookies. Many of them are bars, which are the easiest type of cookie to make because they are done at one time and in one pan. But there are also homey drop cookies to fill the cookie jar and a few exotic entries like biscotti. There is even an easy way to make whimsical gingerbread people.

## How the Cookie Crumbles

Cookies made with mixes are even easier to make than those made from scratch. Use these tips to make you a "smart cookie":

◆ If you don't have enough cooling racks, spread a sheet of wax paper on the counter and sprinkle it with granulated sugar. Move almost-cool cookies to the sheet, and they will cool completely without getting soggy.

◆ If cookies are not removed from the baking sheet within 2 minutes after coming out of the oven, they might stick to the baking sheet. Should this occur, place the sheet back in the oven for 1 minute. The heat will loosen the cookies, and you will be able to remove them easily.

◆ Store crisp cookies loosely covered with wax paper and soft cookies in an airtight tin.

◆ To make rolled cookies thinner and crisper, roll the dough directly on the bottom of a greased and floured baking sheet. Cut the dough into shapes and remove the extra dough from between them.

# Gilding the Lily

Use these easy ways to "dress up" simple cookies:

◆ Chop any form of chocolate finely and place it in a pint-size sealable plastic bag. Submerge the bag in hot tap water, and within 2 minutes the chocolate will be melted. Snip off a small corner of the bag and drizzle cooled cookies with chocolate.

◆ To make chocolate shavings, scrape at a block of chocolate with a vegetable peeler or scrape the block of cool chocolate across the large holes of a box grater.

◆ Brush cooled cookies with a "glue" made from confectioners' sugar and milk. Then press in anything from chopped nuts to tinted coconut.

◆ Dust cooled cookies with either cocoa powder or confectioners' sugar.

◆ Instead of stirring in all the ingredients, such as chocolate chips or nuts, press them on top of the cookies before baking.

## The Least You Need to Know

◆ You can make cookies with cake mixes because they need the same categories of ingredients as cakes, such as flour, sugar, and a leavening agent.

◆ You can decorate cookies before or after baking.

◆ Bar cookies are the easiest to make because they are made in one pan all at once.

◆ Soft cookies should not be stored in the same container as crisp cookies.

# Crunchy Peanut Butter Bars

Prep time: less than 20 minutes   •   Cooking time: 30 minutes   •   Makes 24 bars

1 box yellow cake mix

2 cups crunchy peanut butter

¼ lb. butter, melted

2 eggs

2 cups semisweet chocolate chips

1 (14-oz.) can sweetened condensed milk

1 cup chopped peanuts

Preheat the oven to 350°F. Combine cake mix, 1 cup peanut butter, melted butter, and eggs in a large mixing bowl. Beat with an electric mixer on low speed for 1 minute to combine. Scrape down the sides of the bowl with a rubber spatula, and beat for 1 more minute. The mixture will be a thick dough.

Combine chocolate chips and sweetened condensed milk in a small saucepan over medium heat. Heat, stirring frequently, until chocolate is melted and mixture is glossy. Stir in chopped peanuts and set aside.

Reserve 1½ cups cake mixture. Pat remaining mixture into an even layer in the bottom of an ungreased 9×13-inch pan. Spread remaining 1 cup peanut butter on top. Spread chocolate on top of peanut butter. Crumble reserved crust mixture over chocolate.

Bake in the center of the oven for 25 to 30 minutes or until top is browned. Cool on a wire rack for 30 minutes. Cut into bars.

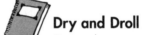 **Dry and Droll**

Peanut butter is an American invention. It was introduced as a health food at the St. Louis World's Fair in 1904.

# Chocolate Caramel Brownies

Prep time: less than 15 minutes • Cooking time: 25 minutes • Makes 24 bars

1 box devil's food cake mix

⅔ cup evaporated milk

12 TB. butter, melted

1 (14-oz.) bag caramels

1½ cups chocolate chips

Preheat the oven to 350°F, and grease a 9×13-inch pan with butter.

Combine cake mix, ⅓ cup evaporated milk, and butter in a mixing bowl. Beat with an electric mixer on low speed for 1 minute or until dough forms. Scrape down the sides of the bowl with a rubber spatula. Press ⅔ mixture into the pan. Bake in the center of the oven for 6 minutes or until set.

### Mix Mastery

You can vary this recipe to suit your tastes. Butterscotch or peanut butter chips work equally well as chocolate, or you can use some other combination.

While brownies are baking, unwrap caramels, if necessary, and combine with remaining ⅓ cup evaporated milk in a small saucepan. Heat over low heat, stirring frequently, until caramels are melted and mixture is smooth.

Remove the pan from the oven, and spread chocolate chips and caramel on top. Piece on remainder of dough mixture to cover caramel. Bake for 15 to 18 minutes. Cool completely on a wire rack before cutting into bars.

# Chocolate Pecan Bars

Prep time: less than 30 minutes   •   Cooking time: 45 minutes   •   Makes 24 bars

**For base:**

1 box chocolate cake mix

3 TB. cocoa powder

¼ lb. butter, melted

1 egg

**For topping:**

1½ cups granulated sugar

⅓ cup water

1 cup heavy cream

4 TB. butter, cut into small pieces

¼ cup bourbon

2 eggs

1½ cups pecan halves, toasted at 350°F for 5 to 7 minutes or until lightly browned

Preheat the oven to 350°F.

Combine cake mix, cocoa powder, ¼ pound butter, and egg in a large mixing bowl. Beat with an electric mixer on low speed for 2 minutes or until dough forms a ball. Scrape down the sides of the bowl with a rubber spatula as necessary. Press mixture into the bottom and 1 inch up the sides of an ungreased 9×13-inch baking pan. Bake in the center of the oven for 15 minutes or until set.

While chocolate crust is baking, combine sugar and water in a small saucepan, and place over medium-high heat. Cook, without stirring, until liquid is golden brown. Turn off heat, and slowly add cream, stirring with a long-handled spoon; mixture will bubble up at first. Once cream has been added, cook caramel over low heat for 2 minutes. Strain mixture into a mixing bowl, and allow it to cool for 10 minutes.

Beat remaining 4 tablespoons butter, bourbon, and eggs into caramel, and whisk until smooth. Stir in pecans. Pour mixture over chocolate crust and spread evenly.

Bake for 20 to 25 minutes or until filling is set and top is lightly browned. Cool on wire rack for 30 minutes, and cut into bars.

 **Mix with Care**

Caramelizing sugar is not difficult, but one pitfall is allowing the sugar to actually reach dark brown before removing the pan from the heat. The liquid and pot are very hot by the time the sugar starts to color, so take the pan off the heat when the syrup is a medium brown; it will continue to cook and change color.

# Oatmeal Jammy Bars

Prep time: less than 15 minutes • Cooking time: 45 minutes • Makes 24 bars

1 box yellow cake mix

2 cups quick oats

12 TB. butter, melted

1 egg

1 tsp. ground cinnamon

1 cup chopped walnuts, toasted in a 350°F oven for 5 minutes

1½ cups raspberry jam

### Mix Mastery

Think of this recipe as a formula, and personalize it to suit your taste. Any flavor of jam will work. I've made it with apricot and blueberry jams, too. Don't use a clear jelly, though. You want the pieces of fruit in there.

Preheat the oven to 375°F, and grease a 9×13-inch baking pan with butter.

Combine cake mix, oats, butter, egg, and cinnamon in a large mixing bowl. Beat with an electric mixer on low speed for 2 minutes or until a ball of dough forms. Scrape down the sides of the bowl with a rubber spatula as necessary. Pat half of mixture firmly into the bottom of the pan. Press walnuts into dough. Spread jam evenly over the top. Sprinkle remaining dough over jam, and press lightly into jam.

Bake in the center of the oven for 35 to 40 minutes or until lightly browned. Cool on a wire rack for 30 minutes. Cut into bars.

# Lemon Squares

Prep time: less than 15 minutes   •   Cooking time: 35 minutes   •   Makes 24 bars

| | |
|---|---|
| 1 yellow cake mix | 4 eggs |
| ¼ lb. butter, melted | 2 cups granulated sugar |
| 1 tsp. pure vanilla extract | ½ cup lemon juice |
| ¾ cup finely chopped blanched almonds | 1 TB. grated lemon zest |

Preheat the oven to 350°F, and grease a 9×13-inch pan with butter.

Reserve ⅓ cup cake mix, and combine remaining cake mix, butter, vanilla, and almonds in a large mixing bowl. Beat with an electric mixer on low speed for 1 minute or until well blended. Scrape down the sides of the bowl with a rubber spatula. Press mixture firmly into the bottom of the pan.

Bake in the center of the oven for 10 to 12 minutes or until lightly browned.

While almond crust is baking, combine reserved cake mix, eggs, sugar, lemon juice, and lemon zest in a mixing bowl. Beat with an electric mixer on medium speed for 2 minutes, scraping the bowl as necessary.

Pour lemon topping over crust, and bake for 20 to 25 minutes or until topping is set and lightly browned. Remove from oven, and cool completely on a wire rack. Cut into bars.

### Mix Mastery

If you prefer lime to lemon, substitute it in equal quantity for your lemon squares. Or for a multi-flavor treat, do half lemon and half lime.

# Key Lime Cheesecake Bars

Prep time: less than 20 minutes • Cooking time: 55 minutes • Makes 24 bars

| | |
|---|---|
| 1 box white cake mix | 1¼ cups granulated sugar |
| ¼ lb. butter, melted | ⅓ cup *key lime* juice |
| 4 eggs | 1 TB. lime zest |
| 3 (8-oz.) pkg. cream cheese, softened | 2 cups sour cream |

Preheat the oven to 350°F, and grease an 11×15-inch jelly roll pan with butter.

Combine cake mix, butter, and 1 egg in a mixing bowl. Mix with an electric mixer on low speed for 1 minute or until mixture forms a ball. Press mixture firmly into the pan, and bake in the center of the oven for 10 to 12 minutes or until lightly brown.

### Ellen on Edibles

**Key limes** are tiny tart limes that are native to the Florida Keys and are also grown in California. They have a distinctive taste that is tarter than lime juice. It's difficult to find key limes in some parts of the country, but you can find bottled juice in many supermarkets and gourmet shops.

While crust is baking, combine cream cheese and 1 cup sugar in a mixing bowl. Beat with an electric mixer on medium speed until light and fluffy. Scrape down the sides of the bowl with a rubber spatula. Add remaining 3 eggs, one at a time, beating well between each addition. Scrape the bowl as necessary. Beat in lime juice and lime zest.

Spread key lime topping over crust. Bake for 30 to 35 minutes or until topping is set in center. While topping is baking, combine sour cream with remaining ¼ cup sugar. Spread mixture over topping, and bake for 5 to 7 minutes or until set.

Remove from oven, and cool to room temperature on a wire rack. Then refrigerate until well chilled, lightly covered with plastic wrap. Cut into bars.

# Hawaiian Bars

Prep time: less than 15 minutes    •    Cooking time: 25 minutes    •    Makes 24 bars

1 box yellow cake mix

¼ lb. butter, melted

¼ cup firmly packed dark brown sugar

2 eggs

1 (8-oz.) can crushed pineapple packed in pineapple juice, juice reserved

¼ cup rum

1 cup chopped macadamia nuts, toasted in a 350°F oven for 5 to 7 minutes or until lightly browned

Preheat the oven to 375°F, and lightly grease a 9×13-inch pan with butter.

Combine cake mix, butter, brown sugar, eggs, pineapple and its juice, and rum in a large mixing bowl. Beat with an electric mixer on low speed for 1 minute to combine. Scrape down the sides of the bowl with a rubber spatula, and beat on medium speed for 2 minutes. Stir in macadamia nuts.

Pat dough into the pan and smooth top. Bake in the center of the oven for 20 to 25 minutes or until lightly browned and a toothpick or cake tester inserted into the center comes out clean.

Cool completely on a wire rack, and then cut into bars.

**Mix with Care**

Canned fruit comes packed in both a heavy sugar syrup and in its own natural juice. For baking, always get the juice-packed fruit unless otherwise instructed. The juice reinforces the flavor of the fruit.

# Butterscotch Brownies

Prep time: less than 15 minutes • Cooking time: 30 minutes • Makes 25 cookies

1 box yellow cake mix

⅓ cup firmly packed dark brown sugar

¼ lb. butter, melted

2 eggs

1 tsp. pure vanilla extract

1 cup butterscotch chips

1 cup chopped walnuts, toasted in a 350°F oven for 5 to 7 minutes or until lightly browned

**Dry and Droll**

The term *brownie* is an American invention, although there are similar rich cookies in many European cultures. The word first appeared in print in a late-nineteenth-century Sears and Roebuck Catalog, which was advertising the baking pan.

Preheat the oven to 350°F, and lightly grease a 9×13-inch baking pan with butter.

Combine cake mix, brown sugar, butter, eggs, and vanilla in a large mixing bowl. Beat with an electric mixer on low speed for 1 minute to combine. Scrape down the sides of the bowl with a rubber spatula, and beat for 2 minutes on medium speed. Scrape the bowl as necessary.

Stir butterscotch chips and walnuts into dough, and scrape dough into the pan, smoothing the top. Bake in the center of the oven for 25 to 30 minutes or until lightly browned and a toothpick or cake tester inserted into the center comes out clean. Cool completely on a wire rack, and cut into bars.

# Oatmeal Cranberry Cookies

Prep time: less than 20 minutes   •   Cooking time: 15 minutes per batch   •   Makes 36 cookies

1 box yellow cake mix

½ cup all-purpose flour

1½ cups quick-cooking oatmeal

12 TB. butter, melted

2 eggs

2 tsp. ground cinnamon

½ tsp. ground ginger

1 tsp. pure vanilla extract

1 cup chopped walnuts, toasted in a 350°F oven for 5 to 7 minutes or until lightly browned

1 cup dried cranberries or raisins

Combine cake mix, flour, oatmeal, butter, eggs, cinnamon, ginger, and vanilla in a large mixing bowl. Beat with an electric mixer on low speed for 1 minute to combine. Scrape down the sides of the bowl with a rubber spatula, and beat on medium speed for 2 minutes.

Fold walnuts and dried cranberries into dough. Form dough into 36 balls, and place them 3 inches apart on ungreased baking sheets. Flatten balls into circles with the bottom of a glass.

Working with 1 filled baking sheet at a time, bake cookies in the center of the oven for 12 to 15 minutes or until lightly browned. Cool cookies on the baking sheet for 1 minute. Transfer to a wire rack with a metal spatula and cool completely.

**Mix with Care**

Soft cookies and crisp cookies should not be stored in the same container. The moisture that makes cookies soft will also make the crisp cookies soft.

# Coconut Drops

Prep time: less than 15 minutes • Cooking time: 12 minutes per batch • Makes 36 cookies

1 box white cake mix

1 (4-serving) box vanilla instant pudding mix

¼ lb. butter, melted

3 eggs

2 tsp. pure vanilla extract

3 cups shredded sweetened coconut

### Mix with Care

If you only have one baking sheet, cool it between batches of cookies by running the back under cold water. If dough is placed on a hot baking sheet, it will spread much too early in the baking cycle.

Preheat the oven to 350°F. Combine cake mix, pudding mix, butter, eggs, and vanilla in a mixing bowl. Beat with an electric mixer on low speed to combine. Raise speed to medium, and beat for 2 minutes, scraping down the sides of the bowl with a rubber spatula as necessary. Stir in coconut.

Drop dough by heaping teaspoons 1½ inches apart onto ungreased baking sheets. Working with 1 filled baking sheet at a time, bake cookies in the center of the oven for 10 to 12 minutes or until lightly browned. Cool cookies on the baking sheet for 1 minute; then transfer to a wire cooling rack to cool completely.

# Almond Biscotti

Prep time: less than 15 minutes    •    Cooking time: 1 hour    •    Makes 24 cookies

1 box yellow cake mix

¼ lb. butter, melted

2 eggs

1 cup all-purpose flour

2 tsp. pure almond extract

¾ cup slivered almonds

Preheat the oven to 350°F, and lightly grease a baking sheet with butter.

Combine cake mix, butter, eggs, flour, and almond extract in a large mixing bowl. Beat with an electric mixer on low speed for 3 to 4 minutes or until dough forms a ball. Scrape down the sides of the bowl with a rubber spatula as necessary. Stir almonds into dough.

Place dough on the baking sheet, and form into 2 rectangles ½ inch high. Bake in the center of the oven for 30 to 35 minutes or until lightly browned and a toothpick or cake tester inserted in the center comes out clean. Cool on a wire rack for 10 minutes.

Using a wide metal spatula, transfer rectangles to cutting board. Cut each into 12 slices, and arrange slices on a baking sheet. Bake in the center of the oven for 10 minutes. Turn off the oven, and leave the baking sheet in the oven for an additional 15 minutes. Transfer biscotti to a wire rack and cool completely.

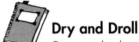

### Dry and Droll

Biscotti, the hard cookie that's a favorite in traditional Tuscan cuisine, means "twice baked," and the name describes the unusual way in which they're made. The first baking is as a loaf; then they are sliced and baked a second time to dry them out.

# Gingerbread People

Prep time: less than 30 minutes • Cooking time: 12 minutes per batch • Makes 18 to 24 cookies

¼ lb. butter, softened

1 egg

1 TB. ground ginger

1 tsp. ground cinnamon

1 tsp. grated nutmeg

½ tsp. ground allspice

¼ cup molasses

1 box yellow cake mix

All-purpose flour for rolling

**Decorations:**

Raisins

Bits of candied fruit

Color-coated chocolate candies

Preheat the oven to 375°F. Combine butter, egg, ginger, cinnamon, nutmeg, allspice, and molasses in a large mixing bowl. Beat with an electric mixer on low speed to combine. Raise speed to medium, and beat for 2 minutes, scraping down the sides of the bowl with a rubber spatula. Add cake mix, and beat on low speed for 2 minutes, scraping the bowl as necessary. The dough should form a ball. Add a few tablespoons water, if necessary, if dough is too dry to hold together.

Place a large sheet of wax paper on a work surface, and sprinkle with a few tablespoons all-purpose flour. Divide dough in half, and form one half into a ball. Place the ball in the center of the wax paper, and flatten it into a pancake. Top pancake with a second sheet of wax paper. Roll dough with a rolling pin to a thickness of ¼ inch. Repeat with second dough ball.

 **Mix with Care**

Although it's tempting, it's not a good idea to take the left-over pieces of dough and re-roll them to create more cookies. Handling the dough twice and adding the flour that is incorporated by rolling can make the cookies tough.

Remove the top sheet of wax paper, and cut out cookies with people-shape cookie cutters. Decorate cookies with raisins, candied fruit, and chocolate candies to suit your taste. Transfer cookies to ungreased baking sheet with a large metal spatula, keeping them 2 inches apart.

Working with 1 filled baking sheet at a time, bake cookies in the center of the oven for 10 to 12 minutes or until lightly browned. Cool cookies on the baking sheet for 1 minute, then transfer cookies to a wire rack to cool completely.

# Fabulous Finales

## In This Chapter

- Homey fresh fruit desserts
- English trifles
- Italian desserts

Here you have an international group of sinfully delicious sweets that run the gamut from homey to haute. You'll find recipes using a cornucopia of succulent fresh fruits. You'll also find custard-layered trifles, a traditional form of English dessert, and some treats drawn from the Italian repertoire.

## Tips for Top Cakes

In addition to using the right pan for the cake, keep these other considerations in mind when baking cakes:

- Turn on the oven before you do anything else. Some ovens take 10 to 15 minutes to preheat to a baking temperature—far longer than it takes to make almost all these cakes.
- If you're using a glass baking pan and not a metal baking pan, reduce the oven temperature by 20 degrees.

◆ Shiny metal pans reflect heat, so cakes baked in these are tender and have a light brown crust. Dark metal or enamel pans absorb heat, so cakes baked in these brown more quickly and develop a crust.

◆ If you're baking more than one dish, allow at least 1 inch of space between pans and between the pans and the oven wall so heat can circulate.

## The Least You Need to Know

◆ Many fresh fruits can be used in cakes.

◆ Trifle is an English dessert that combines cake moistened with liquid and a custard.

◆ Cream should be whipped in a chilled bowl with chilled beaters.

# Deep-Dish Apple Cobbler

Prep time: less than 30 minutes   •   Cooking time: 40 minutes   •   Makes 12 servings

**For crust and topping:**

1 box yellow cake mix

1 cup quick-cooking oats

12 TB. butter, melted

1 cup chopped walnuts or pecans, toasted in a 350°F oven for 5 to 7 minutes or until lightly browned

**For filling:**

8 cups (6 or 7 large) Granny Smith apples, peeled, cored, and thinly sliced

½ cup raisins

½ cup water

¼ cup granulated sugar

3 TB. all-purpose flour

2 tsp. ground cinnamon

½ tsp. ground ginger

Preheat the oven to 350°F, and lightly grease a 9×13-inch baking pan with butter.

For crust and topping, combine cake mix, oats, and butter in a large mixing bowl. Beat with an electric mixer on low speed for 1 minute or until combined. Scrape down the sides of the bowl with a rubber spatula as necessary. Stir in walnuts, and pat half of mixture into the bottom of the prepared pan.

Put apples, raisins, water, sugar, flour, cinnamon, and ginger in a saucepan; toss to combine. Bring to a boil over medium heat, stirring occasionally. Reduce heat to low, and simmer mixture for 5 minutes.

Spread apple mixture over crust, and sprinkle remaining topping over apples. Bake in the center of the oven for 30 to 40 minutes or until lightly browned and apples are tender. Serve hot or at room temperature.

**Dry and Droll**

"Poppin' Fresh," the Pillsbury Doughboy, was the invention of an advertising agency in 1965. Paul Frees, the voice of Boris Badenov in *The Adventures of Rocky and Bullwinkle*, was the original voice of the animated character.

# Rich Apple Cake

Prep time: less than 20 minutes • Cooking time: 50 minutes • Makes 12 servings

**For cake:**

1 box yellow cake mix

1 egg

1 cup sour cream

4 TB. butter, melted

2 tsp. ground cinnamon

1 tsp. pure vanilla extract

**For topping:**

4 cups (3 to 4 medium) Golden Delicious or Jonathan apples, peeled, cored, and thinly sliced

½ cup firmly packed dark brown sugar

1 tsp. ground cinnamon

4 TB. butter, melted

Preheat the oven to 350°F, and lightly grease and flour a 9×13-inch baking pan with butter.

Combine cake mix, egg, sour cream, butter, cinnamon, and vanilla in a large mixing bowl. Beat with an electric mixer on low speed for 1 minute. Scrape down the sides of the bowl with a rubber spatula, and beat for 2 minutes on medium speed or until dough forms a ball. Scrape the bowl as necessary.

Pat dough evenly into the bottom of the prepared pan. Bake in the center of the oven for 10 minutes.

While cake is baking, combine apples, brown sugar, cinnamon, and butter in a mixing bowl. Remove the pan from the oven, and arrange apple slices on top.

Return cake to the oven for 30 to 40 minutes or until cake is browned and apples are tender. Cool on a wire rack for 30 minutes and serve hot or at room temperature.

**Mix Mastery**

> If it matters how the apples in the dish look, the time-honored way of peeling, coring, and then slicing each half or quarter is still the best method. But if the apples are going to be hidden, there's a faster way: Peel the apple and keep turning it in your hand as you cut off slices. Soon all you'll be left with is the core, which you can discard.

# Peach-Cherry Streusel

Prep time: less than 30 minutes   •   Cooking time: 50 minutes   •   Makes 12 servings

**For cake:**

1 box yellow cake mix

⅔ cup orange juice

¼ lb. butter, melted

3 eggs

1 TB. grated orange zest

3 cups (4 medium) peeled and diced ripe peaches

2 TB. all-purpose flour

½ cup dried cherries

**For topping:**

1½ cups all-purpose flour

1 cup firmly packed dark brown sugar

12 TB. butter, softened

1 tsp. ground cinnamon

Pinch salt

Preheat the oven to 350°F, and lightly grease a 9×13-inch baking pan with butter.

Combine cake mix, orange juice, butter, eggs, and orange zest in a large mixing bowl. Beat with an electric mixer on low speed for 1 minute to combine. Scrape down the sides of the bowl with a rubber spatula, and beat for 2 minutes on medium speed or until batter is thick and fluffy. Scrape the bowl as necessary.

Toss peaches with flour, and gently fold peaches and dried cherries into cake batter. Scrape batter into the prepared pan and smooth top. Tap the pan on the countertop to remove any air pockets. Bake in the center of the oven for 30 minutes.

For streusel, combine flour, brown sugar, butter, cinnamon, and salt in a mixing bowl. Mix with a fork or your fingers until mixture is crumbly.

Remove cake from the oven, and sprinkle streusel over top. Return cake to the oven, and bake for an additional 15 to 20 minutes or until toothpick or cake tester inserted into center comes out clean. Serve hot or at room temperature.

**Mix Mastery**

The easiest way to peel peaches is to put them into boiling water for 30 seconds and then remove them from the pan with a slotted spoon. The thin skins will slip right off. Use the same method for peeling tomatoes.

# Blueberry Crumble

Prep time: less than 15 minutes • Cooking time: 50 minutes • Makes 12 servings

**For cake:**

1 box yellow cake mix

1 (8-oz.) pkg. cream cheese, softened

¼ lb. butter, melted

3 eggs

2 TB. lemon juice

1 TB. grated lemon zest

2 pints fresh blueberries, rinsed and picked over to remove twigs

**For topping:**

4 TB. butter, melted

1 cup quick oats

½ cup chopped walnuts or pecans, toasted in a 350°F oven for 5 to 7 minutes or until lightly browned

¼ cup all-purpose flour

1 tsp. ground cinnamon

Pinch of salt

Preheat the oven to 350°F, and grease a 9×13-inch pan with butter.

For cake, combine cake mix, cream cheese, butter, eggs, lemon juice, and lemon zest in a large mixing bowl. Beat with an electric mixer on low speed for 1 minute to combine. Scrape down the sides of the bowl, and beat for 2 minutes on medium speed or until batter is thick and fluffy. Scrape the bowl as necessary.

### Mix with Care

You can use frozen fruit in place of fresh for most baking recipes, but be sure that the fruit is dry-packed and not in a syrup. The extra moisture from the syrup can deflate a cake.

Spread batter into the prepared pan, and sprinkle blueberries evenly over batter.

For topping, combine butter, oats, nuts, flour, cinnamon, and salt in a small bowl. Mix well. Sprinkle topping over blueberries.

Bake in the center of the oven for 40 to 50 minutes or until a toothpick or cake tester inserted into center comes out clean. Cool on a wire rack for 30 minutes. Serve hot or at room temperature.

# Raspberry Lemon Trifle

Prep time: less than 30 minutes,  •  Cooking time: 45 minutes  •  Makes 12 servings
plus 1 day to chill

**For cake:**

1 box yellow cake mix, baked in a 9×13-inch baking pan according to package directions

**For syrup:**

½ cup granulated sugar

⅓ cup lemon juice

¼ cup water

1 tsp. grated lemon zest

**For filling:**

4 eggs

1 cup granulated sugar

⅓ cup lemon juice

¼ lb. butter, softened and cut into 16 pieces

1 TB. grated lemon zest

**For fruit:**

2 pints fresh raspberries

¼ cup granulated sugar

**For topping:**

2 cups whipping cream

½ cup confectioners' sugar

Cut cake in half through the center, and cut each half into strips 2 inches wide. Set aside.

For syrup, combine sugar, lemon juice, water, and lemon zest in a small saucepan. Bring to a boil over medium heat, stirring occasionally. Simmer for 1 minute. Pour syrup into a jar, and refrigerate until cold.

For filling, combine eggs, sugar, and lemon juice in a mixing bowl. Beat with an electric mixer on medium speed for 2 minutes, or until thick and light lemon-colored. Scrape down the sides of the bowl with a rubber spatula as necessary. Transfer mixture to a medium saucepan, and add butter and lemon zest. Place the pan over medium heat, and stir for 10 minutes or until mixture is thick and has the texture of pudding. Scrape filling into a mixing bowl, and press a sheet of plastic wrap directly into the top. Refrigerate until chilled.

For fruit, mash raspberries with sugar and set aside.

To assemble, line a 9×13-inch pan with ⅓ cake strips. Drizzle cake with ⅓ syrup and top with ⅓ filling and ½ berries. Repeat with cake, syrup, filling, and berries for another layer, and then top with cake, syrup, and filling. Cover the pan with plastic wrap, and chill for at least 6 hours, preferably overnight.

To serve, place cream in a chilled mixing bowl. Beat with an electric mixer on medium speed until soft peaks form. Add confectioners' sugar to cream, and beat on high speed until stiff peaks form. Remove trifle from refrigerator, spoon onto plates, and top each serving with whipped cream.

**Mix Mastery**

Adding confectioners' sugar to whipped cream makes it more stable and less likely to become watery than cream whipped with granulated sugar. Confectioners' sugar contains a small amount of cornstarch, which acts as a stabilizing agent.

# Easy Chocolate Mocha Toffee Trifle

Prep time: less than 20 minutes • Cooking time: 45 minutes • Makes 12 servings

**For cake:**

1 box devil's food cake mix, baked according to package directions in a 9×13-inch baking pan

**For syrup:**

½ cup Kahlua or other coffee-flavored liqueur

⅓ cup brewed coffee

**For filling:**

3 cups chilled whipping cream

½ cup confectioners' sugar

3 TB. unsweetened cocoa powder

2 cups chocolate-covered English toffee pieces, crushed

Crumble cake into 1-inch pieces in a mixing bowl. Set aside. Combine Kahlua and coffee and set aside.

 **Mix Mastery**

Cream whips much faster and stronger if everything that touches the cream is well chilled. This includes the beaters as well as the mixing bowl. A metal bowl is better than glass because it holds the chill longer.

Pour cream into a chilled mixing bowl. Beat with an electric mixer on medium speed until soft peaks form. Add confectioners' sugar and cocoa powder. Beat on high speed until stiff peaks form. Fold in crushed toffee pieces.

To assemble, spoon ¼ whipped cream into the bottom of a glass bowl. Top with ⅓ cake pieces. Drizzle with ⅓ syrup. Repeat with cream, cake, and syrup for 2 more layers. Top with remaining ¼ whipped cream. Cover trifle with plastic wrap, and refrigerate for at least 4 hours.

# Cassata

Prep time: less than 30 minutes • Cooking time: 45 minutes • Makes 12 servings

**For cake:**

1 box yellow cake, prepared according to package directions in a 9×13-inch pan

**For syrup:**

½ cup Marsala wine

½ cup granulated sugar

**For filling:**

½ cup dried currants

½ cup Marsala wine

2 (17-oz.) cans dark sweet pitted cherries in syrup, drained, with ¼ cup syrup reserved

2 (15-oz.) containers *ricotta* cheese

¼ cup whipping cream

**For frosting:**

4 TB. (½ stick) butter, cut into thin slices

¼ lb. semisweet chocolate, chopped

½ cup sour cream

Reserved ¼ cup cherry syrup

3 cups confectioners' sugar

Remove cake from the pan, and split across middle into 3 layers. Set aside.

For syrup, combine Marsala and sugar in a small saucepan. Bring to a boil over medium heat, stirring occasionally. Simmer 1 minute. Remove from heat and chill syrup.

For filling, soak dried currants in Marsala for 10 minutes. Cut cherries in half. Combine ricotta and whipping cream in a food processor fitted with a steel blade or in a blender. Purée until smooth. Scrape mixture into a mixing bowl, and stir in currants, Marsala, and cherries. Refrigerate until ready to use.

For frosting, combine butter and chocolate in a microwave-safe dish. Microwave on high power (100 percent) for 20 seconds. Stir and repeat as necessary until mixture is smooth and glossy. Scrape into a mixing bowl, and stir in sour cream and cherry syrup. Beat with an electric mixer on medium speed for 1 minute. Add ½ confectioners' sugar. Beat on low speed to combine. Scrape down the sides of the bowl with a rubber spatula, and add remaining sugar. Beat on low speed for 1 minute, scrape the bowl as necessary, and beat for 2 minutes on medium speed or until smooth.

To assemble, place 1 cake layer on a serving platter, and drizzle with ½ syrup. Top with ½ filling. Repeat with second cake layer and remaining syrup and filling. Top with third cake layer, and frost top and sides with chocolate frosting.

**Ellen on Edibles**

**Ricotta** is a fresh cheese that is smoother than cottage cheese and has a slightly sweet flavor. In Italy, it's made with the whey from cheeses like fresh mozzarella. The name means "recooked," which comes from the fact that the cheese is made by heating the whey.

# Tiramisu

Prep time: less than 30 minutes • Cooking time: 35 minutes • Makes 12 servings

**For cake:**

1 box yellow cake mix

3 eggs

1 cup whole milk

6 TB. butter, melted

1 tsp. pure vanilla extract

**For syrup:**

½ cup hot water

2 TB. instant espresso powder

⅔ cup Kahlua or other coffee-flavored liqueur

**For topping:**

2 (8-oz.) pkg. cream cheese, softened

¼ lb. butter, softened

½ cup granulated sugar

1 tsp. pure vanilla extract

¼ cup unsweetened cocoa powder

Preheat the oven to 350°F, and lightly grease a 9×13-inch baking pan with butter.

For cake, combine cake mix, eggs, milk, butter, and vanilla in a mixing bowl. Beat with an electric mixer on low speed for 1 minute. Scrape down the sides of the bowl with a rubber spatula, and beat on medium speed for 2 minutes. Scrape the bowl as necessary. Scrape batter into the pan, and smooth top with the spatula.

Bake cake in the center of the oven for 30 to 35 minutes or until a toothpick or cake tester inserted into center comes out clean.

### Dry and Droll

*Tiramisu* means "pick me up" in Italian, and the name comes from the strong coffee used to flavor the dish. Legend has it that Tiramisu (pronounced *tear-AHH-mee-soo*) was invented in the 1960s at El Toula, a restaurant in Treviso.

While cake is baking, prepare syrup. Combine water and espresso powder in a mixing bowl. Stir well to dissolve espresso powder. Stir in Kahlua and set aside.

Place baked cake on a cooling rack. Poke holes all over top of cake with a meat fork, and drizzle syrup over cake so it penetrates through holes. Allow cake to cool to room temperature.

For topping, combine cream cheese, butter, sugar, and vanilla in a mixing bowl. Beat with an electric mixer on low speed for 1 minute. Scrape the bowl as necessary. Beat on medium speed for 3 minutes or until light and fluffy. Spread topping over cooled cake, and sprinkle cocoa over top.

# Appendix A

# Glossary

**accoutrement**   An accoutrement is an accompaniment, trapping, or garnish.

**al dente**   Italian for "against the teeth." Refers to pasta (or other ingredient such as rice) that is neither soft nor hard, but just slightly firm against the teeth. This, according to many pasta aficionados, is the perfect way to cook pasta.

**all-purpose flour**   Flour that contains only the inner part of the wheat grain. Usable for all purposes from cakes to gravies.

**allspice**   Named for its flavor echoes of several spices (cinnamon, cloves, nutmeg), allspice is used in many desserts and in rich marinades and stews.

**almonds**   Mild, sweet, and crunchy nuts that combine nicely with creamy and sweet food items.

**amaretto**   A popular almond liqueur.

**anchovies** (also **sardines**)   Tiny, flavorful preserved fish that typically come in cans. The strong flavor from these salted fish is a critical element in many recipes. Anchovies are a traditional garnish for Caesar salad, the dressing of which contains anchovy paste.

**andouille sausage**   A sausage made with highly seasoned pork chitterlings and tripe, and a standard component of many Cajun dishes. *Andouillette* is a similar sausage, although smaller and usually grilled.

**arborio rice**   A plump Italian rice used, among other purposes, for risotto.

**artichoke hearts**   The center part of the artichoke flower, often found canned in grocery stores and used as a stand-alone vegetable dish or as a flavorful base for appetizers or main courses.

**arugula**   A spicy-peppery garden plant with leaves that resemble dandelion leaves and have a distinctive—and very sharp—flavor.

**au gratin**   The quick broiling of a dish before serving to brown the top ingredients. The term is often used as part of a recipe name and implies cheese and a creamy sauce.

**au jus**   French for "with juice," an expression that refers to a dish that is served with juices that result from cooking (as in roast beef).

**baba ghanoush**   A Middle Eastern–style spread composed of eggplant, lemon juice, garlic, olive oil, and tahini.

**bain marie**   A water bath that cooks food gently by surrounding it with simmering water in the oven.

**bake**   To cook in a dry oven. Baking is one of the most popular methods of cooking and is used for everything from roasts, vegetables, and other main courses to desserts such as cakes and pies. Dry-heat cooking often results in a crisping of the exterior of the food being cooked. Moist-heat cooking, through methods such as steaming, poaching, etc., brings a much different, moist quality to the food.

**balsamic vinegar**   Vinegar produced primarily in Italy from a specific type of grape and aged in wood barrels. It is heavier, darker, and sweeter than most vinegars.

**bamboo shoots**   Crunchy, tasty white parts of the growing bamboo plant, often purchased canned.

**barbecue**   This is a loaded word, with different, zealous definitions in different parts of the country. In some cases it is synonymous with grilling (quick-cooking over high heat); in others, to barbecue is to cook something long and slow in a rich liquid (barbecue sauce).

**basil**   A flavorful, almost sweet, resinous herb delicious with tomatoes and in all kinds of Italian or Mediterranean-style dishes.

**baste**   To keep foods moist during cooking by spooning, brushing, or drizzling with a liquid.

**beat**   To quickly mix substances.

**Belgian endive**   A plant that resembles a small, elongated, tightly packed head of romaine lettuce. The thick, crunchy leaves can be broken off and used with dips and spreads.

**blanch**   To place a food in boiling water for about 1 minute (or less) to partially cook the exterior and then submerge in or rinse with cool water to halt the cooking. This is a common method for preparing some vegetables such as asparagus for serving and also for preparing foods for freezing.

**blend**   To completely mix something, usually with a blender or food processor, more slowly than beating.

**boil**   To heat a liquid to a point where water is forced to turn into steam, causing the liquid to bubble. To boil something is to insert it into boiling water. A rapid boil is when a lot of bubbles form on the surface of the liquid.

**bouillon**   Dried essence of stock from chicken, beef, vegetable, or other ingredients. This is a popular starting ingredient for soups as it adds flavor (and often a lot of salt).

**braise**   To cook with the introduction of some liquid, usually over an extended period of time.

**bread flour**   Wheat flour used for bread and other recipes.

**breadcrumbs**   Tiny pieces of crumbled dry bread. Breadcrumbs are an important component in many recipes and are also used as a coating, for example, with breaded chicken breasts.

**brie**   A creamy cow's milk cheese from France with a soft, edible rind and a mild flavor.

**broil**   To cook in a dry oven under the overhead high-heat element.

**broth**   *See* stock.

**brown**   To cook in a skillet, turning, until the surface is brown in color, to lock in the juices.

**brown rice**   Whole-grain rice with a characteristic brown color from the bran coating; more nutritious and flavorful than white rice.

**Cajun cooking**   A style of cooking that combines French and Southern characteristics and includes many highly seasoned stews and meats.

**cake flour**   A high-starch, soft, and fine flour used primarily for cakes.

**canapés**   Bite-size hors d'oeuvres made up of any number of ingredients but prepared individually and usually served on a small piece of bread or toast.

**capicolla**   Seasoned, aged pork shoulder; a traditional component of antipasto dishes.

**caramelize**   The term's original meaning is to cook sugar over low heat until it develops a sweet caramel flavor; however, the term is increasingly gaining use to describe cooking vegetables (especially onions) or meat in butter or oil over low heat until they soften, sweeten, and develop a caramel color. Caramelized onions are a popular addition to many recipes, especially as a pizza topping.

**caraway**   A distinctive spicy seed used for bread, pork, cheese, and cabbage dishes. It is known to reduce stomach upset, which is why it is often paired with, for example, sauerkraut.

**cardamom**   An intense, sweet-smelling spice, common to Indian cooking, used in baking and coffee.

**casserole dishes**   Primarily used in baking, these covered containers hold liquids and solids together and keep moisture around ingredients that might otherwise dry out.

**cayenne**   A fiery spice made from (hot) chili peppers, especially the cayenne chili, a slender, red, and very hot pepper.

**celeriac**   Celery root, which is crisp like a water chestnut when raw, and soft and velvety when cooked.

**ceviche**   A seafood dish in which fresh fish or seafood is marinated for several hours in highly acidic lemon or lime juice, tomato, onion, and cilantro. The acid "cooks" the seafood.

**cheddar**   The ubiquitous hard, cow's milk cheese with a rich, buttery flavor that ranges from mellow to sharp. Originally produced in England, cheddar is now produced worldwide.

**chevre**   Goat cheese, a typically creamy-salty soft cheese delicious by itself or paired with fruits or chutney. Chevres vary in style from mild and creamy to aged, firm, and flavorful. *Artisanal* chevres are usually more expensive and sold in smaller quantities; these are often delicious by themselves. Other chevres produced in quantity are less expensive and often more appropriate for combining with fruit or herbs.

**chickpeas** (also **garbanzo beans**)   The base ingredient in hummus, chickpeas are high in fiber and low in fat, making this a delicious and healthful component of many appetizers and main dishes.

**chiffonade**   Vegetables such as lettuces that are cut into very thin strips.

**chili peppers** (also **chile peppers**)   Any one of many different "hot" peppers, ranging in intensity from the relatively mild ancho pepper to the blisteringly hot habanero.

**chili powder**   A seasoning blend that includes chili pepper, cumin, garlic, and oregano. Proportions vary among different versions, but they all offer a warm, rich flavor.

**chives**   A member of the onion family, chives are found at the grocery store as bunches of long leaves that resemble the green tops of onions. They provide an easy onion flavor to any dish. Chives are very easy to grow, and many people have them in their garden.

**chop**   To cut into pieces, usually qualified by an adverb such as "*coarsely* chopped," or by a size measurement such as "chopped into ½-inch pieces." "Finely chopped" is much closer to mince.

**chorizo**   A spiced pork sausage eaten alone and as a component in many recipes.

**cider vinegar**   Vinegar produced from apple cider, popular in North America.

**cilantro**   A member of the parsley family and used in Mexican cooking and some Asian dishes. Cilantro is what gives some salsas their unique flavor. Use in moderation, as the flavor can overwhelm.

**cinnamon**   A sweet, rich, aromatic spice commonly used in baking or desserts. Cinnamon can also be used for delicious and interesting entrées.

**cloves**   A sweet, strong, almost wintergreen-flavor spice used in baking and with meats such as ham.

**coat**   To cover all sides of a food with a liquid, sauce, or solid.

**converted rice**   White rice that has been subjected to a steam pressure process that keeps the grains separate when cooked.

**core**   To remove the unappetizing middle membranes and seeds of fruit and vegetables.

**coriander**   A rich, warm, spicy herb used in all types of recipes, from African to South American, from entrées to desserts.

**coulis**   A thick paste, often made with vegetables or fruits, used as a sauce for many recipes.

**count**   On packaging of seafood or other foods that come in small sizes, you'll often see a reference to the count, or how many of that item compose 1 pound. For example, 31 to 40 count shrimp are large appetizer shrimp often served with cocktail sauce; 51 to 60 are much smaller.

**couscous**   Granular semolina (durum wheat) that is cooked and used in many Mediterranean and North African dishes.

**cream**   To blend an ingredient to get a soft, creamy liquid or substance.

**crimini mushrooms**   A relative of the white button mushroom but brown in color and with a richer flavor. *See also* portobello mushrooms.

**croutons**   Pieces of bread, usually between ¼ and ½ inch in size, that are sometimes seasoned and baked, broiled, or fried to a crisp texture.

**crudités**   Fresh vegetables served as an appetizer, often all together on one tray.

**cumin**   A fiery, smoky-tasting spice popular in Middle-Eastern and Indian dishes. Cumin is a seed; ground cumin seed is the most common form of the spice used in cooking.

**curing**   A method of preserving uncooked foods, usually meats or fish, by either salting and smoking or pickling.

**curry**   A general term referring to rich, spicy, Indian-style sauces and the dishes prepared with them. Common ingredients include hot pepper, nutmeg, cumin, cinnamon, pepper, and turmeric.

**custard**   A cooked mixture of eggs and milk. Custards are a popular base for desserts.

**dash**   A dash refers to a few drops, usually of a liquid, that is released by a quick shake of, for example, a bottle of hot sauce.

**debeard**   To scrape the fuzzy material off mussels.

**deglaze**   To scrape up the bits of meat and seasoning left in a pan or skillet after cooking. Usually this is done by adding a liquid such as wine or broth and creating a flavorful stock that can be used to create sauces.

**dehydrate**   To remove the natural moisture from foods by drying it at a low temperature.

**devein**   The removal of the dark vein from the back of a large shrimp with a sharp knife.

**dice**   To cut into small cubes about ¼-inch square.

**Dijon mustard**   Hearty, spicy mustard made in the style of the Dijon region of France.

**dill**   A slightly sour, unique herb that is perfect for eggs, cheese dishes, and, of course, vegetables (pickles!).

**double boiler**   A set of two pots designed to nest together, one inside the other, and provide consistent, moist heat for foods that need delicate treatment. The bottom pot holds water (not quite touching the bottom of the top pot); the top pot holds the ingredient you want to heat.

**dredge**   To cover a piece of food with a dry substance such as flour or corn meal.

**dressing**   A liquid mixture usually containing oil, vinegar, and herbs used for seasoning salads and other foods. Also the solid dish commonly called "stuffing" used to stuff turkey and other foods.

**dust**   To sprinkle a dry substance, often a seasoning, over a food or dish.

**emulsion**   A combination of liquid ingredients that do not normally mix well beaten together to create a thick liquid, such as a fat or oil with water. Classic examples are salad dressings and mayonnaise. Creation of an emulsion must be done carefully and rapidly to ensure that particles of one ingredient are suspended in the other.

**entrée**   The main dish in a meal.

**étouffée**   Cajun for "smothered." This savory, rich sauce (often made with crayfish) is served over rice.

**extra-virgin olive oil**   *See* olive oil.

**fennel**   In seed form, a fragrant, licorice-tasting herb. The bulbs have a much milder flavor and a celerylike crunch and are used as a vegetable in salads or cooked recipes.

**feta**   This white, crumbly, salty cheese is popular in Greek cooking, on salads, and on its own. Traditional feta is usually made with sheep's milk, but feta-style cheese can be made from sheep's, cow's, or goat's milk. Its sharp flavor is especially nice with bitter, cured black olives.

**fillet**   A piece of meat or seafood with the bones removed.

**fish basket**   A grill-top metal frame that holds a whole fish intact, making it easier to turn.

**fish poacher**   A long, rectangular pan with a separate metal basket designed to hold a fish either above boiling water for steaming or in simmering liquid for poaching. Fish poachers come in varying sizes up to 24 inches, although an 18-inch version will cover all but the largest meals.

**flake**   To break into thin sections, as with fish.

**floret**   The flower or bud end of broccoli or cauliflower.

**flour**   Grains ground into a meal. Wheat is perhaps the most common flour, an essential component in many breads. Flour is also made from oats, rye, buckwheat, soybeans, etc. Different types of flour serve different purposes. *See also* all-purpose flour; bread flour; cake flour; whole-wheat flour.

**fold**   To combine a dense and light mixture with a circular action from the middle of the bowl.

**fritter**   A food such as apples or corn coated or mixed with batter and deep-fried for a crispy, crunchy exterior.

**fry**   Pan-cooking over high heat with butter or oil.

**fusion**   To blend two or more styles of cooking, such as Chinese and French.

**garlic**   A member of the onion family, a pungent and flavorful element in many savory dishes. A garlic bulb, the form in which garlic is often sold, contains multiple cloves. Each clove, when chopped, provides about 1 teaspoon garlic.

**garnish**   An embellishment not vital to the dish but added to enhance visual appeal.

**ginger**   Available in fresh root or powdered form, ginger adds a pungent, sweet, and spicy quality to a dish. It is a very popular element of many Asian and Indian dishes, among others.

**goulash**   A rich, Hungarian-style meat-and-vegetable stew seasoned with paprika, among other spices.

**grate**   To shave into tiny pieces using a sharp rasp or grater.

**grill**   To cook over high heat, usually over charcoal or gas.

**grind**   To reduce a large, hard substance, often a seasoning such as peppercorns, to the consistency of sand.

**grits**   Coarsely ground grains, usually corn.

**Gruyère**   A rich, sharp cow's milk cheese with a nutty flavor made in Switzerland.

**handful**   An unscientific measurement term that refers to the amount of an ingredient you can hold in your hand.

**haute cuisine**   French for "high cooking." Refers to painstakingly prepared, sometimes exotic, delicious, and complex meals (such as one might find at a high-end traditional French restaurant).

**Havarti**   A creamy, Danish, mild cow's milk cheese perhaps most enjoyed in its herbed versions such as Havarti with dill.

**hazelnut** (also **filbert**)   A sweet nut popular in desserts and, to a lesser degree, in savory dishes.

**hearts of palm**   Firm, elongated, off-white cylinders from the inside of a palm tree stem tip. They are delicious in many recipes.

**herbes de Provence**   A seasoning mix including basil, fennel, marjoram, rosemary, sage, and thyme.

**herbs**   The leaves of flavorful plants characterized by fresh, pungent aromas and flavors, such as parsley, sage, rosemary, and thyme.

**hors d'oeuvre**   French for "outside of work" (the "work" being the main meal). An hors d'oeuvre can be any dish served as a starter before the meal.

**horseradish**   A sharp, spicy root that forms the flavor base in many condiments from cocktail sauce to sharp mustards. It is a natural match with roast beef. The form generally found in grocery stores is prepared horseradish, which contains vinegar and oil, among other ingredients. If you come across pure horseradish, use it much more sparingly than the prepared version, or try cutting it with sour cream.

**hummus**   A thick, Middle Eastern spread made of puréed chickpeas (garbanzo beans), lemon juice, olive oil, garlic, and often tahini (sesame seed paste).

**infusion**   A liquid in which flavorful ingredients such herbs have been soaked or steeped to extract that flavor into the liquid.

**Italian breadcrumbs**   Breadcrumbs that are seasoned with parsley and other herbs, garlic, and Parmesan cheese.

**Italian seasoning** (also **spaghetti sauce seasoning**)   The ubiquitous grocery store blend, which includes basil, oregano, rosemary, and thyme, is a useful seasoning for quick flavor that evokes the "old country" in sauces, meatballs, soups, and vegetable dishes.

**jicama**   A juicy, crunchy, sweet, Central American vegetable that is eaten both raw and cooked. It is available in many large grocery stores as well as from specialty vendors. If you can't find jicama, try substituting sliced water chestnuts.

**julienne**   To slice into very thin pieces.

**key limes**   Very small limes grown primarily in Florida that are known for their tart taste.

**lentils**   Tiny lens-shape pulses used in European, Middle Eastern, and Indian cuisines.

**macerate**   To mix sugar or another sweetener with fruit. The fruit softens, and its juice is released to mix with the sweetener.

**marinate**   To soak meat, seafood, or other food in a seasoned sauce, called a marinade, which is high in acid content. The acids break down the muscle of the meat, making it tender and adding flavor.

**marjoram**   A sweet herb, a cousin of and similar to oregano, popular in Greek, Spanish, and Italian dishes.

**marmalade**   A fruit-and-sugar preserve that contains whole pieces of fruit peel, to achieve simultaneous sweetness (from the sugar) and tartness (from the fruit's natural acids). The most common marmalades are made with citrus fruits such as orange and lemon.

**medallion**   A small round cut, usually of meat or vegetables such as carrots or cucumbers.

**meld**   A combination of *melt* and *weld*, many cooks use this term to describe how flavors blend and spread over time throughout dips and spreads. Melding is often why recipes call for overnight refrigeration and is also why some dishes taste better as leftovers.

**meringue**   A baked mixture of sugar and beaten egg whites, often used as a dessert topping.

**mesclun**   Mixed salad greens, usually containing lettuce and assorted greens such as arugula, cress, endive, and others.

**Mexican cheese blend**   A grated combination of Monterey Jack, pepper Jack, and cheddar cheese used in Mexican and Southwestern cooking.

**mince**   To cut into very small pieces, smaller than diced pieces, about ⅛ inch or smaller.

**mold**   A decorative, shaped metal pan in which contents, such as mousse or gelatin, set up and take the shape of the pan.

**mull** (or **mulled**)   To heat a liquid with the addition of spices and sometimes sweeteners.

**mushrooms**   Any one of a huge variety of *edible* fungi (note emphasis on "edible"; there are also poisonous mushrooms). *See also* crimini mushrooms; porcini mushrooms; portobello mushrooms; shiitake mushrooms; white mushrooms.

**nouvelle cuisine**   *Nouvelle* is French for "new." Refers to a style of cooking that is relatively light in flavor and consistency.

**nutmeg**   A sweet, fragrant, musky spice used primarily in baking.

**nuts**   Shell-covered seeds (or fruits) whose meat is rich in flavor and nutrition. A critical component in many dishes, many nuts are tasty on their own as well. *See also* almonds; hazelnuts; pecans; walnuts.

**olivada**   A simple spread composed of olives, olive oil, and pepper that carries a wealth of flavor.

**olive oil**   A fragrant liquid produced by crushing or pressing olives. Extra-virgin olive oil is the oil produced from the first pressing of a batch of olives; oil is also produced from other pressings after the first. Extra-virgin olive oil is generally considered the most flavorful and highest quality and is the type you want to use when your focus is on the oil itself. Be sure the bottle label reads "extra-virgin."

**olives**   The fruit of the olive tree commonly grown on all sides of the Mediterranean. There are many varieties of olives but two general types: green and black. Black olives are also called "ripe olives."

**oregano**   A fragrant, slightly astringent herb used in Greek, Spanish, and Italian dishes.

**oxidation**   The browning of fruit flesh that happens over time and with exposure to air. Although it's best to prepare fresh fruit dishes just before serving, sometimes that's not possible. If you need to cut apples in advance, minimize oxidation by rubbing the cut surfaces with a lemon half.

**pan-broil**   Quick-cooking over high heat in a skillet with a minimum of butter or oil. (Frying, on the other hand, uses more butter or oil.)

**pancetta**   Salted, seasoned bacon; an important element in many Italian-style dishes.

**paprika**   A rich, red, warm, earthy spice that also lends a rich red color to many dishes.

**parboil**   To partially cook in boiling water or broth. Parboiling is similar to blanching, although blanched foods are quickly cooled with cold water.

**pare**   To scrape away the skin of a food, usually a vegetable, as part of preparation for serving or cooking.

**Parmesan**   A hard, dry, flavorful cheese primarily used grated or shredded as a seasoning for Italian-style dishes.

**parsley**   A fresh-tasting green leafy herb used to add color and interest to just about any savory dish. Often used as a garnish just before serving.

**pâté**   A savory loaf that contains meats, spices, and often a lot of fat, served cold spread or sliced on crusty bread or crackers. Pâtés can also be made from poultry and seafood.

**peanuts**   The nutritious and high-fat seeds of the peanut plant that are sold shelled or unshelled and in a variety of preparations, including peanut butter and peanut oil. Some people are allergic to peanuts, so care should be taken with their inclusion in recipes.

**pecans**   Rich, buttery nuts native to North America. Their flavor, a terrific addition to appetizers, is at least partially due to their high unsaturated fat content.

**pepper**   A biting and pungent seasoning, freshly ground pepper is a must for many dishes and adds an extra level of flavor and taste.

**peppercorns**   Large, round, dried berries that are ground to produce pepper.

**pesto**   A thick spread or sauce made with fresh basil leaves, garlic, olive oil, pine nuts, and Parmesan cheese. Other new versions are made with other herbs. Rich and flavorful, pesto can be made at home or purchased in a grocery store and used on anything from appetizers to pasta and other main dishes.

**pickle**   A food, usually a vegetable such as a cucumber, that has been pickled in brine.

**pilaf**   A rice dish in which the rice is browned in butter or oil, then cooked in a flavorful liquid such as a broth, often with the addition of meats or vegetables. The rice absorbs the broth, resulting in a savory dish.

**pinch**   An unscientific measurement term that refers to the amount of an ingredient—typically a dry, granular substance such as an herb or seasoning—you can hold between your finger and thumb.

**pine nuts** (also **pignoli** or **piñon**)   Nuts grown on pine trees, that are rich (read: high fat), flavorful, and, yes, a bit pine-y. Pine nuts are a traditional component of pesto, and they add a wonderful hearty crunch to many other recipes.

**pita bread**   A flat, hollow wheat bread that can be used for sandwiches or sliced, pizza-style, into slices. Pita bread is terrific soft with dips, or baked or broiled as a vehicle for other ingredients.

**pizza stone**   Preheated with the oven, a pizza stone cooks a crust to a delicious, crispy, pizza-parlor texture. It also holds heat well, so a pizza removed from the oven on the stone will stay hot for as long as a half-hour at the table. Can also be used for other baking needs, including bread.

**plantain**   A relative of the banana, a plantain is larger, milder in flavor, and used as a staple in many Latin American dishes.

**poach**   To cook a food in simmering liquid, such as water, wine, or broth.

**porcini mushrooms**   Rich and flavorful mushrooms used in rice and Italian-style dishes.

**portobello mushrooms**   A mature and larger form of the smaller crimini mushroom, portobellos are brownish, chewy, and flavorful. They are trendy served as whole caps, grilled, and as thin sautéed slices. *See also* crimini mushrooms.

**preheat**   To turn on an oven, broiler, or other cooking appliance in advance of cooking so the temperature will be at the desired level when the assembled dish is ready for cooking.

**prosciutto**   Dry, salt-cured ham, rich and evocative of Italy. Prosciutto is popular in many simple dishes in which its unique flavor is allowed to shine.

**purée**   To reduce a food to a thick, creamy texture, usually using a blender or food processor.

**ragout** (pronounced *rag-OO*)   A thick, spicy stew.

**red pepper flakes**   Hot yet rich, crushed red pepper, used in moderation, brings flavor and interest to many savory dishes.

**reduce**   To heat a broth or sauce to remove some of the water content, resulting in more concentrated flavor and color.

**refried beans** (also **refritos**)   Twice-cooked beans—most often pinto beans—softened into a thick paste and often seasoned with peppers and spices. Most refried beans include lard, but many fat-free, lard-free versions are available.

**render**   To cook a meat to the point where its fat melts and can be removed.

**reserve**   To hold a specified ingredient for another use later in the recipe.

**rice vinegar**   Vinegar produced from fermented rice or rice wine, popular in Asian-style dishes.

**ricotta**   A fresh Italian cheese that is smoother than cottage cheese and has a slightly sweet flavor.

**risotto**   A popular Italian rice dish made by browning arborio rice in butter or oil, then slowly adding liquid to cook the rice, resulting in a creamy texture.

**roast**   To cook something uncovered in an oven.

**Roquefort**   A world-famous (French) creamy but sharp sheep's milk cheese containing blue lines of mold, making it a "blue cheese."

**rosemary**   A pungent, sweet herb used with chicken, pork, fish, and especially lamb. A little of it goes a long way.

**roulade**   A rolled food that can be sweet or savory and has contrasting layers of colors and textures.

**roux**   A mixture of butter or another fat source and flour used to thicken liquids such as sauces.

**saffron**   A famous spice made from the stamens of crocus flowers. Saffron lends a dramatic yellow color and distinctive flavor to a dish. Only a tiny amount needs to be used, which is good because saffron is very expensive.

**sage**   An herb with a fruity, musty, lemon-rind scent and "sunny" flavor. It is a terrific addition to many dishes.

**salsa**   A style of mixing fresh vegetables and/or fresh fruit in a coarse chop. Salsa can be spicy or not, fruit-based or not, and served as a starter on its own (with chips, for example) or as a companion to a main course.

**sauté**   Pan-cooking over lower heat than used for frying.

**savory**   A popular herb with a fresh, woody taste.

**scant**   A measurement modification that specifies "include no extra," as in 1 scant teaspoon.

**Scoville scale**   A scale used to measure the "hot" in hot peppers. The lower the Scoville units, the more mild the pepper. Ancho peppers, which are mildly hot, are about 3,000 Scovilles; Thai hot peppers are about 6,000; and some of the more daring peppers such as Tears of Fire and habanero are 30,000 Scovilles or more.

**scrapple**   A sausagelike mixture of seasoned pork and cornmeal that is formed into loaves and sliced for cooking.

**sear**   To quickly brown the exterior of a food over high heat to preserve interior moisture (that's why many meat recipes involve searing).

**shallot**   A member of the onion family that grows in a bulb somewhat like garlic and has a milder onion flavor. When a recipe calls for shallot, you use the entire bulb. (They might or might not have cloves.)

**shellfish**   A broad range of seafood, including clams, mussels, oysters, crabs, shrimp, and lobster. Some people are allergic to shellfish, so care should be taken with its inclusion in recipes.

**shiitake mushrooms**   Large (about 5 inches), dark brown mushrooms originally from the Far East with a hearty, meaty flavor that can be grilled or used as a component in other recipes and as a flavoring source for broth. They can be used dried or fresh.

**shred**   To cut into many long, thin slices.

**silverskin**   The almost iridescent membrane surrounding certain parts of a meat tenderloin.

**simmer**   To boil gently so the liquid barely bubbles.

**skewers**   Thin wooden or metal sticks, usually about eight inches long, that are perfect for assembling kebabs, dipping food pieces into hot sauces, or serving single-bite food items with a bit of panache.

**skillet** (also **frying pan**)   A generally heavy, flat metal pan with a handle designed to cook food over heat on a stovetop or campfire.

**skim**   To remove fat from the top of liquid.

**slice**   To cut into thin pieces.

**slow cooker**   An electric countertop device with a lidded container that maintains a low temperature and slowly cooks its contents, often over several hours or a full day.

**steam**   To suspend a food over boiling water and allow the heat of the steam (water vapor) to cook the food. Steaming is a very quick cooking method that preserves the flavor and texture of a food.

**stew**   To slowly cook pieces of food submerged in a liquid. Also a dish that has been prepared by this method.

**Stilton**   The famous English blue cheese, delicious with toasted nuts and renowned for its pairing with Port wine.

**stir-fry**   To cook food in a wok or skillet over high heat, moving and turning the food quickly to cook all sides.

**stock**   A flavorful broth made by cooking meats and/or vegetables with seasonings until the liquid absorbs these flavors. This liquid is then strained and the solids discarded. Stock can be eaten by itself or used as a base for soups, stews, sauces, risotto, or many other recipes.

**strata**   A savory bread pudding made with eggs and cheese.

**stripe**   To scrape off a fruit's or vegetable's skin in lengthwise strokes, leaving a "stripe" of the skin between each scrape.

**succotash**   A cooked vegetable dish usually made of corn and peppers.

**sweat**   To cook vegetables covered over low heat to soften them.

**tahini**   A paste made from sesame seeds that is used to flavor many Middle Eastern recipes, especially baba ghanoush and hummus.

**tamarind**   A sweet, pungent, flavorful fruit used in Indian-style sauces and curries.

**tapenade**   A thick, chunky spread made from savory ingredients such as olives, lemon juice, and anchovies. Adventuresome grocery and gourmet stores are likely to have different versions focusing on specific ingredients, from olives to peppers and mushrooms.

**tarragon**   A sour-sweet, rich-smelling herb perfect with seafood, vegetables (especially asparagus), chicken, and pork.

**thyme**   A minty, zesty herb whose leaves are used in a wide range of recipes.

**toast**   To heat something, usually bread, so it is browned and crisp.

**toast points** (also **toast triangles**)   Pieces of toast with the crusts removed that are then cut on the diagonal from each corner, resulting in four triangle-shape pieces.

**tofu**   A cheeselike substance made from soybeans and soy milk. Flavorful and nutritious, tofu is an important component of foods across the globe, especially from the Far East.

**tomatillo**   A small, round fruit with a distinctive spicy flavor reminiscent of its cousin, the tomato. Tomatillos are a traditional component of many south-of-the-border dishes. To use, remove the papery outer skin, rinse off any sticky residue, and chop like a tomato.

**tripe**   The stomach of a cow.

**turmeric**   A spicy, pungent yellow root used in many dishes, especially Indian cuisine, for color and flavor. Turmeric is the source of the brilliant yellow color in many prepared mustards.

**twist**   A twist (as in lemon or other citrus fruit twist) is simply an attractive way to garnish an appetizer or other dish. Cut a thin (about $\frac{1}{8}$-inch-thick) cross-section slice of a lemon, for example. Then take that slice and cut from the center out to the edge of the slice on one side. Pick up the piece of lemon and pull apart the two cut ends in opposite directions.

**veal**   Meat from a calf, generally characterized by mild flavor and tenderness. Certain cuts of veal, such as cutlets and scaloppini, are well suited to quick-cooking.

**vegetable steamer**   An insert for a large saucepan. Also a special pot with tiny holes in the bottom designed to fit on another pot to hold food to be steamed above boiling water. The insert is generally less expensive and resembles a metal poppy flower that expands to touch the sides of the pot and has small legs. *See also* steam.

**venison**   Meat from deer or other large wild game animals.

**vichy**   A classic vegetable dish of carrots cooked in water and sugar.

**vinegar**   An acidic liquid widely used as dressing and seasoning. Many cuisines use vinegars made from different source materials. *See also* balsamic vinegar; cider vinegar; rice vinegar; white vinegar; wine vinegar.

**walnuts**   Grown worldwide, walnuts bring a rich, slightly woody flavor to all types of food. For the quick cook, walnuts are available chopped and ready to go at your grocery store. They are delicious toasted and make fine accompaniments to cheeses.

**water chestnuts**   Actually a tuber, water chestnuts are a popular element in many types of Asian-style cooking. The flesh is white, crunchy, and juicy, and the vegetable holds its texture whether cool or hot.

**whisk**   To rapidly mix, introducing air to the mixture.

**white mushrooms**   Ubiquitous button mushrooms. When fresh, they will have an earthy smell and an appealing "soft crunch." White mushrooms are delicious raw in salads, marinated, sautéed, and as component ingredients in many recipes.

**white vinegar**   The most common type of vinegar found on grocery store shelves. It is produced from grain.

**whole-wheat flour**   Wheat flour that contains the entire grain.

**wild rice**   Actually a grain with a rich, nutty flavor, popular as an unusual and nutritious side dish.

**wine vinegar**   Vinegar produced from red or white wine.

**Worcestershire sauce**   Originally developed in India and containing tamarind, this spicy sauce is used as a seasoning for many meats and other dishes.

**yeast**   Tiny fungi that, when mixed with water, sugar, flour, and heat, release carbon dioxide bubbles, which, in turn, raise bread. The yeast also provides that wonderful warm, rich smell and flavor.

**zest**   Small slivers of peel, usually from a citrus fruit such as lemon, lime, or orange.

# Metric Conversion Charts

The scientifically precise calculations needed for baking are not necessary when cooking conventionally or in a slow cooker. This chart is designed for general cooking. If making conversions for baking, grab your calculator and compute the exact figure.

## Converting Ounces to Grams

The numbers in the following table are approximate. To reach the exact amount of grams, multiply the number of ounces by 28.35.

| Ounces | Grams | Ounces | Grams |
| --- | --- | --- | --- |
| 1 oz. | 30 g | 9 oz. | 250 g |
| 2 oz. | 60 g | 10 oz. | 285 g |
| 3 oz. | 85 g | 11 oz. | 300 g |
| 4 oz. | 115 g | 12 oz. | 340 g |
| 5 oz. | 140 g | 13 oz. | 370 g |
| 6 oz. | 180 g | 14 oz. | 400 g |
| 7 oz. | 200 g | 15 oz. | 425 g |
| 8 oz. | 225 g | 16 oz. | 450 g |

# Converting Quarts to Liters

The numbers in the following table are approximate. To reach the exact amount of liters, multiply the number of quarts by 0.95.

| Quarts | Liters | Quarts | Liters |
|---|---|---|---|
| 1 cup (¼ qt.) | ¼ L | 4 qt. | 3¾ L |
| 1 pint (½ qt.) | ½ L | 5 qt. | 4¾ L |
| 1 qt. | 1 L | 6 qt. | 5½ L |
| 2 qt. | 2 L | 7 qt. | 6½ L |
| 2½ qt. | 2½ L | 8 qt. | 7½ L |
| 3 qt. | 2¾ L | | |

# Converting Pounds to Grams and Kilograms

The numbers in the following table are approximate. To reach the exact amount of kilograms, multiply the number of pounds by 453.6.

| Pounds | Grams; Kilograms | Pounds | Grams; Kilograms |
|---|---|---|---|
| 1 lb. | 450 g | 5 lb. | 2¼ kg |
| 1½ lb. | 675 g | 5½ lb. | 2½ kg |
| 2 lb. | 900 g | 6 lb. | 2¾ kg |
| 2½ lb. | 1,125 g; 1¼ kg | 6½ lb. | 3 kg |
| 3 lb. | 1,350 g | 7 lb. | 3¼ kg |
| 3½ lb. | 1,500 g; 1½ kg | 7½ lb. | 3½ kg |
| 4 lb. | 1,800 g | 8 lb. | 3¾ kg |
| 4½ lb. | 2 kg | | |

# Converting Fahrenheit to Celsius

The numbers in the following table are approximate. To reach the exact temperature, subtract 32 from the Fahrenheit reading, multiply the number by 5, then divide by 9.

| Fahrenheit | Celsius | Fahrenheit | Celsius |
|------------|---------|------------|---------|
| 170°F | 77°C | 350°F | 180°C |
| 180°F | 82°C | 375°F | 190°C |
| 190°F | 88°C | 400°F | 205°C |
| 200°F | 95°C | 425°F | 220°C |
| 225°F | 110°C | 450°F | 230°C |
| 250°F | 120°C | 475°F | 245°C |
| 300°F | 150°C | 500°F | 260°C |
| 325°F | 165°C | | |

# Converting Inches to Centimeters

The numbers in the following table are approximate. To reach the exact number of centimeters, multiply the number of inches by 2.54.

| Inches | Centimeters | Inches | Centimeters |
|--------|-------------|--------|-------------|
| ½ in. | 1.5 cm | 7 in. | 18 cm |
| 1 in. | 2.5 cm | 8 in. | 20 cm |
| 2 in. | 5 cm | 9 in. | 23 cm |
| 3 in. | 8 cm | 10 in. | 25 cm |
| 4 in. | 10 cm | 11 in. | 28 cm |
| 5 in. | 13 cm | 12 in. | 30 cm |
| 6 in. | 15 cm | | |

# Measurement Tables

## Table of Weights and Measures of Common Ingredients

| Food | Quantity | Yield |
| --- | --- | --- |
| Apples | 1 lb. | 2½ to 3 cups, sliced |
| Bananas | 1 medium | 1 cup, sliced |
| Blueberries | 1 lb. | 3⅓ cups |
| Butter | ¼ lb. (1 stick) | 8 TB. |
| Chocolate, morsels | 12 oz. | 2 cups |
| Chocolate, bulk | 1 oz. | 3 TB. grated |
| Cocoa powder | 1 oz. | ¼ cup |
| Coconut, flaked | 7 oz. | 2½ cups |
| Cream | ½ pt. | 1 cup, 2 cups whipped |
| Cream cheese | 8 oz. | 1 cup |
| Flour | 1 lb. | 4 cups |
| Lemons | 1 medium | 3 TB. juice |
| Milk | 1 qt. | 4 cups |
| Molasses | 12 oz. | 1½ cups |
| Pecans | 6 oz. | 1½ cups |

*continues*

# Table of Weights and Measures of Common Ingredients (continued)

| Food | Quantity | Yield |
|------|----------|-------|
| Raisins | 1 lb. | 3 cups |
| Strawberries | 1 pt. | 1½ cups, sliced |
| Sugar, brown | 1 lb. | 2¼ cups, packed |
| Sugar, confectioners' | 1 lb. | 4 cups |
| Sugar, granulated | 1 lb. | 2¼ cups |

## Table of Liquid Measurements

| | | |
|------|------|------|
| Pinch | = | less than ⅛ tsp. |
| 3 tsp. | = | 1 TB. |
| 2 TB. | = | 1 oz. |
| 8 TB. | = | ½ cup |
| 2 cups | = | 1 pint |
| 1 quart | = | 2 pints |

# Index